The Reinecke Diary

Terence James

Michael Terence
Publishing

First published in paperback by
Michael Terence Publishing in 2020
www.mtp.agency

ISBN 9781800940499

*For the Lady Patricia, for her keeping me on an even keel,
giving me a fair course in life's stormy seas.*

PART ONE

1

March 1941

Fingers of terror wrapped their icy cold grasp tightly around his heart, stopping him breathing, causing his numbed hands to fumble with the release handle. It could not be happening, not to him… not now! This aircraft, one of finest machines the Reich aviation minds could produce, it should not be crippled in this way. Fire now raging through the front section of the narrow cockpit, fanned by the loud roaring of the wind driven through the gaping holes in the canopy, it was like a blow torch searing all that it touched.

Oberleutnant Frick was already dead, his body forced back in the pilot's seat, his head arched back at the moment of death with his skull an unrecognisable tattered mash of bone and blood. Schroder, the bombardier in the seat beside him, in agony, wrestling with the controls as the one functioning engine screamed in metal torment as it began to tear itself apart under the strain. With both of his hands badly burned by the crackling flames it could be only moments before he lost control. *'GET OUT!'* He yelled desperately at the two remaining men in the rear of the cockpit… The body of the fifth crew member, Hartnung, clearly beyond help, lay bleeding heaped near the ventral machine gun position, both legs severed below the knee his moans could not be heard, drowned out by the cacophony of sound in and around the stricken aircraft.

Schroder gave one last effort, with all of his strength heaving back on the stick to raise the bomber's nose a fraction, *'NOW, GO.'* The bomber's belly escape hatch suddenly came free and was immediately torn away snapping from its hinges as it fell away into the night. Another roaring gale now blasted inwards pushing the two men back into the body of the aircraft. Young Frick jumped first, his trembling hand prematurely jerking at the release mechanism, his parachute opening immediately, but before his body could clear the fuselage the chute canopy it billowed and caught on the tail fin dragging him screaming twirling and spinning into the slip stream.

Ernst Dorn watched helplessly as his friend died before his eyes, then with another sickening lurch the aircraft told him there was no time left for thinking. Grasping both sides of the trap door he jumped clear into the dark mouth of the void below. Gripping his parachute release handle, he watched as the world span around him as he fell away, the roar of the burning aircraft being replaced by the rush of wind generated by his headlong tumbling plunge earthwards. A shaking nervous hand yanked with desperation on the release handle, nothing... On the second attempt his body was jerked abruptly upright as the chute snapped opened above him. Both shoulders felt as if they were being torn from their sockets and his left leg hurt like hell. Above him the noise of the burning bomber receded, then seemed to pick up then droned on out of hearing. For a moment he thought maybe it would have been better to stay with Schroder and to have taken his chances with the aircraft. Craning his head, he could no longer see any sign of the bomber, an eerie silence enveloped him, only broken by the rustling of the wind as he hung beneath the shroud of the chute above. Dorn now swinging from side to side gripped the parachute lines with both hands as he tried to control the swing, pulling hard on the left side seemed to slow the movement and at last he appeared to be falling in some degree of order.

Staring hard below into the darkness, it took a while before features began to emerge, first the surface of the sea beckoned with white crested waves far below, then as his chute drifted with the wind he could see that he was crossing a coastline into a countryside in darkness. Off to his left the glimmer of light from the sea faded as he was carried inland, whilst immediately below the ground was still shrouded several hundred metres beneath his feet. From horizon to horizon there was only a blackness interrupted here and there by patches of grey. They had been hit by a night fighter over the sea, their heading had been a westwards course at an altitude of about two thousand metres, this must mean that they had drifted over land after being hit. This land below was enemy England.

Without warning his decent earthwards seemed to have accelerated, suddenly landscape features appeared, he was dropping into a forest or a wood at an alarming speed. The first branches of tall treetops whipped him as he crashed through, then a bone jarring series of crunches as he snapped branches before coming to rest swinging from the harness trapped in the branches above him.

The sudden agony was intense, his left knee felt as if a giant had stepped upon it with incredible pain lancing through the joint and upper thigh. Blood was running into his right eye from a deep wound to his forehead. Raising his right gloved hand to wipe the blood away Dorn screamed as his right shoulder joint crunched with the movement as it dragged broken bone on bone. The swinging had ceased, he now hung silently suspended in his harness from the tree above. The raging pain in his leg now was all consuming to the point where he was close to losing consciousness. Dorn tried again, this time with his left hand to explore his injuries, working the glove off against his body he grunted with pain as he tried to reach the leg. What he discovered was that a jagged piece of bone protruding through the material of his flying suit above the knee, strangely there was no feeling, no sensation other than that the leg felt cold and wet. Any further movement brought unbearable bolts of knifing red-hot agony from both the leg and his shoulder. It seemed better to try to just keep as still as possible, and wait for help…?

Help? What help and from whom? Trying to clear his mind, he remembered painfully that as he had been part of a bombing mission over an enemy country in time of war, what possible mercy could he expect from whoever found him? Time seemed to slow and stand still, he began to drift in and out of consciousness, a coldness throughout his entire being caused him to begin to shiver. Gradually he became aware of the dull light beginning to steal through the tops of the leafless trees around him. He was only about two metres off the ground, but descending was impossible, he could not free himself from the harness that had earlier saved his life. A cold but gentle breeze stirred the branches turning Dorn slowly in its chilling caress. As the dawn light increased twenty-two-year-old Oberfeldwebel Dorn, felt tears begin to trickle down his cheeks, involuntary he voiced the word 'Mutti' but there was only silence from the bare trees around him.

As Dorn, suspended by his parachute had plummeted earthwards, so Schroder's battle to keep the Heinkel flying level was being lost. Despite all of his efforts and with his strength exhausted the nose dipped for the last time. He stared in numbed horror through the remains of the wind screen as the angry sea relentlessly rose up to meet him. A moment before the aircraft struck the water as he reacted automatically putting his hands across his face in a human but feeble attempt to avert the sight of the impact, a final irrelevant fleeting thought entered his mind in that last second, 'Who will look after Mitzi and her puppies…?' Then it hit the water…

The fuselage of the Heinkel broke up on impact with the surface of the sea, shattered into a thousand pieces by the sheer velocity as the aircraft disintegrated scattering the debris across the surface of the wave tossed green water. Within moments it had gone, sinking beneath the surface taking with it the bodies of the crew, except for Frick whose trailing body had hit the water a millisecond after the bomber. One fragment from the nose which had been bearing the painted picture of a winged Dachshund floated, floated lingering a few seconds before disappearing forever. Of the five-man crew only Frick's remains would be found when they would be recovered from the sea having been driven in by the tide to finally drift ashore a month later.

2

North Wales
Friday 7th January 1944
Late Evening

The back door of the ale house opening onto the narrow alleyway banged noisily open, momentarily lighting the pale face of the skinny youth standing on the wet cobbles of the back entry for a second before the blackout curtain was replaced and darkness returned. The outline of the man stood only feet from the youth, then waiting moments for his eyes to grow accustomed to the darkness, he swore and shouted into the gloom, 'Where are you brat?' He scowled and a damp lock of his thick black hair fell over his face. His question was answered quietly from the dark, 'Here Uncle Ifan, I'm in right in front of you.' At which the man lumbered forward, staggered then reaching and grasping the boy's shoulder breathing the rank smell of stale beer into his face and demanded, 'How much did you get?' The skinny youth fumbled in his pockets and produced a handful of copper coins, 'One and six Uncle Ifan,' the boy had then tipped the money into the outstretched big bony hand held menacingly inches in front of his face.

The money was grabbed out of his hand and followed by a slap across the face which was delivered without warning so suddenly and viciously that it stunned him. 'You bad little bugger, where's the rest of it?' The angry voice ranted at him, 'If you think to thief it for yourself, I'll skin the hide off you.' The youth's face stung, a mark beginning to appear that would later glow red, a tear formed in his eyes, but not from the pain, but from the humiliation. Knowing what could come next, he began to offer, 'The Yanks didn't want much today, most of them stayed in case of the rain, honest Uncle Ifan.' He ducked as the expected second blow came but it missed causing Ifan to stagger again. 'Get home,' he shouted, pocketing the handful of coppers he threw another blow at the shadows, 'I'll deal with you later, and your bitch mother!' With that he searched and found the door again to the ale house, and, with more than enough for another three pints went back to his friends in the warmth and tobacco smoke of the public bar.

Huw Henryd Thomas, stood silently in the falling rain, seething, the anger in his stomach burned as hot as the handprint on his thirteen-year-old face. Helplessness, a forlorn feeling of inadequacy, of impotence. It was not his fault his own Da' had been killed, not his fault that his mother, left alone with him as an infant had fallen for the guiles and charm of his Dad's workmate, Ifan Evans. Who had pretended to be so kind, so generous, so helpful to the vulnerable pretty grief-stricken young widow when William Thomas's broken body was brought home to be washed then put into his suit ready to be laid in his coffin. Every day he had dutifully, called his cap reverently held in his hands when he knocked at their door. Then, when the months had passed, he made his bid and moved into the cottage at Bryn Morfa where Huw and his mother lived, his Dad's home. Oh, there had been some kind of ceremony, not in church but his mam had a piece of paper which said Ifan was her new husband and Huw was to call him Uncle Ifan. Then, within the first year, baby Ellen had been born, followed then by Dafydd and now baby Megan who was just six months old. Ifan Evans didn't work, he had managed to get himself sacked from the gas works not long after Dafydd was born, he got something called the Dole and did odd jobs on the sly, scrounged his way around so ensuring that he never went short of his beer and cigarette money, even when they had no food on the table. Ifan had told Huw in no uncertain terms that he had to contribute or he was out, that he didn't want Will Thomas's son as a blight in his life and there was always the threat of the local 'Crafnant Home' for unwanted brats if he, Huw, didn't do exactly as he was told. Huw had ran the half mile home, his thin but strong wiry legs pumping him along the wide avenue the hobnails on his boots clattering on the paving stones, then past the guard post and barrier of the sprawling American compound of Nissen huts occupying most of the flat land to left side of the road, then on across the beach road to where the Bryn Morfa cottages lay at right angles to the concrete sea wall which ran only yards from the front door. Entering the gate which served all four of the cottages, he made his way to one of the two communal outside toilets which served the six families of cottage dwellers, let himself in, put the bolt on the door and stood in the darkness wiping his face with the sleeve of his torn jumper. He fumbled in the darkness for the candle in its brass holder and for the box of matches on the shelf on the rear wall. It took three matches before the stump of the candle caught and flickered into a long yellow flame.

The light revealed the clean whitewashed interior, with red and blue quarry tiled floor, the neatly torn stack of pages of a newspaper hanging conveniently from a hook. The cottage house holders took turns in their pride in keeping their shared privy facilities as comfortable and as sanitary as was possible. Huw took stock, his too long flannel shorts were also torn, though well-worn they were sturdy and warm, they were the result of his mother's recent trips to the jumble sales at the church hall in town, from the pockets he brought out three penny coins, these would be the latest recent addition to his savings. In the candlelight he carefully removed a brick from behind the toilet seat by touch and placed these coins in beside the others he had been depositing there since his earnings from the Yanks had begun. Nearly two shillings! He was rich, but this was his emergency money, if Ifan, one day, decided to carry out his Crafnant threat then Huw needed his escape money to be ready when that day came as he knew surely that it would with Ifan's unpredictable and violent temper.

Huw lifted the latch to the cottage door, the light from the fire lit the room within with the few pieces of furniture gathered near the range fireplace. His mother sat at the fireside in a creaking rocking chair nursing baby Ellen. 'Huw is that you?' she said softly without turning her head. 'Yes Mam, sorry I'm late…' His mother turned and looked at him fondly with her pinched white face, 'There's some bread and a little dripping on the table, I won't ask where you've been lad but you must keep out of trouble, you know what HE's like…' Huw came closer to the warmth of the fire and his mother noticed the mark on his face. Before she could word the question, he interjected, 'I fell in the dark Ma, I'm OK honest I am, just stupid and clumsy like the teachers say…' She ran her fingers gently through his blond curly hair then stroked his cheek, 'Oh my son, how I wish that it were different,' she whispered in his ear. 'It'll be going to get better Mam, I've found some new Yanks and one of my best ones is called Jonesey and he says he's Welsh, from a place called Pitts… Pitts something… ah *Pittsburgh*…! They're really good to me Mam, as their best messenger, I'll get you one of them chocolate bars from Jonesey tomorrow, I promise, they call them *'Hershey's'* bars Mam. A little later, having downed the bread and fatty dripping he climbed the rickety stairs to the small bedroom which he shared with the other two children. His place was at the bottom end of the wide bed, he undressed putting his clothes on the one wooden chair then climbed into bed carefully so as not to disturb the toddler Dafydd and six-year-old Megan who were sound asleep. Pulling the thin army blankets around him, they had no sheets, he curled up shivering with the cold and stared up at the ceiling in the above, 'one day' he promised himself, then turned on his side listened to the rising wind outside and waited for the inevitable return of drunken Ifan, when the weekly Friday ritual after the pub would begin again.

3

The Irish Sea Friday
7th January 1944
20.00hrs

Bruno Reinecke ducked involuntarily as a ton of green sea water cascaded down upon the bridge of the conning tower pummeling the four crewmen on watch. Even with the oilskins fastened tight, a scarf tied over his head keeping his cap on and a towel around his neck, he was soaked through and cold to the bone. The U-boat's bows plunged down yet again to disappeared under the next wall of green water rising metres above them. And so, it had gone on for nearly thirty-six hours of bad weather and angry seas.

Below, throughout body of the submarine, an organised chaos reigned as the crewman each fought with their duties in the roller coaster conditions caused by the boat's twisting and corkscrewing motion through the water. In each of the sections from the bow torpedo room to the stern electric motor room the duty crew went about their work as best they could. Willi Pöhl, the galley cook swore as the boat bucked as a wave hit, causing him to spill the dixie container of lukewarm soup he was carrying onto the soaked steel of the deck plates. Further aft in the diesel engine room Hartmann, the first engineer officer with his six man team was tending his beloved diesels, despite the roar and gurgle of the exhausts he contentedly smiled to himself as he wiped an oily rag over the covers, grunting with a professional's pleasure as his hearing noted with satisfaction that they were tuned and running smoothly with the revolutions set for standard running speed ahead.

Pöhl ducked through the bulkhead hatch into the diesel engine room and with one hand offered a chunk of fat salami sausage and then a tin mug of soup and shouted, 'It's pea again Heini, so don't bother to complain…'

Hartmann reached for mug, steadying himself with one hand on the

9

warm engine cover pushing hip cap back from his sweating brow, his diesel engine room kingdom being the warmest section of the boat even in this weather, nodded and shouted back, 'How goes it topside?'

Pöhl grinned, 'The Boss is one hell of a mood, so what's new. We're off course it seems, and he blames everyone including Remischke's, for being behind whatever schedule we are supposed to be working to. How are your babies?'

Hartmann took a deep draft of the soup then a bite of sausage, screwed up his face before answering through a half full mouth, 'Purring… there was some problem with the inlet valve adjustment on number one but its running ok now, otherwise, we're in good shape, at least mechanically…! Hey, see to the boys next Pöhl, I've got things to do.' Pöhl dutifully served each of the six men of Hartmann's watch crew their meal.

Both men were silent amid the diesel engine room din and clatter, the past day and a half had been testing. Alternate running, on the surface with the boat like a living beast bucking and rolling at the mercy of the waves, then with some comparative respite when dived to periscope depth where running submerged, was a little more steady with limited motion where the 'off watch' could try to get some rest from their four hours on and four off duties.

With another nod, Pöhl served the other crewmen then wended his way forward ducking the wet clothing hanging from the overhead piping to dry. Dishing out the sausage and mugs of soup while he tried to keep his footing as the slippery metal of the deck canted and moved under him, to each crewman in the bow to stern connected compartments of the boat. The forward torpedo room seemed to be having the worst of it, bearing the brunt of the falling and rising as they ground plunging and nosing into the turbulent waters. The U-boat's weapons officer, Walter Janeschitz, like Pöhl, at twenty-eight years old was one of the boat's '*Old men,*' unlike Pöhl however, he was although well respected, neither a patient nor a forgiving man, especially the crewmen subordinates under his command. 'Is this the bloody best you can do Pöhl, two days of this filth, it's pig food?' More expletives followed and the crew members watched in amusement for Pöhl reaction as this daily ritual played out. Positioning himself against one of the starboard torpedoes slung in its cradle, he looked about the cramped confines of the bow torpedo room as if seeing it for the first time. 'Your right,' he said laconically, 'it's a disgrace to the heroic men of the Kriegsmarine to be treated in this way,

I will file your report immediately with the Kapitän for his most urgent attention.'

In the command room amidships, the boat's navigating officer, Johannes Remischke was bent cramped over the small cluttered chart table secured against the starboard pressure hull. He straightened up his bent six-foot frame painfully, a tall man in a U-boat was never comfortable. As another fresh deluge as litres of sea water poured down from the control tower sloshing to the bilges the boat struggled to come back on an even keel, Remischke grabbed the edge of the chart table just as Pöhl struggled through the command room hatch bearing his soup and sausage in time to get a soaking from the falling water. Remischke, pointing the dividers still in his right hand at Pöhl said aloud, 'Is that what I think it is Willi, we could smell something festering in the galley all morning?' Pöhl had been made a suitable relay but the humour had gone out of him, worn thin by the same remarks. Instead he merely served each man at his duty station, with, 'Plenty left if you can stomach it…!' Then made his way aft to the rear of the main command centre dodging the stored salamis sausages, the bags of onions and vegetables hanging from and festooning the overhead pipe works as he went. Hartmann, balancing with the pitching and rolling deck beneath his feet, for the moment, went back towards the rear and to some small peace, in his galley, his personal kingdom where the *'Galley Slave'* reigned supreme just aft of the command room.

Aloft, on the bridge above the central section of the tower, Reinecke took another long careful sweep of the sleet obscured horizon through the bridge binoculars, 'Nothing…' replacing the cover to the heavy duty binoculars and turning to his first officer Oberleutnant Georg Leiter, he shouted, 'Keep her on this heading for ten more minutes, North by East, then bring her five degrees to starboard on new course heading East by East, clear?' Both men with water streaming down their faces lunged for the steel rail on the front edge of the bridge as the boat heeled over to port under another incoming wave. 'Clear Herr Kaleu,' Leiter, bracing his foot on the steel footrest below the rail shouted back, his words whipped away by the wind. Reinecke paused, glanced at the other two lookouts aft then nodded, shouting again above the howling wind, 'Ok, I'm going below, keep alert.' He turned to the opened hatch in the middle of the bridge, steadied himself for a moment against the sky periscope shaft, then unslinging the binoculars from around his neck he climbed into the opening then slid down the ladder inside the conning tower to the upper control room. A quick check with the two crewmen stationed there, then ordering one aloft, a senior midshipman, to take Reinecke's place as the fourth watchman on the bridge. He continued his downward progress sliding down the last few rungs into the command room below bringing with him a welter of seawater. Reinecke took off his peaked cap and shook it vigorously then removing the sodden towel from his neck before ducking through the forward hatch into the small compartment housing Feldwebel Szasz, the radio operator was seated hunched over his equipment, one hand fixing his headset which was covering both of his ears as he moved the dials on the set. 'Anything Szasz?' Reinecke asked touching the sonar man on the shoulder. 'Nothing Herr Kaleu, the Tommie's don't like this weather either.' Came the reply. 'Ok, but let me know anything immediately, even a whisper, in a few minutes we submerge again.' Szasz answered, 'Clear Herr Kaleu,' then turned back to his equipment. Reinecke unpeeled his black shiny oilskin, moving again a mere step to the right into the next tiny compartment to where he found Lodz, the hydrophone operator, deeply engrossed in slowly moving his tracking wheel back and forth scanning ahead and listening for the minutest trace of sounds. Lodz, his earphones fixed to his ears, turned as his Kapitän entered to stand beside him in the confined space. 'How goes it Rudi?' He quizzed the man with a smile of encouragement, 'Anything moving out there?' 'Nothing Herr Kaleu,' the hydrophone operator lifted the one earpiece to reply, 'there were some small but indistinct distant echoes a little while ago, way off to port, I've tracked for them repeatedly but they never came back, and that was…,' looking down at his watch and then at then at his notes, 'nearly two hours ago Herr Kaleu.' Reinecke, critically aware that these were the ears of the boat thought for a moment before adding seriously, 'Then keep vigilant Rudi, I'm relying on you for warning of any sign or sound of surface craft however small.' There was no need to reply, the words carried implicit meaning which both men mutually understood, there was no margin at all for error no matter how minute that might be.

Reinecke returned to the command room joining the navigating officer Remischke, at the chart table. 'How near are we according to your latest figures Johann?' Remischke looked up from the chart he was studying then at the pencilled calculations in his notebook. 'By my reckoning, best guess is that we are within forty nautical miles if we can maintain this course and speed in this weather, what worries me is we are now entering shallow waters, sandbanks, there won't be much water under the keel if we run into any trouble Herr Kaleu.' Remischke said the last words slowly and with deliberation. 'I know Johann, I know…'

Reinecke thought back to his briefing before the mission, this was still too early to tell even his first officer, there was much he forbidden to share as yet with either officers and crew, even though they were risking their lives by trusting to his judgement. The time would come, and very soon enough to enlighten them to just what lay before them. He stared fixedly at his navigator nodded, then replaced his sodden cap and raised an eyebrow adding, 'The Tommies lost one of their own boats near here back in 39, dived with a tube open to the sea, lost the boat and the crew, with her nose first stuck on the bottom, her tail stuck out of the water for days.' Remischke's face looked uncertain as he heard this, Reinecke returned the worried look of the navigating officer who then voiced his reaction to this piece of history, 'Fills me with joy Herr Kaleu,' he smiled, 'Then can this really be done, so close to the surface and to the enemy's coast here, the Tommies patrols have total control of both sea and the air, with us so nearly in their back garden?' 'I'll let you into a little secret Johann, it's been done before, Kapitän sur see Max Valentiner of U- 38 took his boat in there, stayed three days and nights then got away.' Remischke looked puzzled, 'I don't know the name 'Valentiner' Herr Kaleu, with which flotilla does he serve?' Reinecke dropped his gaze to the chart, breathing out he patted Remischke's arm, 'Don't be concerned, that was in August 1915, for your interest Johann; there was another trip earlier, U-27 under Korvettenkapitän Bernd Weggener in June of the same year so it has been done and we are going to do it again Johann.' Remischke, struggling to get the words out adding to his earlier concern, 'Herr Kaleu, that was nearly thirty years ago, the Tommies have better ships, better technology now…!' 'Yes indeed,' Reinecke interrupted before he could go on, 'but now like then, what is in our favour, is surprise, they don't expect us Johann, the Tommies have become complacent and don't seem to learn from the past.' Remischke didn't look convinced at all by the explanation and persisted, 'What happened to the Valentiner and Weggener mission's Herr Kaleu?'

Reinecke decided this was enough, it was tempting towards negative thinking which would serve no purpose as they were already totally committed, 'Not now Johann, you don't need to know right now other than it *is* possible to get a U boat in and out of these waters without Tommy noticing. Just do your part and get us in there, when we have done what it is we have come this far to do, then we can go home, this is, as you are aware, only stage one. I'll be in my cabin speaking with our guests after we go to periscope depth, so we'll need to talk again later, then Johann, and only then will I brief all of you, the crew and officers about stage two of the mission. Now, bring us onto this new heading.' He repeated the same new course details given to Leiter minutes before, Remischke added some additional relevant precise points to the first officer, expanding further on each detail of the instructions, that they would be blowing ballast and adjusting the trim to run semi submerged at six metres, he reached over and for emphasis tapped the gauge at eye level marked '*Tiefenmesser,*' as he continued to speak to Leiter. Reinecke wanted it made absolutely clear that the boat would be running at a steady seven knots at a depth where the decks were only partially submerged just a metre below the surface. With only the conning tower exposed above the water with the waves washing over the casing, this would in effect be cutting the boat's visible silhouette down to a minimum so reducing the risk of detection from any vigilant eyes. This is a must, whilst maintaining an air flow from the outside to the crew and the diesel engines through the open hatch. A difficult undertaking normally in good weather, more hazardous with the present wave conditions at the surface.

Satisfied that Remischke had been given everything he needed to know at least for the next twenty minutes of the running the boat, Reinecke, putting his wet cap back on the crown of his head turned back to the centre of the command space, then through the open bulk head hatch making his way to the small curtained off section of his Kapitän's quarters across the companion way to the hydrophone and radio rooms. Perhaps he was being a little hard on his officers, Leiter and Remischke were not juveniles, with the other crew they were as a body all experienced and reliable good men, treating them with so little confidence was a result of the tensions he felt within himself. Reinecke knew this, yet he could not afford any uncertainty at this time, there was too much at stake. They must lie silent on the bottom for one more time during this last day, tensions would be high he knew this, yet this had to be done the die had been cast for this vital manoeuvre weeks ago, they had no choice, would have to endure this last test of nerves, to overcome their personal fears, he told himself not entirely convinced by his own attempts to quieten the devils of uncertainty nagging at his mind.

The next part was going to be difficult, the men he was going to speak with were not U-Boat crew, nor were they Kriegsmarine servicemen, they were from a much different arm of the German war machine and only subject under his command by a temporary agreement and then, only when the boat was at sea…

As he made his way forward, acknowledging each crewman as he went, Reinecke thoughts went back to that memorable day when he had been summoned to Rennes, where this voyage had really begun and when this fateful madness had really started to unfold into a nightmare.

4

St. Nazaire

December 28th, 1943

The sealed orders had been delivered to his commanding officer at the Lorient base where his U-boat was presently laid up undergoing an engine refit having returned with a bent main propeller shaft, had fouled a sunken wreck, on what had been otherwise a pointless uneventful patrol in the Bay of Biscay. The boat had needed extensive repairs and the crew were given an unheard of ten days' leave! With this incredible gift from the gods, a slice of the cake of good fortune, Reinecke had contemplated using this leave to journey home to his village of Österndorf, set in the beautiful Brixental, a valley in the alpine mountains of Northern Austria. However, the fates had played him a different unkind hand. Korvettenkapitän Müller, his flotilla commander, had summoned Reinecke immediately and with some urgency to attend him at his office base that morning.

On arrival at the headquarters base unit, Reinecke had made his way to Müller's office, and was greeted by the smartly uniformed female clerk who greeted him without even asking his name. 'Herr Korvettenkapitän Müller is expecting you Herr Kapitän Reinecke,' she knocked on the office door, announced his name and then held it open for Reinecke to enter, saying 'Please…' Then stepped aside for Reinecke to pass, she smiled then left closing the door behind her. Behind a large ornate antique desk in the former small French customs office a tall imposing figure rose to greet him. 'Ah, Reinecke, so glad you could come so quickly, do sit down.' Korvettenkapitän Piening, at thirty-eight years of age cut an impressive figure in his immaculate Kriegsmarine uniform, he was not wearing a cap so didn't demand the salute Reinecke was usually required to give. He was known for his brusque but efficient manner and got down to the business in hand immediately. 'I was asked, from the highest level I can tell you, to recommend an experienced officer and crew for a one-off mission. I chose you, not because you are my top scoring ace, but because you have the knack of getting the job done without the glory hunting that seems to affect so many of my U-boat commanders. Don't ask any questions Reinecke, I can't give you the answers. You are to leave, for Rennes, immediately. There is a car and driver waiting for you outside,' he stopped and looked at his watch, 'You will be there in three hours, you are expected, all I have for you is this,' he passed an envelope to Reinecke, 'Inside are your transport papers and orders for anyone who may stop you on route. You will not speak with anyone on the way, and don't try to quiz the driver, he has explicit instructions to deliver you to your destination in good order. Clear?'

Reinecke looked at the envelope in his hand, he noted with some alarm, written across in large bold red letters were the words, *'STRENG GEHEIME'* beneath was the stamp of the 'SS,' Schutz Staffel. 'Herr Korvettenkapitän…' He began and was abruptly stopped before he could utter another word with Müller quickly raising his hand. 'I've told you Reinecke, I can tell you nothing, and yes, as you have already noticed, this is not the business of the Kriegsmarine, you have been summoned by the offices of the SS, that's all I know. If it is any small consolation, it's not because you are in any trouble, your services are needed. Now, on your way and good luck to you whatever this is about.' Müller, reached over and briefly shook Reinecke's hand and making it clear that was the end of the discussion as he sat back in his chair.

Reinecke walked down the steps from customs office the building, sure enough a civilian Renault car was parked at the foot of the stairs with an SS corporal holding the door open, as Reinecke approached he saluted, an army salute oddly not the Nazi straight arm as would normally be expected, Reinecke returned the salute and took his place in the rear of the vehicle. With no conversation or small talk the driver drove off, then with some obvious skills and avoiding the military traffic wound the car through back streets then on negotiating the roads out of St. Nazaire heading eastwards in the main direction towards to Rennes.

It was a long, tedious but uneventful journey with frequent detours along quiet back roads broken only when the driver halted the vehicle under trees when he assumed what were potentially hostile aircraft detected in the grey skies overhead. They had arrived in the early evening with light beginning to fade, the car driven up to the front steps of an impressive chateau in a wood covered estate Reinecke guessed they must be still a kilometre or two outside Rennes. The driver jumped out and smartly opened the door for Reinecke, saluted crisply saying, 'I will be waiting for you when you need me Herr. Kaleu.' He then without another word drove the car away leaving Reinecke alone to mount the steps to where SS black-uniformed guards stood either side of the entrance. Reinecke presented his papers and was marched into the wide imposing entrance hall of the chateau to a desk where two uniformed female attendants were seated. Again he presented his paperwork and the senior attendant reached across and pressed a button on her desk, almost immediately a door to his right opened and an adjutant NCO with the rank of Oberscharfuhrer appeared, after a glance at Reinecke's papers he gave a curt salute nodded and said, 'You are expected Herr Kaleu, please follow me…' Reinecke walked after the NCO, whose boots clicking methodically on the polished wooden floor echoed leading him along a series of dark corridors until coming to a halt outside a massive set of polished oak double doors. He knocked once, went inside to appear moments later beckoning Reinecke into the chamber beyond. Whatever Reinecke had imagined he might expect to lay within, that which was to greet his eyes was a colourful surprise. A large green leather topped desk stood in the middle of the high-ceilinged room, in front two deep red leather padded chairs with a matching generously proportioned sofa standing a little further back. The last light from the late evening sun filtered in through two sets of French doors leading to a garden terrace, high above an ornate candelabra hung from its elaborate ceiling brass fixture, a large detailed coloured map of Europe covered most of one wall. In front of a near two-metre-high ornamental stone fireplace, stood a tall bare headed man with neatly trimmed white curly hair wearing a grey green field uniform. Reinecke took in the oak leaf clusters on the black collar tabs of the uniform, those of a Gruppenfuhrer of the SS (or Leutnant General), he stood warming his hands behind him, his back to the open fire. He looked up as Reinecke entered preparing the obligatory salute.

'Ah, my dear Reinecke, don't bother with that, 'he waved away Reinecke's hand held at the brim of his white crowned Kriegsmarine peaked cap, 'so very pleased to see you, no formalities here please, do come in,' he strode over and shook Reinecke's hand with a slow but firm grip. 'My name is Konrad Leibnitz, and, as I'm sure that you can already have noticed, my rank is that of Gruppenfuhrer.' Reinecke, stunned at the lack of formality removed his cap and placed it under his arm and stood at ease. Leibnitz animated with a shrug of impatience didn't wait for a response and hurried on. 'Now… here… Reinecke, make yourself comfortable,' he added sincerely assuming a pleasant even affable manner pointing to a deep red leathered button cushioned armchair in front of the desk, 'A drink perhaps to warm you up after your journey, cognac perhaps?' He asked while making his way to a well-stocked open ornate cocktail cabinet set at the side of the room. Reinecke, his thoughts still in a state of bemused curiosity noted that there had been no offer of permission to smoke and at this point, would dearly have welcomed a cigarette rather than alcohol. Leibnitz's voice and tone sounded genuinely welcoming, friendly even, at odds with the uniform which he wore and the vast gap between their individual ranks. The man's beaming face was reminiscent of a favourite rustic uncle, with his short grey hair over ruddy weathered features. Reinecke, still harbouring the feelings of uneasiness at what was to come next, gazed at his immaculately turned out host, sharply contrasting with his own grubby appearance, he was conscious of the stubble adorning his own cheeks whilst the other's skin had the sheen of polish which only comes from a whetted razor. He thought him to be in his mid to late fifties at least yet with the trim figure of an athlete.

Reinecke accepted the offered seat and sitting down at the same time unbuttoning his Kriegsmarine overcoat. Liebnitz returned and proffered a large brandy balloon with a generous measure of mellow liquid filling the bowl of the glass. Reinecke looked up at the older man, waiting for him to begin to speak first as by now his senses were struggling to comprehend what could possibly be the reason or cause for him being summoned to the presence of such a high ranking officer of the SS…? The older man seated himself comfortably behind his desk, smiling sympathetically at Reinecke's discomfort, his puzzled expression suggested with some degree of accuracy his feelings of trepidation, 'My dear Reinecke, judging by your looks, you've probably spent the last few hours trying to understand for what reason or purpose you have been ordered here, you haven't the remotest idea have you?' He halted a moment indicating Reinecke's untouched glass. 'Here now, drink your cognac, it's one of the few luxuries I have been able to lay my hands on here, what do you think of the quality?'

'It's very good Sir,' Reinecke said quietly, swilling the cognac warming around the glass with the heat of hid hand before sipping at the amber liquid, 'but you are right Herr Gruppenfuhrer, I am at a loss, to understand why I am here, I'm U-boat personnel, what could the SS possibly want with me?'

Leibnitz leaned against the desk, his face taking on a serious look, the mood changing somewhat abruptly, then, with slow and precisely modulated words he began. 'Good! I am relieved to hear that you have been held in a state of blissful ignorance, it's far better that way or indeed for the most part of this mission that you remain so,' Leibnitz look became more fixed, 'You, and I, for my part too, have become players in a little scheme dreamed up by certain parties at offices of the Reichfuhrer, with the sanction of my '*boss*' you might say. In some sense you may be given to rightly consider that we are each a game piece being played upon a larger board than we at our level, can either understand or truly comprehend at this time.' Leibnitz metred out the next words with the same deliberation. 'What this fascinating intrigue involves in the most simplest of terms, my dear Reinecke, is that what we may refer to as a very special consignment of goods needs to be delivered to a clandestine destination, the 'which' and the 'where' of this will become clearly apparent to you later. A what we have been given charge over is an especially important cargo indeed, with the highest degree of security surrounding both its contents and its ultimate destination. The safeguarding of these goods and their valuable contents and nature is down to me, the delivery of these precious articles, it has been strongly suggested, could be entrusted to your safe keeping!' Leibnitz leant across and tapped a buff folder on the desk before him with a red diagonal stripe across the front,' Here is your dossier Reinecke, and including those of your men. You were selected for having a history of a cool calculating mind rather than a foolhardy glory hunter as so many of your fellow commanders have proven to be. No, there was some suggestion of your being, shall we say, less than enthusiastic regarding your recent missions, a little too timid or cautious according to one source? However, on balance with the particular requirements of what is to be attempted, here we will look at your historical successes in conserving the lives of your men and that of your command with clear thinking, we will concentrate on those sterling aspects of your reputation for getting your given assignments successfully completed with little needless risk. In this case, specifically important in this one I am offering you, that these attributes and skills are considered as highly desirable, this is why you are sitting here today Reinecke.

There was a momentary heavily pregnant pause before Leibnitz, drawing a deep breath continued. This novel assignment then, and your so-called cargo Reinecke, its method and means of delivery, whole and intact, is to effected by you with your boat as both the means and the vector, for the conveyance and the perilous but necessary sea voyage of getting it where it must finally arrive. This, I must emphasise, is to be carried out with both the minimum degree of detection and any possible risk to your mission, as to what you will carry, these demand the utmost degree of maximum secrecy with a 'needs to know only,' clearly stamped upon the mind of every individual involved, at every step of the way.' Leibnitz smiled briefly before continuing, 'In essence you are to take on the role of a smuggler of old, brave the elements and the excise men to bring your contraband ashore. There is here a temptation perhaps to imagine the romanticisms of an English novel, hero with his piratical craft, however, what we are ordered to bring about, the part you are being asked to play, is critically and deadly serious. It may, indeed if it is successful, influence and change the lives of hundreds of thousands of people for many years to come. If it fails then it may see you and your precious cargo of goods consigned to the bottom of the sea, failure is not therefore an option to contemplate. Do I make myself perfectly clear Reinecke before we go on?' He then sat himself back behind the desk, leant back in his chair, sipping his own cognac, allowing his words to take effect whilst taking careful note of Reinecke's every expression and his reaction.

Reinecke took his time before answering, a host of questions were already urgently forming in his mind. He gazed too wondering at the contents of the dossier-file on the general's desk, 'I'm not sure how I can make any valid comment Herr Gruppenfuhrer, without knowing what this mission entails or involves, what is to be expected of me and of my men…'

Leibnitz nodded, 'Quite right, then let's make things a little clearer for you.' As he said the words, he cleared the two-metre-long desk in front of him and reached behind his chair produced a leather map case of large proportions. Extracting two large charts he unfolded these and placed them upon the desk spreading each out with his hands, weighting the corners with a heavy glass ashtray and the brass inkwell on the desk. 'Here, Reinecke, I need your expert opinion on setting the course this projected voyage that you and your boat are to take…'

The two charts were laid one on top of the other, Reinecke stood glass in hand went over to stand before the desk noting immediately the legend in the top margins of the first chart, '*British Admiralty*' the chart itself being a large scale nautical map of the Western English Channel with depth soundings and navigational marking for shipping, it included the coastal area off St. Nazaire. Leibnitz stated, 'Obviously this is where your present base lies, and where you will commence your journey, now here, this is more problematic…' He lifted away the first chart and underneath revealed another Admiralty chart, this one being of a southern section of the Irish Sea, the Isle of Man and the western coastline of Britain the part he then pointed to being the waters off the uneven of coast of Wales. Both men stared intently at the chart, then Leibnitz reached again into the map case bringing out a large brown envelope, 'These are a fairly recent series of high level aerial photographs, courtesy of the Luftwaffe, this gives pictorial imagery to your eventual landfall site what is obviously an enemy coastline.' The three photographs were a little grainy showing a three fingered like projections into the sea from a rocky headland. Leibnitz turned back to the second chart, 'See, you can see how these reflect the outline on the chart, it also shows a concrete installation of some kind, we believe it may be an aircraft radar warning station but the intelligence is limited.'

Reinecke pored over the photographs, then the chart, 'And what are these…?' He said pointing to two red coloured cross markings penned at points where the coast met the sea on both the photographs and on the chart.

Leibnitz leant over the chart, 'Here, and here these are lighthouse stations, we do have good reliable intelligence that these are only activated when the Tommies are expecting shipping which too valuable to lose on the rocks, so they only illuminate at set times when notified there is sea traffic crossing their paths. The northern most, 'South Stack' protects the shipping lanes here, 'He said pointing to the sea off Holyhead mountain and the Isle of Man, the second and the more important as far as you are concerned is here, the '*Würm,*' this is a headland running north westerly for three and a half kilometres out into the bay as you can see, these features are limestone cliffs nearly two hundred metres high above the shallow waters on the approach, however, at the location where your vessel is to touch land at your projected landfall site, the covering cliff face above rises just a hundred metres above sea level.

'I need to know what your thinking is on how this can be done, as you can see an exploratory course has already been plotted out of your base at St. Nazaire into the waters of the approaches to the channel, then north eastwards to off the coast of Ireland where it then follows an eastwards line to here…' He jabbed a finger again at an island off the coast of North Wales. 'This is the island of Mona; the set course rounds the northern tip of the island before continuing to this point.' He again pointed the finger, this time at a headland reaching out into the Liverpool Bay, this as given in the photograph detail, is your target destination Reinecke…'

Reinecke took in the pencilled red line of the outlined course and bent over the chart tracing the path with his own fingers, it was the course a weekend sailor might have plotted, rudimentary and basic with no little consideration for a submerged vessel. 'Herr Gruppenfuhrer, if we tried to follow this course setting, we wouldn't survive the first day! No, we need to rethink here not the most direct of routes, but the one that is navigable part on the surface and part submerged. Look, these lines give the depths between the coast of Ireland and that of Britain, here, in the middle we have perhaps one hundred and twenty metres, near this coastal area,' he pointed to Wales, 'The sea bed here shelves into depths of around only twenty metres, this is shallow water for a U-boat, this we need to keep in mind when plotting the course, running in darkness on the surface where possible to conserve fuel, lying submerged in shallow water during day light hours between navigational points, here, here and here…' Reinecke sketched a course across the chart that bore little resemblance to the original red line. 'We would need to calculate the distances between each point to allow for fuel consumption, for how far we could run on the surface at a comfortable ten knots to conserve resources and then to get us there submerged for the final run into the location you have marked here, and, it must be done during a no moon period, darkness here will be a valuable ally. There is some work to be done on this if it is to be given a fair chance of success Herr Gruppenfuhrer, and that is without taking the presence of the Tommies in their own waters into the equation.' Reinecke rose and stood back from the charts.

Leibnitz rested his elbows on the desk cupping his chin in one hand with the other resting under his elbow his fingers framing his mouth in thought, 'Of course you are right Reinecke, I would not have expected you to have accepted this original course, in fact I would have been deeply disappointed if you had been too accommodating for what was so obviously a naïvely considered scheme of approach. You must forgive me Reinecke, in a short while I must temporarily excuse myself. I have an important meeting scheduled in a few minutes, a discussion over early dinner with my staff officer, this I can't cancel, however, there is a sense of immediate urgency about actioning this matter expediently and with as little delay as is possible, 'he indicated towards the open charts, 'I need to hear what you have to say and how we can cooperate our thinking, there isn't a great deal of time before the date set to perform this minor this… shall we say, miracle? Now, what do you need from me to make this work?' Leibnitz looked expectantly at Reinecke, then down at his watch.

'Some thinking time, a slide rule, these charts and some paper Herr Gruppenfuhrer, give me at least a couple of hours to outline just for the rudimentary basics at this stage, then, when I've found a better solution, I can tell you more of what I think.' Reinecke was feeling at some ease at this moment, in his own element of taking into account the projected routes, the tides and currents in the waters of the Irish seas, in the recent past he had some earned some hard won hair raising experiences of running the gauntlet of British warships in the *Irish Lake.* 'Good advance planning was a vital asset to any such dangerous navigation, the ability to adapt, at a moment's notice to unforeseen deviations from set plans being an absolute must.

Liebnitz stood and rand the bell on the wall behind his desk, 'Take as long as you need Reinecke, I'm going to leave you alone in here to do your calculations. I will have coffee and something to eat brought to you. Shall we meet again at say nine later tonight for an update? And I will want to introduce you to your passengers for the voyage.'

'Passengers…?' Reinecke began to reply but was stopped by a curt wave of the hand.

'Later Reinecke, let me know if there's anything you need, Oberscharfuhrer Hartmann, whom you met earlier, he will be stationed outside this door at all times, if you need anything just ask. Until later then…' Leibnitz left the room closing the door after him.

Reinecke took off his hat, removed his coat unbuttoned his uniform jacket easing into the comfortable chair. Within minutes Hartmann appeared with everything Reinecke had requested and more… Seating himself at Leibnitz's desk he, looked around taking in his surroundings, it was really rather plain with no personalised ornaments or decorations apart from the wall map, old antique furnishings, all functional, no personal touch here, he mused. Reinecke smiled to himself at this twist of fate, at the incongruity of the impossible and ridiculous situation he now found himself part of. Sitting here with all manner of comfort while the world outside was so busy tearing itself apart, seated at the desk of a Gruppenfuhrer of the SS with refreshments on demand, it must be a dream, or a nightmare perhaps and one he couldn't seem to wake from!

After a brief pause to collect his thoughts, Reinecke settled down in the chair, if it was a dream he thought then he would play along with it enjoy the moment, then biting into a sandwich savouring the taste of the strong French cheese reminded himself that in a dream, there is no sense of taste… Turning to the photographs, charts and note paper provided staring stark and blank on the desk before him, he picked up a pen and began to focus his attention on the works needed on the charts.

It was just after nine when Leibnitz reappeared, he appeared quite relaxed as he came through the door straightening his uniform jacket. 'Ah, Reinecke, how goes it, have you made any progress?' He said making his way to stand beside the chair where Reinecke had risen to attention when the door opened. 'Sit down, sit down, has Hartmann looked after you?' He waved away the salute Reinecke had automatically given, then pointed to the remains of Reinecke's supper.

Reinecke resumed his seat, 'He has, I have been well looked after Herr Gruppenfuhrer.

'Then what have you been able to put together, I want the truth, can this be done?' There was an edge to his voice, his face was serious now with the genial smile for the moment disappearing.

'It can I believe Herr Gruppenfuhrer, though I don't know what we will be carrying so I have concentrated upon the logistics of sailing from St. Nazaire to the target area in the Irish Sea. Based on what you have given me on the charts and bearing in mind the presence of hostile units of the Royal Navy and their air force, this is what I have as a very basic projection of how this could be achieved.' Reinecke replaced the to chart on the desk, 'From the point of embarking at St. Nazaire to the landfall we envisage will need the voyage to be carried out in stages, lying on the bottom during the day, then maximum running at night. To achieve this we would need to take a series of dog leg routes for most of the journey, from here, to here, then to here then here,' he pointed to each location in turn on the chart. These would be subject to adaptations depending on what we find when we are at sea.' Reinecke looked up to see if Leibnitz's look was one of approval.

'That is an improvement, but you have extended the times between navigational points, is this adding to your overall sailing time…?'

'It is, though this is absolutely necessary if we are to avoid the 'hot spots' where both surface vessels and aircraft patrol will be concentrated, this course will take a little longer but is a safer route to take.' Again,

Reinecke awaited approval before continuing.

'Then how long will you be at sea, if this is to be done well it must be clearly evident from what is required from you will be that the landfall must be accomplished at night, under cover of darkness during a no moon period, how will this affect your figures?' Leibnitz pointed to the proposed route Reinecke had outlined.

'Then this is what I suggest Herr Gruppenfuhrer, we sail under the cover of darkness, we will cover a maximum estimated in total one thousand seven hundred and twenty kilometres to the target area. This includes the laying on the bottom for as long as is possible during the day before surfacing to recharge the batteries. My estimate of the journey time has to be here an approximation, therefore I am looking at a minimum of seventy-two hours with a margin of a further ten depending upon the weather conditions and the currents,' Reinecke sitting back added, 'This has to be only an a considered estimate, we would need to sit down with a great deal more care to look at the final logistics, fuel oil also has to be taken into consideration with enough reserves for deviations if they occur, I will want to bring my boat and my officers and men home in one piece when this is over Herr Gruppenfuhrer, for us this cannot be a one way journey.'

Leibnitz looked again at the map and asking to see Reinecke's handwritten notes, 'These are impressive at such short notice, you are to be congratulated Reinecke...'

Reinecke broke in, 'I can't own any original thoughts for this Herr Gruppenfuhrer, these strategies were employed by Korvettenkapitän Gunther Prien back in 1939, a memorable mission when he infiltrated Scapa Flow with U-47 and sank a British capital ship, the Royal Oak. His book, *"Mein Weg nach Scapa Flow"* is a standard reading manual for all U-boat personnel...'

'And modesty too Reinecke,' beamed Leibnitz, 'I remember Prien, he was presented to the Fuhrer for his remarkable achievements, awarded the oak leaves to his knight's cross too, however, while we may have a different mission, this one might be considered as even more important in the current climate of things. Then we needed heroes and an old British battleship was fine at that time, now we are beginning to think more of survival,' Leibnitz shook his head then hurried on. 'So, you will cover the sea voyage in four days putting some estimated near thousand and eight hundred kilometres under your keel on the outward-bound journey. Then we need to get down to work beginning tomorrow to refine your draft ideas and come up with some specific figures. Now my dear Reinecke, I want to introduce you to your two companions on this voyage, I have waiting in the ante room, Sturmbannfuhrer Jurgen Breitfeld and Hauptsturmfuhrer Max Schumann, I think that the three of you are going to get along fine…!'

Leibnitz did not wait for any reply from Reinecke, walking across the room opening the door he called to the orderly standing patiently outside, 'Hartmann, kindly fetch Herr Kapitän Reinecke's guests and bring me another bottle of the good cognac from my quarters.' Turning back to Reinecke he said, 'Don't judge these books by their covers Reinecke, they, like yourself have been selected for their skills and expertise in their individual fields of experience and specialism.' He moved back to his desk and sat down heavily, 'This could be a long night ahead of us Reinecke, 'Please feel free to smoke is you wish, you may find these useful,' he smiled as he pulled from the desk drawer a carved wooden cigarette box, pushed the same and the ashtray across the desk in Reinecke's direction, 'The cigarettes you may find to your taste, they are American liberated when one of their transport aircraft came down last week, in Italy. The local security commander is an old friend of mine and sent me three cartons for my birthday…!'

Reinecke reached to the box opened it finding inside a number of crush packs of the American Lucky Strike brand, 'Help yourself, … take a packet, you may need them for later.' Leibnitz said nodding towards the box and its contents. Reinecke did as he was bid, opened a packet, savouring the smell of the American toasted tobacco, extracting and putting a filtered cigarette to his lips, flicking his lighter open lit it and inhaled the smoke deeply. It was a luxury unlike the rubbish issue provided for the German servicemen.

In a very short time Hartmann reappeared having knocked on the door, entered leading two men into room, 'Mein Herrn, Breitfeld und Schumann, Herr Gruppenfuhrer…'

Reinecke rose from his chair while Leibnitz indicated to the leather sofa to the two newcomers, 'Gentlemen, please be seated, may I introduce to you Kapitän Bruno Reinecke of the Kriegsmarine, I believe that I have told you about him so it will be good for you to at last meet him in the flesh…'

Before the two men sat, Reinecke shook hands with each taking his time in turn to take in the two individuals and their bearing. These were not what he had expected, in his imagination he had already formed the likely picture of two daunting stalwarts of the elite SS, black-uniformed, formally correct and at least two metres tall. The reality was in fact far removed from this image of superior examples of the Reich's finest manhood. The taller man, Breitfeld, was about the right height for the SS stereotype, dressed in a grey casual suit, yet however, with thin receding hair he resembled more the looks of a university professor. 'This is Sturmbannfuhrer Jurgen Breitfeld of Amt V1a foreign section, our expert in clandestine things and intelligence.' The man did not smile just raised his eyebrows in a condescending manner, his face remaining a pale mask devoid of any warmth or emotion, 'Kapitänleutnant Reinecke, we have heard a great deal about you.' The handshake was a touch rather than a grip of hands.

'And this is Hauptsturmfuhrer Max Schumann who comes to us from the RSHA in Berlin no less, who has exceptional talents in the world of economics and international finances and Reich economy, is not that so Schumann?' Schumann smiled and nodded, he stood a head shorter than his companion, again it was a stretch of the imagination to picture him in the black garb of the SS, his frame, though slim was not that of the muscular asphalt soldier. Short dark hair with a complexion that looked as if it had not seen the sun for a while, dressed in a lounge jacket and matching well cut trousers appeared as if he were ready to go to his club rather than any serious meeting of minds… However, both men's handshakes were markedly varied, whilst Breitfeld's had been effete and limp so Schumann's had been firm and powerful, with each of the owners stares unflinchingly holding Reinecke's eyes as they were introduced. The introductions over the two SS men seated themselves on the leather couch, Reinecke turned his chair and Leibnitz began to run through what was to be done. Even as they were speaking, he went on adding further, 'Both Herr Breitfeld and Herr Schumann have excellent command of the English language, both are accomplished fluent speakers with Herr Breitfeld being an Oxford graduate. The U-367, your boat, is receiving some modifications for the voyage, stores and provisions will be reaching St. Nazaire before the end of this week, the 'consignment' itself will leave from here under SS escort with Herr Breitfeld and Herr Schumann in charge to oversee the safe delivery to the U-boot base. Once there they will be loaded on under their personal supervision.

Reinecke's curiosity was aroused, when the two newcomers had been presented, no salutes had been exchanged nor did they appear to be expected, during the exchanges which had followed neither of the men had deferred to Leibnitz rank, despite his superiority, Why? Leibnitz himself tending to direct his dialogue in a matter of fact almost too familiar a manner, again, why? The only explanation which would seem logical was that given each man's specialism, then they could have been given nominal SS ranks appropriate to their roles purely for this operation? The RSHA was filled with grey sinister corners where figures of intrigue and espionage lurked finding fertile minds to dream up the widest of hair-brained schemes for their masters. He would return to this irksome question many times in the days to come.

Leibnitz, unperturbed ensuring each member of his captive audience was supplied with generous measures of the rare cognac Hartmann had brought along with his 'guests,' There followed, with each nursing their glass of amber fluid, a detailed discussion of the arrangements which had been made to receive them at their destination, Reinecke was surprised to hear that there was to be an Irish element to the operation, 'That, my dear Reinecke is our insurance, out plan B already worked out in advance should there be any unforeseen difficulties with the intended destination.' Leibnitz continued stating that they would each be given sealed orders before setting out from St. Nazaire, these to be opened only once they were at sea and not before. Reinecke asked about the destination landfall their reception, those who they were to meet them and what assistance they would be expected to give to the mission? Leibnitz leaned forward in his chair, then in a conspiratorial manner added, 'Ah, now this you may find surprising, it's not only the Irish who have a grudge against the English, the men meeting you are also of Celtic origin who have several hundreds of years resisting their English oppressors, they are of the Welsh Reinecke, a hardy people…'

Reinecke's thinking was momentarily stunned, confounded by this last statement, unable to resist the temptation to ask what appeared an obvious question he blurted out, 'The Welsh Herr Gruppenfuhrer…? Are these people to be considered at all reliable, I'm not sure I have even heard of their antagonism to the English before, they are neighbours surely, they share the same island…!'

Leibnitz's face became deadly serious, 'You know Reinecke, you have tended to underestimate what our intelligence services can do. These are the patriots of an oppressed people, there are those amongst them that who had made overtures to us before hostilities began with

England, they, like their Irish counterparts have been seeking separation from the government ruling from London for a long time, for them this is a chance to hit back in a common cause…'

Reinecke was becoming more concerned as each stage of the details were laid out, at the same time a tiredness crept over him, his concentration beginning to drift despite the gravity of the moment, 'This is foolish surely, to rely upon these… untried people… who on inspection, may be just a band of radicals… this reliance… for so important a mission…?' This was then to be the composition of their reception committee, a band of unknowns with dubious motivations, Reinecke groaned inwardly as another problematic facet of the practicalities began to shape unpleasantly in his mind. Yet, to challenge the wisdom of the gods of the RHSA would be considered a sacrilege.

Leibnitz stopped him, glancing at Reinecke's face then looking at his watch he said, 'Gentlemen, it's after 01.00hrs, I'm going to suggest we continue this conversation in the morning when we are all refreshed, shall we say a briefing then at 09.00hrs? Excellent, then I wish you pleasant dreams, we have much to do tomorrow, zero hour for your mission begins in five days time… Goodnight…!' Without saying more Leibnitz called for Hartmann, who came in to take each of the three men to lead them to their respective rooms.

Next morning, less than six hours had elapsed when Reinecke was woken by the orderly Hartmann's soft knocking at the door of his room, he called for him to enter and Hartmann came in carrying with him a tray furnished with a tall coffee jug and cup, under his arm was a brown paper bundle, setting both down on the dressing table near to the window, 'The Herr Gruppenfuhrer thought as you have no luggage these would make you more comfortable. I am to remind you your meeting is in forty-five minutes Herr Kapitän…' Then as quietly as he had entered, he withdrew. For a few moments Reinecke speculated whether the man could be related in any way to the Hartmann his engineering officer on the U-367? Then no, this man had no sense of humour where Heini was good company, even in bad weather. Reinecke reached for his uniform trousers, slipped these on then inspected the parcel. It was a set of new officer's white issue vest and under shorts, he laughed, even in these circumstances the SS were so particular about personal hygiene that they touchingly had gone to these extraordinary lengths for his comfort.

Showered and spruced up in his newly provided under wear, he was back downstairs to join the others at 08.300 for a light breakfast in the room they had occupied the evening before.

Leibnitz wasted no time in getting started and they gathered around his desk poring first over the maps and photographs then the lists of logistical notes for undertaking the cruise to their landfall on the enemy occupied coast of Wales. By the afternoon Leibnitz appeared satisfied that each knew their role for the cruise part of the voyage to their destination. Reinecke's calculations formulated their planning would see that after loading and preparation, the U-367 would sail under cover of darkness on the evening tide from St. Nazaire 16.30hrs on the night of the Monday 3rd January 1944, a no moon period.

Reinecke had pinpointed the specific locations on the chart to show his intended course with circles drawn with the latitude and longitude references with the approximate time of arrival at each stage. Nominally they would be outward bound on a night passage, mainly be running at a maximum speed on the surface of around 17 knots, sea and tide allowing for deviations, maintaining speed through the hours of darkness, at this time of year this being between 16.30 hrs until 08.00 the following morning. The crew and passengers would rest up mostly during part of the day when Reinecke intended to lie on the bottom submerged, before surfacing they would run at periscope depth at about 16 metres cruising at 7 knots to eat up some of the distance to be covered below the surface. This, if all went according to plan, would see them off their landfall at the end of the day after four nights at sea.

There seemed to be little more to be said regarding the planning for the sea voyage, Reinecke had one important thing on his mind, 'Who, Herr Gruppenfuhrer, is to be in overall command of this mission?'

Leibnitz looked up from the chart, 'At sea Reinecke, it's you naturally, you know what you are doing with your vessel, your role is to plan and execute the sailing effectively to ensure safe arrival. Then, once on land for stage two of the mission, then this falls Sturmbannfuhrer Breitfeld, once the landfall has been achieved then his authority is absolute, do I make myself perfectly clear, there must be no squabbles about command, this has to be understood, nothing is to be allowed to jeopardise the mission in any way...?'

Reinecke had some misgivings about this but saw little point in raising them as a debate, the orders were already set in stone, he would get them there in good order, then when his part was over, he would bring both his boat and his crew home as safely as he possibly could.

The rest, the part he was not privy to, was up to Breitfeld, Schumann and who ever their associates were to pull off their part of the mission whatever that may entail…

'And now gentlemen, I expect you have been wondering what your precious cargo looks like, yes…?' he looked from one to the other like an expectant teacher who had just posed his math class a puzzle, 'Well, now follow me please…' Beaming he led the way to another similar sized room in the same corridor, armed sentries stood either side jerking to attention as Leibnitz drew near, he withdrew a bunch of keys from his pocket and inserted two into locks set one above the other, with a flourish he threw the door open, Gentlemen, please…!'

They stood quietly in the half light as Leibnitz closed the door behind them then turned on the light switch, the room was suddenly brilliantly illuminated. The one window had a grille of steel bars across set into the stonework. In the middle of the floor a green canvass sheet covered a mound about four metres in length and a metre in height, walking around the covered mound Reinecke estimated another metre in width… a long regular shaped oblong? Leibnitz put his hands on his hips, 'So, gentlemen, here is your treasure for transportation, now…,' he picked up a corner of the canvass and pulled it aside revealing two lines of uniformly crafted sturdy crates two crates deep some twelve in total. Each crate measured a metre in length, forty or so centimetres in depth and similar in width, Reinecke immediately thought of the exact similar kind of wooden cases K98 military rifles were packed in for transport, each having a rope handle at either end. Unusually there were no visible letter marking to be seen, only a number stencilled in black on the corner of each, numbering one to twelve. To him they were rather reminiscent of small coffins…

Reinecke and the two SS men waited in silence, was Leibnitz going to disclose whatever was contained within or were they just to stand and contemplate, 'Herr Gruppenfuhrer, are we permitted to ask what these contain, they could be anything, art treasures perhaps…?' Reinecke quietly enquired.

'No, no you are not permitted, art treasures rest assured, have already been removed by Herr Goering, no, Breitfeld is the only person authorised to have the inventory of contents, in this my dear Reinecke you do not have a bill of lading for your cargo, officially… it does not exist!'

Reinecke reached for one of the rope handles and tugged tentatively, 'I will need to know the weight for when we take these on board, unlike a surface ship every kilogramme needs to be carefully spread out and balanced so that it doesn't alter the trim when we are submerged Herr Gruppenfuhrer.'

Liebnitz agreed nodding his head, 'You are quite right, at the dockside you will be given a copy of the weight manifest only for each crate, no two are alike or of the same weight, contents or packing, as this is a needs to know vital detail so here you must work closely with Breitfeld. One of the adjustments being made to your vessel is the unloading of your reload torpedoes, you will sail with only the those already loaded in the forward torpedo tubes, this will more than compensate for the weight of your cargo when it is loaded on board.'

Reinecke looked aghast, they would reduce the boats fighting ability, the loss of all of the reload torpedoes would leave them defenceless once the loaded tubes had been fired, 'I must protest Herr Gruppenfuhrer, if we lose these we lose the ability to retaliate if we are attacked, the cargo and the lives of all will be needlessly compromised. There is space in the bow torpedo room without stripping us of our fighting potential…'

Leibnitz considered Reinecke's statement, there was an element of truth in what he had said, if the weapons were needed to protect the cargo rather than excess baggage it might pose a problem if he were questioned about this point at a later date. 'A fair point Reinecke, then we will compromise, losing you only half of your reloads and their weight, this should strengthen your resolve in keeping well clear and out of any physical contact with any hostile enemy units you may encounter. Now gentlemen, we return to the charts for a final check. After which, Reinecke will be leaving us for St. Nazaire, I'm sure you are anxious to be back with your men for a secure briefing of their impending excursion in the Irish sea. I think gentlemen, time dinner we've all worked up an appetite.'

Dinner…? Reinecke didn't feel like dinner at all, as a matter of fact he felt a feeling of sickening nausea clenching at his intestines, this juggernaut of an operation was increasingly becoming fraught with one potential disaster after another rearing in his consciousness. The ill-will he had tried to suppress toward the two SS men resurfaced, neither of them had batted an eye when any significant question had been posed regarding the practical difficulties that they would encounter, he made a mental note to be wary of both men until they and their cargo were delivered. Passengers in name and passengers in reality with no place on a U-boat at sea. He followed Leibnitz and the others back to the briefing room with a growing sense of trepidation. He felt a deep and all-consuming realisation that he had no control over the events which had caught him up so utterly in their madness, the events themselves had taken on a lives of their own which now was controlling both him and the lives of his crew, fate or destiny had begun to show its hand and he was helpless to change the chosen path in which it was leading.

The following morning Reinecke took his leave from Leibnitz on the steps of the chateau, as he shook Reinecke's hand the Gruppenfuhrer solemnly held the grasp for a moment, 'Make no mistake Reinecke, your mission is one of the utmost importance, what you carry if the equivalent to a Veltungswaffe except this has a more deep and profound effect than the explosive devices being dropped on London, those merely blew holes in the ground, damaged buildings indiscriminately killed people, this will dislocate the Allies thinking throwing out of gear their preparations for their second front and their ability to wage war for the foreseeable future. I'm not a man to fantasise nor to put my faith in false hopes, we all have known the seriousness of our current predicament at this time for some time, the Russians are pressing on our eastern borders, the Allies in North Africa and now Italy, nineteen forty-three was disastrous year for us, we need to buy time to regroup our forces if we are to survive at all in the next years of this conflict. There, my dear Reinecke, I have already spoken far too much, I, like you now, are the servants of the offices of the RSHA, what I have told you is in the highest of confidence, it is not to be shared with anyone, including your officers and men! If this adventure does not come off then the fewer people who know the implications, for now and in the long term future the better, the less knowledge you have of this may preserve your sanity, it has cost me mine I assure you. Your God go with Reinecke, don't fail. Aufwiedersehn ...' He turned and marched smartly back up the steps and was gone. Miraculously the same SS driver brought the tired old Renault car to meet him, within minutes, in silence once again, they were on their way returning on the road back to St. Nazaire with Reinecke deep in thought around the possible inferences and meanings Leibnitz had hinted with his final words.

5

The Irish Sea

Friday 7th to 8th January 1944

21.15hrs

Reinecke resumed his way forward through the control room, stopping briefly to check with steuermann controlling the boat's course and direction and the mechaniker in charge of the forward dive planes, satisfied he reached his cabin, drawing the curtain aside he looked down at Breitfeld and Schumann seated on his bunk. Both looked ill, Reinecke smiled inwardly, the green complexion of both men testified to their discomfort, in a weak moment of sadistic malice for their past arrogance during the voyage he jovially said, 'Greetings gentlemen, we are now less than an hour from our rendezvous with your friends, may I suggest you have something to eat before we dive for the initial approach, you may feel better with something in your stomachs...!' He surveyed the sorry sight the two men presented, both clad in stained thick naval type sweaters with thick trouser and sea boots, they were a parody of any semblance to Kriegsmarine sailors.

Breitfeld turned a sickly face towards Reinecke spitting out his words, 'Then I shall be relieved to get off this accursed pig boat Reinecke, it stinks like a sewer, no, no food, I can wait until we reach land.'

Schumann fared no better, there were marks on his sweater from his last bout of vomiting in the full bucket on the deck in front of him, he merely shook his head in agreement with Breitfeld, 'How long before we land Reinecke, I will want to check our cargo, you will need to give us some of the crew to lend a hand with the unloading...?'

Reinecke remembered four days previously when shortly after they had sailed and had dived for the first time, Schumann had tried to use the 'heads,' this despite being told that only buckets were to be used when the boat was submerged. The U-367 common to her V11C class had only two heads or toilets, one aft, next to the galley which was used mainly as a storage space for the extra food and necessities, the other forward head located the port side of the crew living quarters, this was the one Schumann had sneaked in to use. The blow back from the unequal water pressure when Schumann had operated the discharge handle had flooded the deck with effluence which oozed and slopped until it trickled into the bilges, the smell had been over powering and still lingered with the smell of sweat, cabbage and vomit pervading the entire boat much to the annoyance of the officers and men. To the U-boat men this had not been of great concern, these were the aromas peculiar to a submarine, to Breitfeld and Schumann it was hell perpetuating their discomfort many times over in the days which followed.

Their days at sea had been a torment, both men had been repeatedly seasick, when they had spent the day light hours submerged, on the three days when they had lain on the bottom a hundred metres deep in silence for nearly eight hours, they had moaned continually when the rest of the crew took the opportunity to try to get some rest, to sleep where ever they could. Neither Breitfeld or Schumann could comprehend why they were not allowed on the bridge in the evenings when they surfaced, to smoke! Reinecke had tried very hard to explain that if they met any trouble and had he had to give the order to 'crash dive,' then they would have only seconds to clear the bridge before they plunged beneath the waves. Breitfeld thought he, Reinecke, had made this up just to spite him, of this he was certain!

Reinecke continued advising the two men, keeping his disgust of both under control, 'Within the hour, I would suggest then that you both dress accordingly, we will have a period of smooth running when we submerge for a short while, when we surface again it will be rough and very cold, it's snowing up top and although the sea is calming for the present, it won't last long. If you have to check on the cargo then do so now, when we reach land the forward torpedo loading hatch will be used to bring the crates up on deck, if you haven't forgotten the order in which they were stowed on board then you will remember that they will be taken off in the exactly same order and sequence as was arranged Breitfeld…?'

Breitfeld had little to say, Schumann seemed keen to check one last time that the numbered sequence was scheduled in their dock side briefing in St. Nazaire, there under arc lights in the U-boat pen, Schumann and Breitfeld had overseen the loading of each crate, ticking off the numbers in Breitfeld's note book which he carried with him at all times. The contents of the crates had remained an insistent mystery guarded by the two, though Reinecke had observed that the SS soldiers of the escort when carrying the crates on board had struggled with the weight of at least two of the cases where the others, though exactly the same appeared to have far less bulk and were more manageable.

Reinecke pushed his cap back on his head, 'I'll be back with you and continue our discussion when we are on the final approach.' He threw a mock salute and made his way back into the control room, donning his sea clothes once again climbed up to the bridge.

'Kapitän on the bridge!' Shouted Oberleutnant Georg Leiter sur Zee, U-367's first officer made way for him as he took over command.

'Anything to report...?' Reinecke shouted back adjusting his binoculars around his neck sweeping the seas around them.

'Nothing Herr Kaleu, visibility is still down to a few metres though the sea is calming fast now, we're making a steady sixteen knots, fair to constant over the last hour.'

Reinecke took a last look around, 'Clear the bridge, take her down, periscope depth Georg, one third ahead both bring to her 5 degrees to port steady as she goes ring below.' As the last man down the metal rungs he mentally was counting off the seconds after having closing the conning tower hatch above him; he was satisfied with the twenty-seven seconds it had taken for the waves to wash over the steel decks and the boat begin to glide like serpent beneath the surface. Below, in the engine room, Hartmann engaged the main engine clutch throwing the lever which switched the engines over from diesel to electric power. A relative silence descended, the clatter and roar of the diesels replaced by the hum of the two battery driven motors as they engaged on either side of the hull. Power for the boat's propellers now coming from the electric motor room one bulkhead back astern of the diesel motor room. Hartmann wasted no time in getting to work with his men on maintenance work on the diesel engines, metres away the six men now running the electric motors bent to their tasks. At the foot of the bridge ladder Reinecke looked around the expectant faces of the officers and men crowed in the confined space of the control room. 'Right gentlemen, we are closing with our destination, if you want refreshments, ask Pöhl to serve them at your stations, otherwise I want silence throughout the boat we are now in Tommy's back yard from now on, let's hope he's tucked up in bed...!' There was an obedient chorus of laughter then each man returned to his duties.

Reinecke looked down at the marine chronometer in its polished wooden case, the words 'CHRONOMETER HAMBURG' in brass on its face, the time reading 20.30hrs, he checked the reading against his watch assuring himself it was set to synchronise with English maritime reading, the unthinkable possibility of arriving in the right place at the wrong time had already occurred to him. Bracing himself against the central column he ordered, 'Up periscope' moving to the shaft of the 'sky' telescope as it began to rise through the deck housing, fixing his cap on the back of his head he grasped the handles as the periscope shaft slid smoothly into position, Reinecke calling, 'Red lighting in the boat…' the control room lighting switched down into an eerie red glow.

Swinging the view finder through a full 360o arc the horizons showed little other than the steady snow flurries and waves washing against the periscope lens, visibility poor, down to a few metres, they would have to rely on instruments for accurate navigating. Reinecke continued with his vigil for twenty-five minutes on this heading repeatedly issuing a stream of calls to the navigating officer and sonar man for updates.

'Bearing…?'

'South by south east, heading on one hundred and eighty-five degrees, Herr Kaleu!'

'Depth sounding…?'

'Forty-five metres under the keel decreasing Herr Kaleu!'

'Contacts…?'

'Contacts clear, nothing showing Herr Kaleu!'

'Speed…?'

'Seven and a half knots Herr Kaleu…'

Reinecke snapped closed the periscope handles, he had made his decision, 'Take her up to seven metres, standby watch crew for the bridge.'

The U-367s conning tower broke the surface of the water, disappeared then broke again to run with only the top two three metres showing above the waves. The bridge grew taking up their watch positions with Reinecke and Leiter taking station side by side. 'The next bit is going to be interesting Georg, if the Tommies don't get us then their rocks may feel patriotic and sink us for fun...!'

Leiter wasn't so sure it would be that simple, they were heading towards a land mass they couldn't see in relatively too shallow water for a submarine to freely manoeuvre with any true flexibility, a crash dive if ordered, would see their nose dig into the sea bed, a minor miscalculation in heading would bring them onto rocks in the darkness. The margins for error were very narrowly limited with catastrophe awaiting as a reward for any slip of judgement. Leiter liked neither the mission nor the purpose or its secrecy insisted upon by Reinecke, all the officers had been given was their destination unlike any routine patrol where these details would have been shared by the captain. Neither did he or any of the crew take to the two ominously shrouded figures they had brought with them, they didn't speak other than to demand, they kept themselves apart as much as they could given the crowded conditions on board where it was impossible to avoid contact. He shivered, it was not just the cold, he felt anxiety and tension grip his being with a sudden urge needing to use the head.

Reinecke strained his eyes forward into the dark murk ahead, the flurries of snow had occasional patches of vision where for a moment he could make out in the near distance the darker outline or silhouette of mountains. They were closing with the coast now. He rang down, 'Slow ahead both. Steady on this heading, give me depth and bearing again?' The information was relayed to him through the speaking tube to the bridge, assimilating the flow of information, now his attention becoming fixed firmly on the water ahead as he searched for recognisable features from the charts and briefings in Rennes.

Reinecke looked at his watch, 23. 45hrs, it was time to start the show. 'Below! Give the order to Szasz to send the signal...!'

Below in his radio compartment, Szasz received the command and turned his dials tuning to the frequency Reinecke had written for him. Picking up the mouthpiece he pressed the transmit button, then in English, 'Ragnar, repeat, Ragnar...' He repeated the message three times then sat back, switching the headphones to receive awaiting a reply. It came after three minutes. *'Loki'...' 'Loki'...*

6

The Irish Sea
Saturday 8th January 1944
18.00hrs

The squat little fishing smack 'Lady Patricia,' topped another wave then slid wallowing down the rear of the crest into the trough beyond. At her helm her master, Mick Lewis, span the wheel to take her bows head on into the next twenty-footer. As the unexpected winter storm had raged now for nearly four hours with little abate in the weather conditions, man and boat were being pushed to their limits. Beyond the glass of the tiny wheelhouse, the lashing rain seemed made of myriad streaks of vertical sleet spears blotting out any view beyond a dozen yards. Unusually for a small vessel at sea in these conditions and at night, she was running without lights, he had doused the oil lamps in of both the starboard and port navigation lights and that of the mast head lamp he had shut an hour earlier. They were in darkness except for the dim orange glow inside the wheelhouse.

The shipping forecast for the Irish Sea had been poor, for sleet and rain with squalls gusting at thirty knot winds around the Isle of Man to the North of where they presently were underway in the Liverpool Bay. These conditions were worse than he had expected but nothing he hadn't encountered in these waters before. What was worrying him, however, would be the delay caused by the lack of visibility in reaching the rendezvous off the Welsh coast, still some nautical miles ahead in the darkness. By dead reckoning, with the time on the wheelhouse nautical clock and a glance at the binnacle of the compass, he estimated another hour, at the best at a speed of about 5 knots.

The wheelhouse door banged open and Finn Kearney, the Lady Pat's mate clambered in his black oilskins running with water. In the dim light of the wheelhouse lamp his weathered worn and bearded face broke into grin, 'I've brought you something to keep out the cold, with a flourish he produced a bottle of Jameson's from a pocket inside his sea jacket adding, 'Only a drop mind in yer tea, I would na want you wanderin' off now would I…?' The big man cocked his head waiting for the obvious answer from his friend and the Lady Pat's owner.

Lewis, mentally had made some rough calculations, noted the clock reading of 23.50hrs then he nodded at Finn to top up his tea mug. 'We're about an hour to go in this wind, are you and the boy ready below?' His thoughts turned to his sixteen-year-old son below, Gerry, his deck hand and only other crew member this night. In his forty-eight years Lewis had fathered four fine sons, now only Gerry remained after first the sickness, then the 'troubles' when the English had taken the lives of both of the older boys. Molly would never forgive him if anything happened to their only surviving lad, she had called him 'Her late lamb' with Gerry having been born after several miscarriages in the twenty eighth year of her life. Though she too, worn out and broken had now lain in her grave these past eight years an exhausted old woman long before her time.

It seemed as if it were only yesterday that he had received the letter with the Dublin post mark. Which was odd as he could count the letters he had received after Molly's death on the fingers of one hand. The handwritten instruction in neat cursive writing had been brief to the point with no explanations. To meet his brother-in-law Riordan, off the evening eight o'clock train at Greystones, that he would be bearing some family news too important to be put in a letter. By itself this was a mystery as Molly had no living brothers when she died, she and Lewis had named their own first born after Riordan, Molly's older brother who had been killed fighting for the British on the on the Somme in 1916.

And so he had made the meeting. The week before, closing the door which had no lock, leaving his tiny fisherman's cottage in the dark of the evening he had walked down into Greystone village past the quayside where his boat was moored, then trudging through the rain the mile to the tiny station set beside the sea just south of Greystones, until he had stood on in the cold drifting rain from the sea on downline platform and turning up the collar of his sea jacket waited for the Dublin train to arrive.

As he stood stamping his feet to ward off the cold, he sheltered against the seawall, then cast his mind back to year before, the Summer of forty three, it had been August when a flight of three American Mitchell bombers had come in low having somehow wandered well away from the course to their airfield on Anglesey across the water in the

North of Wales. They had droned crossed the coast near Greystones. Out of fuel, eventually one had pancaked had landed near Tinnhich on the slope of the mountain above the town, another had made a good landing in a field forty miles away and had been immediately impounded with its crew by the Garda. But the third had flown straight into the hill above Delgany bursting into flames. Mick and Finn had been in the quay in Greystones fueling the Lady Pat' when it had flown above them low over town, with only feet to spare before the engines had cut and the aircraft went into a shallow dive before disappearing out of sight towards Delgany. Then they heard the explosion… Grabbing Finn's motor bike they had raced to the scene of the crash. The exhaust roared as Finn, with Mick hanging on the pillion seat his hands firmly planted on Finn's shoulders, they had nursed the old 500cc machine along the winding leafy lanes inland in the direction of the village of Delgany. The pall of oily smoke rising above the trees a clear marker to where the aircraft had come down, within minutes they were at the scene.

The burning wreckage had been scattered over a wide area of open farmland. As they had drawn near to the left of the main crash site, Mick had noticed that the whole section of the front section of the aircraft had smashed on impact but the machine gun turret had been torn clear on, then bounced on another hundred yards coming to rest leaning to one side but upright and relatively intact. Finn brought his machine to rest close to the battered turret and Mick stepped clear of the bike and ran across the field to where he had seen the body of the front turret gunner who lay on his back half way out of the rear of the turret, his feet and legs were still trapped inside. He was clearly beyond all hope and Mick absently crossed himself as he reached the dead man. He bent over the corpse and took in the youthful face, the wide staring eyes and open mouth, 'To be sure, you're own Mammy wouldn't recognise you now son…' He muttered as he closed the man's eyes. Then, he saw the handle of the pistol, it was sticking out of a holster under the open flying jacket. Mick had quickly unbuckled it and was holding the pistol in its holster in his hands when Finn came up behind him. 'Well, then.' He said, 'this boy'll have no use further for it to be sure now will he Finn? And, when they get here, the Garda and the army lads will take everything anyway including this beauty.' With that he'd tucked the weapon into the deep pocket of his sea coat, and after a few brief minutes, there being nothing to be done for the lad or his mates, there were no survivors to tend, they rode back to Greystone leaving the site for the military.

At Greystones, the train had been late, as was usual. The tired old tank engine, with its rods clanking as it coasted to a halt the two ancient wooden carriages coupled behind. Only three passengers had alighted from the train. The third and last, a tall gaunt looking man, who for some reason reminded Lewis as having the funeral air of an undertaker, who, dressed all in black, a formal long coat and wearing a bowler hat and with what appeared to be a leather case in his right hand was now left standing on the platform as the smoke and steam drifted was cleared by the wind coming in off the sea.

'You'll be Lewis?' the undertaker image had said with clipped tones and peering from behind his gold rimmed spectacles. 'I am he,' Lewis replied, his stomach churning at the thought of whatever intrigue he may be getting himself into just by being here. So many long years ago he had sworn his allegiance to the cause and vengeance after the brutal killing of his two beloved sons, Duncan and Rory, innocent victims of the 'Tans,' the murderers brought in by the English to squash the people under their reign of martial law. Duncan had been but six years old, his brother Rory a mere four when they died that terrible Summer's day in 1921. Molly, on a day trip to Dublin had left the boys playing in the street outside the shop in town, hadn't heard the screams before the blast had blown in the windows, she was left bloodied and dazed lying amidst the broken glass, her hearing would never recover. A bomb left in a pram, one of the investigating Tans seeing a pram left alone in the road had panicked, pushing the device away from the pair of Royal Irish Constabulary members standing in the road in the direction of the small crowd of passers-by on the pavement where it had detonated with devastating effect amongst the innocent people. Mick had been at sea on a fishing trip when it had happened, it was not until The Lady Patricia reached harbour and had tied up, then meeting the priest waiting for him with the news, standing silently on the quay as they had docked. Mick heard from Father Kelly that tragedy had befallen his family whilst he was away, that it had struck his young family again for the second time in less than twelve months. His first born, Riordan, had been taken by the Spanish flu the year before, one of twenty-three thousand who had succumbed to the epidemic.

Walking back from the grave side, beside himself with grief trying to hold and bear up a fragile Molly, her head covered by a shawl, whose heart had been broken, already an old woman at her twenty-one years of age. He had sworn aloud to God, and all who were capable of hearing that he would not rest until the debt was paid for the murder of his two lovely boys. Father Kelly had put his hand upon Mick's shoulder, 'Take care now Michael, come and see me in a day or two when you've seen to Molly, she needs you at her side this day lad, you both need time to mourn your loss.' Mick then had felt only anger, through the tears in his eyes he could see only a red mist. 'I'll let you know when I need you father, until then just let me be…' He had shrugged off the elderly priest's hand and walked on with both he and Molly suffocated in the deepest pit of misery and despair they neither could have imagined, beyond the touch of all, except Finn. Who, despite being told in no uncertain terms that he was not needed, stuck by the couple through the pain of the weeks which were to inevitably follow the children's funeral. But there had been no closure, no end to the anger and the bile of bitterness in Mick's soul.

Nothing had happened following his erratic attempts to make contact with the movement driven by his desperate need for justice. Then when he did, it was a surreal event, in shadows giving his pledge to grey faceless men, his undying oath to serve. The weeks had turned into months and then years with nothing following on from his induction other than the recall of the repeated instruction, 'Be ready.' So, Mick had held himself ready, biding his time to be called… And so it was until now. The 'undertaker' face lifted the small leather case which he carried and without a word handed it over a to Lewis, who, surprised by the unexpected weight of the case, nearly dropped it. 'Have a care now Lewis, you'll no want to damage this!' The undertaker's voice had risen a note.

Lewis looked into the face of the man shadowed under the bowler hat, 'What do you want of me?' He had asked quietly. The other, dipping his head glancing slowly from side to side as if to make sure that he was not over heard, leant forward and continued more softly, 'You'll do exactly what *this* tells you to do, it's all in there, then afterwards I'll be in touch, no questions now, is it clear?'

Lewis looked down at the leather case resting in his rough seaman's hands, 'Will I need to be talking with you when I read whatever's in this?' His words seemed to hang in the air before the undertaker curtly replied one more time. 'You said you were ready to serve Lewis, now is the time to honour that promise. Do what you're asked to do, it's well within your experience and capability as a mariner. Then, only then, we'll be in contact you. God be with you this night Lewis.' With that he turned on his heel and strode off into the falling rain, crossing the line to wait for the upline Dublin train and disappeared out of Lewis's life.

At home, alone in the privacy of his cottage kitchen with the curtains closed, with the wind whistling at the windows, and, thank God, Gerry away out for the night with his mates, he had sat own and placed the small leather suitcase type bag on the table. It was firmly made with good quality heavy leather about two feet in length eighteen inches across and six in depth with two locking metal clasps to the front of it, Lewis unclipped the locks and opened the case. On the top lay a large buff coloured envelope, he lifted this out first to reveal beneath on the front of a compact radio, the letters 'FUNKWERK Neunstadt' were stamped on a small copper plate in the right-hand top corner. In the side section, a wire loomed two-piece headset, and mouthpiece were neatly folded in a purpose made recess covered in a layer of rubberised cloth. Lewis took a minute to take in what he was seeing. He, running his fingers over the polished knobs at the front of the set, touched on what appeared to be a folding aerial looped from side to side in the top of the case, then closing the lid and set it to one side. He sat contemplating the case for a moment then turned his attention to his attention to the envelope. Taking it carefully in his hands and mentally weighing the contents, he slit open the top edge and peered within, then lifting the envelope emptied it out. From it, onto the rough wooden kitchen table fell a thick bundle of new bank notes, more than he had ever seen at one time, 'There must be hundreds here,' he muttered quietly to himself, 'and what are these?' The next was a sheaf of typed documents with some handwritten papers fastened with a large paper clip, the last a carefully folded nautical chart. Examination of the latter took his breath away, now, he had some inclination of what he had to do. Sitting by the light of the hurricane lamp at the centre of the table with his reading glasses perched on the end of his nose he read through the papers, turning each one over with deliberate care then digesting the next with the agonisingly slow growing realisation of the full portent of that which lay before him. Pouring himself a generous measure of his depleted bottle of Irish whiskey, recorking the bottle he slowly and purposely he filled his pipe tamping the tobacco down, the match flared, then drawing the aromatic tobacco smoke in deeply, Lewis exhaled slowly firmly closing his eyes reflected upon his myriad of questioning troubled thoughts.

With only a matter of days to both mentally and physically prepare for the task ahead, he knew that it was going to be a proving challenge to of all of his years of experience, his seamanship, his ability as a skipper, as an test to the obligations made to himself, to his pledge and sworn oath, to his own self-regard, of himself as man honourable to his word and his beliefs. There was little of no choice in the choosing of his crew and reliable ship mates for the voyage which lay ahead, he would need Finn, the Lady Patricia's mate and his lifelong friend, he couldn't involve Eamon, his deck hand, the lad had a wife and three young children. That left his own boy, Gerry. Although only eighteen he had spent much of his young life at his father's side as deck hand on the Lady Pat.' Mick took paternal pride in young Gerry's natural flair with things mechanical, the boy had applied himself enthusiastically to get to know the vessel intimately, from her broad backside to her snub of a wooden prow his keen eye had noted how things fitted together and made for her running at sea. Gerry had taken a keen interest in the basic practical mechanics and workings of the marine engine, then applied his hard-won acquired skills to the intricacies and temperamental foibles of The Lady Pat's diesel engine. His talents and knowledge were proven over and over again when urgent running repairs were needed at sea when turning back to land would be both time consuming and costly. The boy would have to stand in, take Eamon's place on this trip, though, with the dangers which lay ahead Mick's conscience continued to plague him, could only agonise over his final choice, it would have to be the three of them. There was some small relief, he was not being asked to be involved in any killing. Yet the awesome and appalling weight of the burden of responsibility for the course of events which now must follow, the consequence of that which he had begun all of those years ago, fell upon him. Like a shroud, the pall draining both his mind and his strength of will. There could be no turning back, no way out nor any way to disassociate himself from the events of which he had now set in motion. He was sure that he heard the *Devil* laugh softly in the darkness... The undertaker and those for whom he worked would not allow for the jumping of ship at this or any other time, would be without mercy and totally unforgiving, no excuse would be accepted nor would their retribution merely be satisfied with his head alone if he betrayed the cause, he was already in too deep for that. The only small consolation was the resolution that he had made with himself, that when the debt for his boys had been paid by the English, then please God, there could be no more pain a man could bear in one life...

He sat back in his creaking chair and running his fingers through his thick grey hair, reflecting with some self-incriminating anxieties upon the onerous task which lay before him. The onus of personal responsibility weighed heavily upon Lewis, not just for himself, but for the others whom he must now, out of necessity implicate, draw in to become involved to play a part in carrying out this undertaking of his making. If there was to be even the slimmest chance of success, then it rested upon a team effort to carry it off, not one man alone. It was an imperative not a choice, there had to be more than one set of hands to pull this together to make what seemed an impossibility on paper, happen in reality. An ordeal, a dangerous venture fraught with a multitude of hazards to overcome both on land and sea, to navigate and adapt to with only himself with the knowledge of what had begun this nightmare and in that, he, as the prime mover would be held to account whether they failed or succeeded. And, all this including the risk to the two most important things left in his life, that of his boat, the Lady Pat,' his livelihood, and the survival of his close knit but as yet unwitting crew, including his only surviving son Gerry. Yet Gerry was eighteen, a man now, when Mick had been but a year older, he had fathered his first child with Molly. His eyes rose to the sepia tinted picture on the kitchen dresser, 'Oh Molly, me lovely girl,' he breathed sadly, 'what have I done?'

7

A Resort Town in North Wales
The Morning of Saturday January 8th

The jeep rounded the corner of the wide tree lined main street of the Victorian coastal resort town and pulled up outside the busy little café frontage. The painted banner above the door announced in foot high lettering, AMERICAN RED CROSS, beneath were the words, 'The Doughnut Dugout' with the Red Cross flags pinned at either side with the American Stars and Stripes flag fluttering proudly from a pole above. The meeting place for off duty servicemen other ranks and NCOs. The three occupants climbed out through the open sides onto the wide wet pavement, the driver being the last out, pulling on his fatigue cap cut the engine and whistled at two girls walking past, 'Hey, honey, how're doing…?' The taller, prettier of the two stopped for moment twirled her floral dress despite the cold then shouted back, 'Hi Yank, got any gum chum?' The small dark American nimbly trotted over and attempted to chat with the two girls who both moments later erupted into juvenile laughter and giggles, then promptly ran off arm in arm. He walked back to his companions his hands thrust deep in his pockets shrugging his bowed shoulders, 'Jeez you guys, these broads don't speak American!' He declared visible ruffled by the put down.

'Common Dutch, leave them alone, they are not *broads*, they're only kids,' his companion, Jonesey, mouthed laconically drawled while chewing on a fat cigar, straightening his tie, turning back to the door of the servicemen's coffee shop he added, 'You missed that tram by inches, you losing concentration again…?' Pfc Van Der Hool, known as 'Dutch,' straightened up and lit a cigarette, 'No sir, I missed it by a mile, not my fault they drive on the wrong side of the road here!' The third young GI, Smitty, shook his head and unfastened his greatcoat as they crossed the wide pavement. 'You know, I never knew it could rain so much and now the buzz is they're telling us it could turn into snow any time, I'm going to write my Ma about this country's lousy weather, she sent me more socks for Christmas… Anyway, you guys heard there's a dance tonight at the Winter Gardens?' 'Yep, there'll be lots of pretty girls too Jonesey, hey, why you tell the kid you were Welsh, you'll confuse the life out of him?' Jonesey smiled, indulge me Smitty, 'There's truth in that, my grandpa came from somewhere in the south of this country, lots of Jones's there he told me. All worked in the mines just like he did, came to Pittsburgh to work with coal in the steel works back in the 80s so I guess I have some claim to being a descendant of a native, here come home to the old country…' He thought for a moment then went on, 'We came from the 'clean part' of town, reminds me a little of this place, and January is our coldest month back home, but not as wet as this.'

They walked across to the door under the elegant Victorian wrought iron canopy above the sidewalk through door of the Donut Dugout to be greeted with a chorus of 'Hi's' then shouts of, 'hey guys shut the door…' came from the dozen servicemen dressed like themselves in fatigues crowded around the square deal tables sitting on folding wooden chairs which served as furniture in the small cramped but friendly atmosphere of the eating area. The pleasing aroma of coffee, doughnuts and waffles hung in the air mingling with the haze of cigarette smoke while a radio was playing lively dance band music through the wall loudspeaker. Finding table near the window Smitty sat down, idly noticing a pair of seagulls strutting across the sidewalk like they owned it, they snatching at a piece of doughnut some fool had tossed in the road, Smitty though that so typical of this town, they were everywhere, then idly waited for his two companions who were chatting to the other guys as they stood in line waiting to be served by the white-uniformed Red Cross ladies at the bar.

Jonesey and Smitty returned to the table carrying a tray with coffee cups and a pile of doughnuts on a plate. Dutch reached for a crushed packet of 'Lucky Strike' from his uniform top pocket and offered it to his companions. 'Thanks Dutch, I'll stick with the cigars' Jonesey said, 'they go with the new image' he added taping the sergeant's stripes on his left arm. Smitty took one of the offered cigarettes and flipped open his Zippo, then asked 'Are you getting serious with Peggy? He posed the questioning inhaling the tobacco smoke. Jonesey had been walking out with Peggy now for some weeks and his absences from his buddies were becoming noticeable. 'I guess so,' his reply was thoughtful, 'You may have to look after yourselves tonight, Peggy and I have a date so we're going to the dance together.' 'Gee whizz Jonesey, that's serious stuff…!' Dutch said leaning across the table and taking two of the doughnuts from the pile, 'That's 'going steady' they call it, next thing you'll be meeting her folks. The wireless radio began to play an old Al Bowly version of the Wizard of Oz hit, 'Somewhere over the rainbow,' Jonesey's gaze drifted absently across the road as he remembered his own rainbow some just weeks before when he and the boys had met Peggy and her friends for the first time.

They had been standing at the corner of the big church next to the department store on the main street like the three Musketeers when half a dozen giggling girls had come out through door of the store. Jonesey had been in the middle of trying to count out the heavy new-fangled money from one hand to another at the same time trying to light a cigar, he had then managed to drop most of the copper and silver coins jingling to the sidewalk where they rolled in every direction. As he had bent to retrieve the scattered money, one of the girls had stopped one rolling coin with her foot, picked up and with a smile on her face had walked over to return it to its owner. 'Hey Yank, you've dropped your spending money,' she said flashing a smile at him. 'Why, thank you Ma'am, that's real kind of you. Just getting used to your pounds and pennies is sure difficult, I'm no Yank. I'm from Pittsburgh Penn, these are my buddies, this is Smitty, he's from Green Bay, Wisconsin, and here this Dutch, now he's a real yank from Chicago…!' Peggy smiled again and straightened her dress, 'Well that's some chat up line Mr Pittsburgh, only just said 'hello' and you've already given your histories, I suppose you'll be telling us next that you're all cowboys, now what's the problem your having with the money…?'

Dutch and Smitty had joined them and three of the other girls lingered nearby while they talked. The three men looked at each other, Jonesey saying, 'Sorry Ma'am, none of us are cowboys though Dutch says that he sat on a horse once. It seems you have so many coins here Ma'am. These big heavy ones are ok, but then twelve of them make this silver one and these others…?' Jonesey opened his hand with it palm upwards showing the collection of thrupenny bits, half pennies and six pence coins, 'And we haven't gotten on to the paper notes yet,' he grinned and attempted to explain the confusion that he and most of his young countrymen were having adjusting to the British currency. Peggy, with a that look of infinite patience often reserved for small children, laughed as the three men stood in each their naïve embarrassment. 'Right, let's start again, I'm not a 'Ma'am. I'm Peggy, and these are my friends Alice, Sue and Lisa. Look, we're on our half an hour lunch break, if it would help, we'll try to explain these to you over a quick cup of tea?' And so, it had began though the 'cup of tea' had been a disaster with none of the young men enjoying the taste of the strange brew with milk instead of lemon. They did however declare that they had enjoyed the 'unique' and different taste… Then, as they were leaving the girls at the twee little tea shop on the main street, Jonesey had asked Peggy if he could see her again, to his surprise she had said 'Yes, tomorrow?' Before going back with her friends to their work at the store. In those few minutes Jonesey had been taken by her easy going warmth, the easy laugh raised at the silliest of things he had said and even some of Dutch's ridiculous comments about the 'English customs,' and, touchingly by the way dimples appeared in her cheeks when she smiled. The next day at lunch time, Jonesey had been there waiting for her in at the same spot by the corner of the church, in fact he had been standing there for nearly half an hour when Peggy appeared.

In their long weeks together, whenever he was off duty, or she not at work in the store they had strolled along the beaches near the town, just talking over a wide range of things and topics in the many pleasant days that had followed. On one of these walks, he with his greatcoat buttoned up, she with her gloves, coat and scarf, she had leant against him and put her head on his shoulder as if it were the most natural thing in the world on a empty beach, with the sea birds calling, the rhythmic sound of the waves lapping at the shore in their ears. Jonesey felt a warmth course through him, a pleasant kind of glow, something he had never felt before, not even with any of the few pretty girls he had dated back home. Peggy had said to him that with his NCOs peaked service cap he looked like an officer, they both had laughed, then he had kissed her. It was sudden and very gentle, as she drew away the wind rustling her hair, she had lowered her head and looking up at him through deep blue eyes and demurely whispered 'That was very special, Jonesey, believe me I haven't done that before, do you forgive me?' He put his forehead against hers, 'I do Baby Snooks, you just got in there first…!' They had walked on, this time hand in hand.

One time, when they were strolling the promenade on the north shore, it had suddenly began to rain, Peggy had brought no coat so Jonesey took off his own issue great coat and put it gently on her shoulders. Jonesey's coat cut, for his near six feet and broad frame drowned her smaller person, with the hem nearly touching the floor as her five feet four-inch petit body was engulfed by the heavy material. Jonesey stood back and surveyed the result. 'You look like a tent Peggy,' he had said. They both had laughed at the unintended slip, then ran holding hands to one of the near shelters on the prom.

In their long talks, sometimes sitting in one of the quaint Victoria beach shelters on the north shore of the Bay, Jonesey learnt that Peggy lived with her widowed mother and two sisters. Norah, at nineteen being the oldest was engaged to Bob, a gunner in the Royal Artillery stationed with an anti-aircraft unit while Doreen was only fourteen and still at school. Peggy's father, a railway worker, had been tragically killed on the railway when he was hit by a train on something called a level crossing some years before. Mr Owen had left his wife taken care of, with the three-bedroomed cottage they rented paid for in advance for at least ten years out of his pension and her widow's railway man's compensation. In turn Jonesey told her about his childhood in Pittsburgh, the clean end of the town that is he had emphasised, where he had grown up with his two brothers, attended the local grade school then the high where he had graduated and was going on to study engineering when Pearl Harbour had brought America into the war. Shortly after Pearl in the December of 41, he had enlisted like many of his countrymen instead of waiting for the draft. Had made corporal pretty quickly after basic training then sergeant after nearly a year at Bragg. He had met Smitty and Dutch when they were assigned to his training platoon which had then graduated to a rifle company before embarking State side on a troop ship for the crossing of the pond to the European theatre of operations. Landing at the port of Liverpool the next stage there had been the journey by crowded steam train to the resort town where they were to be stationed ready for the assault on Europe, when it came…!

The best and most moving memorable occasion had been only weeks before, when Peggy's mother, who Jonesey had only just met the one time, had invited him to join them and the family their Christmas Dinner. He had arrived in his best uniform bearing gifts, a fruit cake his mother had sent from the States and a case of beer from the PX. He had arrived to find Norah's 'Gunner Bob' already seated in an armchair by the fire, he had leapt up and vigorously pumped Jonesey's hand, 'Merry Christmas Jonesey, will you have a brown ale?' Jonesey wasn't quite sure what a 'brown ale was but readily agreed. Gunner Bob had too brought extras for the table and they had performed that peculiar British custom of silence, all gathered around a tiny wireless plugged into their one light fitting to hear their King's speech His goodwill message to the nation, then the progress of the war with mainly the good news that the Germans were suffering defeats on all fronts. As they had feasted on the large roasted chicken and the home grown vegetables somehow procured by Mrs Owen, she had leant across the table with a glass in her hand and said, 'Jonesey, I need to ask you a question, don't want to embarrass our Peg' but we can't keep calling you just 'Jonesey' it's not right, what's your Christian name lad?' Jonesey had known this had to come at some time, pushing his chair back he raised his glass, 'Here's to you Mrs Owen, you can call me *Lem'* Ma'am, all those around the table acknowledged the toast, then he went on, 'Well, it's like this, my Mom, when she was carrying me, took to reading and the last the book was, 'Gulliver's Travels,' you all know that one?' They nodded that they did. 'Well' my Mom was so taken with the book that when I was born in the hospital and they asked for a name for me, she said 'Lemuel,' so that's how I got the name, now *you* can call me Lem, but outside the guys either call me 'Serg,' or just Jonesey…!' More toasts had been made, then they had chatted animatedly over the meal, at one point Jonesey attempting with some difficulty, to explain to Gunner Bob, the finer tactics of American Football where he played a forward at high school, Bob had sat with his back beret still tucked under his shoulder epaulette entranced. The family, and Bob, had pressed Jonesey for more stories about his hometown Stateside, his schooling and his plans for the future. In fact, they had asked about just everything. At times Jonesey felt a little embarrassed at missing the point some of Bob's remarks, his Newcastle accent he had to really concentrate upon to translate into terms he understood. But they pressed him for still more eager for any firsthand accounts of the world he had so recently left, so, as modestly as he could he related the journeys that he and his friends and comrades, Dutch, and Smitty had made before finding themselves together then being posted to England. Young Megan asked about Dutch, 'Was he really from Holland?' She had naively wanted to know. Jonesey explained that his name really was Jacob Van der Hool, but as this was such a mouthful that he had been nick named 'Dutch,' at boot camp and that name had stuck. Peggy had added that she, and the other girls, had found his dark thick hair, olive complexion and good looks attractive until he opened his mouth in his Chicago speak, said that they had thought that he might be descended from Italian origins, whereas Smitty, with his shock of blond hair more like a Swede or Norwegian. All Jonesey could do on that one was to say that there was some truth in this as, Smitty, otherwise known as Pfc Walter Smittsohn had farming grandparents who hailed originally from near Gottenberg in Sweden before emigrating to the US and to Green Bay. The afternoon and evening had finished on a high note with each of the Owen girls taking it in turns to read from Dicken's 'A Christmas Carol,' which had held everyone spellbound. Taking their leave and thanks to Mrs Owen, both he and Gunner Bob had each received a present, a woollen balaclava knitted with her own hands! Both men thanked her in the appropriate manner with both harbouring private thoughts about what to do and where to be seen with such a gift. Then he and Bob, had taken a walk with their girls along the seawall before returning for a last good night by the cottage gates. It had been a wonderful day, Jonesey wondered what his Mom would make of Peggy and her family? With a sigh, which bordered on a touch of homesickness, he joined Bob for the walk back into town.

While these thoughts were still pleasantly occupying his conscious thinking in the front spaces of his mind, Jonesey's memories of these recent events were dispelled momentarily when the music in the Donut Dugout was turned up with a popular Miller number loudly playing. The guys, having persuaded the red cross ladies to turn up the volume, were beating time with their feet and singing along with the lyrics to 'Chattanooga Choo Choo,' bringing his warm meanderings abruptly to an end from the receding rosy recollections of the recent Christmas. Those meaningful new friendships that had been so formed in the friendly atmosphere at Peggy's home. And, the boy Huw, to whom he had been introduced by Peggy as a neighbour's son who brought the driftwood he found on the nearby beach to the Owen's home fire for a couple of coppers. The lad had been fascinated by the American badges and stripes on Jonesey's uniform and had promptly asked for one. Politely refusing but not wanting to offend, Jonesey had asked him if he knew anyone who could show him around the town and Huw, enthusiastically, had been more than willing to give him a walking guided tour the next day. This had taken place with Dutch and Smitty not without protest, being dragged along with them. At the end of a trek around the town's main sites of interest including the pier and the gasworks, it had been Dutch's idea to adopt Huw as their *'Gopher,'* he could go for this and go for that when he was needed and they would pay him for his services, a mutual arrangement to which Huw readily agreed, as a potential source of pocket money.

Jonesey sighed inwardly, as the noise as more American servicemen now had crowded into the small confines of the Dugout, persisted in encroaching on the pleasure he was enjoying with his thoughts. However, the arrival of yet more uniformed bodies, had as well as diverting his train of thoughts from these pleasantries, in turn had raised other recent memories, brought back the series of events that had led to him and his buddies fetching up here in this quaint Victorian Bay resort in the first place. Their present place and purpose in the world, it was no holiday, this was no boy's camp and his mind drifted again to some of those other earlier events and their meanings as those of which he had spoken of so light heartedly to Peggy and her family, there was a serious side.

Jonesey thought back on those early days. The GIs, the dough boys, the majority of them draftees, called when Uncle Sam had blown the bugle of patriotic fervour. Many would be hard pressed to show you on a map where Japan was, where Germany sat on the map of Europe. Yet they had arrived, believing themselves, as told by the propaganda, as crusaders, the new saviours coming to aid of the tired, weary and beleaguered people of mainland Britain. Eventually, when the paper checks were done, all present and accounted for, after passing through the city of Chester in ancient wooden rolling stock behind a grimy steam locomotive they had passed into North Wales! Then having been taken on down the branch line towards the end of the line seaside resort town with all heads hanging out of the windows. The whistle blowing just before they came into the station with the smoke and soot in their eyes as they had craned to get a first glimpse of their new home. He remembered what Peggy had said on how the locals who had been watching when his platoon and others had formed up inside the station on the platforms before moving off, had gathered in groups, pretty young girls, mature looking women and older ones with aprons on, by gangs of kids and other casual passers to whom, Peggy had said, 'were amazed at the quiet sound of a hundred feet in their rubber soled boots made instead of the rhythmic crunch-crunch-crunch of the hob-nailed British leather ammunition boots of other troops.'

He had noticed a niggling feeling somewhere deep in himself, just a feeling, a strange sensation that something was not quite right, leaving him feeling somewhat uncomfortably for no particular reason. When his platoon had marched out, with he, as platoon sergeant at its head picking up the cadence of the step at the front of his men with the, 'Hup, two three four, Hup, two three four' spoken beat as they had swung into easy step with each man carrying his gear with his rifle slung on his shoulder. Just a feeling perhaps, something not exactly as expected. These thoughts nagged at him. Strangely, a number of his men had later remarked that they too had noticed where although the women they passed had shouted and waved happily at the newcomers, what few men were to be seen seemed were appearing to stand silently and just watch as the hundreds of American troops passed on by in their squads up their main street, and through into their town. So, it had been all along the route to their base and the compound assembly area near the West shore of the Bay town, a mixed welcome.

Returning to present once again he found Smitty and Dutch were arguing over the importance of what they had studied at high school and usefulness in their daily lives, with Dutch ridiculing Smitty's earnest and obvious interests in academics. 'So, your telling me that this guy, an old Greek, sits in his bath-tub when an apple falls on his head and he shouts, *"Found it!"*, is that wat you're telling me is important?'

'No, no! You're missing it completely Dutch, education broadens the mind' a frustrated Smitty persisted, 'it's really important, how you goin' to impress any girl when all you got to talk about is junk?'

'Well some junk is ok, girls ain't interested in college talk in these parts, they wanna hear about good times, music, dancing and having a ball…' Dutch fired back exasperated at the direction the discussion had taken.

'Ok, Mr Wise guy, there's a movie on this afternoon in the church hall, they're showing Bob Hope in 'The Cat and the Canary' again, wanna come to kill a couple of hours?'

'We've seen that already,' Jonesey chipped in with mock seriousness, then looking at his watch said 'but if you two want to go and get 'educated' some more then be my guests, me, I'm going to take a walk and stretch my legs.'

They broke up on leaving the Donut Dugout with Dutch and Smitty continuing their debate on route for the matinee performance at the church hall. Jonesey, wanting some time to himself, always drawn back to the attraction of the sea he decided to walk the beach where he and Peggy had enjoyed some quiet hours together. He arranged with the guys to pick them up later and deliver them to the compound for evening 'chow time.'

8

Saturday January 8th Afternoon

Huw Henryd Thomas stood in the gravel and ash of the roadway beneath the looming shadow of the drum shaped massive gasholder, its three stages inflated by the gas within it rose nearly a hundred feet above him blotting out the grey sky. The rain had stopped, and it was overcast though he could see clearly gazing up as he had done so many times. This was where it had happened, where Ifan Evans had said Huw's Da,' his work friend Will,' had fallen to his death in this place all those years ago. Scanning the rust streaked and greasy sides with the iron Jacob's ladders fixed to the ascending walls of each drum section, to Huw it looked foreboding even in daylight. Ifan had said that it had happened in the dark, that his Dad had fallen from the walk way on the very top and Huw could clearly see the outline of the steel handrail which circled the top, even from down here… His two friends, Henry and Ronnie, fellow members of the 'Gassy Arabs gang,' were dressed like him in the similar worn tatty jumpers and knee length shorts, the uniform of poorer boys. They were enthusiastically kicking a football across the road then bouncing it against the brick wall of the gasworks building. 'Hoy! Clear off all of you!' Two boiler suited men appeared at the railings of the works gates shouting and moved the boys on.

The tallest of the three boys grabbed the ball and ran past the men and stuck his tongue out, 'C'mon, race you to the dump…' He cried then sped off with the other two in pursuit, Huw's hob nailed boots scraping on the road surface. At the end of the road near the entrance to the town dump they halted and regained their breath. Henry, the oldest and the biggest of the youths, wiped his nose with the back of his sleeve, threw a stone at the flocks of Herring Gulls foraging around and over in the dump then said 'Let's go and see the Yanks, they'll be coming out now and there's nothing else to do in town.' After a few moments' argument, with Huw secretly not wanting to share any of the rewards and advantages which he earned for being a 'Gopher' messenger for the new Americans, they were after all 'His' Yanks. Henry's more assertive choice of what to do for the afternoon won and they set off to walk the half a mile to where the American compound in the part of town that was situated near to Huw's home at Bryn Morfa in the lea of the mountain which reared its massive lime stone head land nearly seven hundred feet above the town. The Americans had adopted and created a cluster of matt black painted their ten men Nissen huts in neat rows with a central office area, their all-important PX, and a motor pool lay on land that had been only an empty field before the coming of the military and the war. The wide tree lined Victorian avenue boasted well-to-do housing on the one side whilst across the road, when in Edwardian times the buyer's money had run out and the prospective development of impressive hotels had failed to materialise. It had left an imposing broad carriage way designed for two lanes of horse drawn traffic with a central cultivated area its entire appearing both asymmetrical and unbalanced. When the GIs came, this layout had suited their needs for a convenient base close to the town. Even so, now with so many new batches of Americans arriving weekly, some had been billeted out to stay with local families. Jonesey was one of these.

The three boys stood on the corner and watched as jeeps came and went, then four large six wheeled trucks arrived in a convoy loaded down with supplies and provisions for the troops. Henry decided he bored and was going home, after a moment Ronnie, the third member of the Gassy Arab gang left to follow him leaving Huw standing on his own. He worried about his silly promise to his mother, had he been too hasty promising something which he didn't have, how could he face her if he failed and what would her disappointment be like? In the fading light of the afternoon Huw spotted a jeep with Jonesey and his two friends approaching the guard post. Huw waved frantically to get his attention. The jeep pulled up and Jonesey craned round in the driving seat, 'Hiya young Huw, how's it going?' Huw leaned into the jeep, 'Wow, can I have a ride Jonesey?' He asked earnestly with all of the enthusiasm of young boys for things mechanical. 'Not today Huw, but I've got a job for you.' He reached into his coat and produced a white envelope, 'Would you take this to Peggy, it's important she gets it quickly?' Huw had no hesitation, Peggy and her family lived next door but one at number three in the Bryn Morfa cottages. 'Sure thing Jonesey, do it right now cos I'm going home.' Jonesey searched in his coat pocket for some coins. 'Jonesey,' Huw hesitated, 'could I have one of those Hershey's instead of my pennies?' he said, almost beggingly. Jonesey laughed, 'Ok, it's a deal if you mean one of these?' Producing from the same pocket a blue and white wrapped chocolate bar! Huw was delighted and felt a warm glow of expectation spread throughout his body. 'Oh, thank you Jonesey, I'll take this to Peggy right now.' He said reaching for the letter, then wiping his hands on his shorts he put his hand out for the chocolate, 'This is great Jonesey, it's not for me it's for my Mam honest.' Jonesey looked at the thin pale youth and could see instantly that the boy earnestly meant exactly what he had said, therefore knew without a doubt that Peggy would get his note about the dance tonight pretty quickly. 'Thanks Huw, appreciate that, look, tomorrow I'll have another bar for you, but this time for yourself, what do you say?' Huw really didn't know what to say, he actually felt embarrassed, in his short life there hadn't been a great deal of kindness shown, any rewards or gifts had always been earned the hard way, no one gave anything away for free in Huw's cold and sometimes cruel world. Yet there was a deeply instilled honesty in Huw's make up, something good that he had inherited from his Da' his Mam had said. 'Thanks Jonesey, I'll work for it I promise.' Huw said now itching to be on his way before the January darkness fell. Huw raced off crossing the avenue onto the beach road, he thought quickly, much as he wanted to get home with his present for his Mam burning in his hand, he worried that it would melt before he got there, he had the letter for Peggy in the other hand and that job must be done first. Looking up at a blackening sky Huw reached the road gate to the cottages.

Jonesey watched the boy go, he felt a genuine concern to see this kid, dressed always in thread bare clothes, like something out of a Dickens hard luck story, so willing to please, yet with that persisting air of mournful sadness and poverty hanging over him like an enveloping mantle of unhappiness, a kind of melancholy that shouldn't be there in any kid of that age. This was the first time Jonesey had noticed the boy's face break into a real smile, that troubled him for some reason, that there was something going on behind the sadness, a cause or reason which maybe or somehow could be changed? Gunning the engine of the open topped jeep he looked heavenwards as the first heavy drops of sleet began to fall. 'C'mon Jonesey shake the lead' the soldier on guard duty at the entrance called over. 'Yeah,' said Dutch from the back seat, 'There's a real storm coming up, and I need to get my good duds fixed for tonight…'

Jonesey steered the jeep in through the gates, dropping his two companions outside their enlisted men's hut, then drove on over to the motor pool. Fixing up the hood on the jeep before he went into the office and spoke briefly with the Pfc on duty. Then, handing over two dollars, he signed out the jeep to himself for, 'Early morning duties on the 9th January 1944.' One of the small perks of being a technical sergeant first class, he thought to himself as he drove out from the compound once again then the short drive across town to where he was billeted as an NCO in civilian quarters. It was a welcoming if quaint family home in a quiet little street off the town centre. Jonesey, if all went well, aimed to pick up Peggy at 19.00hrs, time to kill in the two hours before for the dance was due to start. That was if the kid, true to his promise had delivered the message as he had said that he would. He parked up outside the little semidetached house, pocketed the jeep keys and carrying the two tins of peaches for the family knocked at the door. They, the elderly Mr and Mrs Hughes, his billeting family, really appreciated these little luxuries which the dough boys brought with them.

9

Saturday January 8th Evening

17.15hrs

Huw had opened the gate then closing it behind him to save the banging it would inevitably cause in the strengthening wind, hesitated for a second then knocked on the door of number three whilst he wiped the front of each of his boots on the back of his socks. The door opened and the widow Owen peered out, 'Bless me it's young Huw! What are doing out there in the cold lad?' She beckoned Huw to come inside but he was itching to get home. 'Sorry Mrs Owen,' Huw blurted out, 'Is Peggy in please?' Mrs Owen shook her head then disappeared to be replaced in a moment by her seventeen-year-old daughter Peggy. 'Hello Huw Bach,' she smiled at Huw and his heart melted. Peggy was a pretty girl, Huw thought that she had the face of an angel with a halo of blond curly hair, had always been kind to him and had added the title 'Bach' (Small or little in Welsh) to his name years before, 'Aren't you coming in, Huw it's freezing out there?' Peggy asked with genuine concern. 'No Peg,' he replied, 'I got to get home, but I've got a note for you from Jonesey, he said it was important.' Peggy took the envelope from his hand, 'Thanks Huw, now get off with you before you get soaked, I'll see you tomorrow.'

Beaming with pleasure Huw ran the few steps to his own door and opened the latch. Inside a drama was in progress, Ifan was stood before the fire putting on his coat, his face livid with temper. Huw's mother stood beside the fireside range comforting baby Ellen who was crying, Megan and Dafydd were curled up on the chair, Megan, her arm around Dafydd was sobbing as her brother whose face was hidden clung to her. 'Just as well you decided to turn up Brat…!' Ifan shouted immediately he caught sight of the boy. His rage boiling over as he screamed at his wife, 'Now, get it clear, I'm going and I'm not coming back, you can stick it here with your brood and starve for all I care.' Huw's mother was pleading, 'But Ifan, what have we done, I've given you everything…' 'Your everything you bitch? These snivelling brats and your moaning on and on and on, well I'm getting a new life free from the lot of you and it starts tonight, so bawl all you like woman, I'm leaving for good.' Ifan threw a glare at Huw which turned his blood to ice.' And you can get out of my way,' he thrust Huw's mother and the baby aside causing her to bang her head on the wall with the force of the push. Huw darted forward. 'Don't hurt my Mam Ifan,' Huw heard himself shout and was rewarded by a blow to the side of his head which sent him reeling across Megan and Dafydd. 'Gutter scum!,' Ifan screamed and hit Huw again, 'I'll teach you to raise your hand to me...!' Huw's mother tried to intervene only to be slapped across her face. 'IFAN, not his head, leave the boy alone!' Ifan bellowed in unrestrained anger and laughed as the blue veins stood out from his forehead in temper, 'Who do you think you are Bitch? He's going to get what he's had coming for years. *Darling* Will's useless whelp...!' Huw sprang forward desperately grabbing Ifan around the waist, 'You leave my Mam alone.' His strangled words came out strangely loud but shrill, but he was quickly beaten back, over powered by Ifan's greater strength which now held him firmly gripped around the throat and his back against the wall, Ifan's dark face thrust so close that his nose touched Huw's. Spittle flew from Ifan's mouth, his lips were drawn back from his teeth in a snarl, as flecks of spit spattered onto Huw's face as spat out. 'Think you're clever BRAT, think you know everything? Your beloved Dad, your Mam's the darling Will? Well, I've got some news for you see, about that day, the day so important to you, when he 'fell' that you whinge on and on so much about. Well, BRAT; he didn't fall, SEE! I know, I was there, and he fell because it was me that pushed-him!'

The silence was thunderous, moments passed before Ifan released Huw leaving him gasping for breath as he tried to grasp what had just been said. His mother stood with the back of one hand across her mouth, Huw registered her scream of tortured anguish and pain, the 'NO!' Issued from her like a wail from a tormented soul of the possessed. The children had stopped crying, were silent and still, each was frozen in time in this hideous cameo created by Ifan's heart stopping and devastating revelation. The spell was broken when Huw, galvanised by the outrage of pure hatred, this time dove head down for Ifan again. Almost leisurely, the gleam of madness now in his eyes, Ifan stuck him hard across the face. The force of the blow causing Huw to momentarily lose consciousness as he fell backwards against the wall. Huw was vaguely aware of the figure of Ifan, picking up his packed bag, when Huw saw to his dismay that the bag Ifan was taking had belonged was

Will's, his father's old army kit bag. Glaring around for one last venomous look at his sobbing wife and her terrified children, Ifan hawked spat at Huw in vicious contempt, then with his long black overcoat flapping around his knees stormed out into the night swearing as he went, leaving the empty door wide open to the angry wind. Huw's senses reeled, his vision faded, then he blacked out.

Huw slowly came round, his head ached but his vision was clearing, he was sitting on the floor with his back against the wall, his mother, having closed the cottage door, was bending over him still holding the baby in her arms. 'Oh, Huw, I'm so sorry.' She sobbed as she put a dampened cloth to his forehead. Huw's twelve-year-old mind staggering under the weight of realisation, with the enormity of what Ifan had said that he had purposely done, to Huw's father, to Will Thomas, his Da.'

Huw struggled to his feet shaking his head, there was the coppery taste of blood in his mouth. He took in the sight of his mother, the three children in the flickering poor light given off by the fire, and then suddenly, surprising himself, the anger came upon him with the heat of a furnace. Ifan would not get away with this, Huw could not let him go free for what he had done. Even though if part of him felt the relief for himself and to his family at no longer having to have this vile, unpredictable and vicious animal in their home. He knew what he had to do, somehow, he must find Ifan and see him punished, by the police, that's what they did wasn't it, punished criminals and Ifan was a criminal? That would come later. Huw grabbed his coat from the handrail at the bottom of the stairs, it didn't fit, Mam said that he hadn't "grown into it", he hadn't yet but it would have to do.

His mother rose trembling and shaking, looking like a frightened mouse as she often was when the devil was here, 'What are doing Huw, you mustn't go out, he might come back!' She was clearly beside herself with worry, four children, no money, what would she do? Huw found the present of the precious Hershey bar still in his pocket, with an unsteady hand he offered it to his mother, 'Give it the kids, I'll be back soon Mam, I promise.' With that and not wanting to get into a row with his already distraught mother, he went out into the night. Pausing outside number three he banged on the for the second time that night. Norah, Peggy's older sister came to the door, 'What' the matter Huw? She said taking in his appearance and then anxiously called back over her shoulder, 'Bob, come here a minute,' she was joined by her fiancé who Huw knew as 'Bob the gunner' in his army battle dress. 'God, Huw you're a mess,' he said, 'What have you been up to?' Huw didn't want to waste any more time, 'Sorry Norah, me Mam's not good, could you come over and help her?' 'Of course, Huw, let me get my coat, 'Peggy, Mum' she shouted into the house, 'Come quickly, Mrs Evans needs our help. Ok Huw, we're coming now, where are you going Huw?'

Huw shouted, 'Going for my mates.' turned and ran, didn't want to wait for the awkward questions that must come. Much as he knew that Peggy and her family would take care of his Mam, the talking would have to wait and anyway embarrassingly the Owens family already knew just what a bullying brute Ifan could be. He took off on the road back into town, there was a house up on the higher slopes of the mountain where the old quarry men's cottages were clustered around and along the mountain road higher up above the buildings of the main town, this was where Ifan had his so-called friends, where the brothers Bill and Reg Martin had their home, villains by name and by nature so people said. The Martin brothers were drinking friends of Ifan, he had earned money from them doing whatever under handed dealings he could to make beer money to swill down his throat. They had a small lorry, a familiar enough sight round the town and Huw knew that sometimes Ifan had helped them collecting the scrap metal which was their main business in the immediate area, they had a yard down by the gas works where they collected all manner of junk. Huw also knew Ifan had other shady friends, but this was as good a place to start as any. The sleet was falling quite heavily now he pulled his collar up as he trudged through the beginnings of slush forming at the side of the road. He tried hard to formulate some kind of plan in his mind, he'd already had a hiding from Ifan and if he were caught it would be more of the same rather than any vengeance his puny arms could inflict on the man. He must think clearly, though his head still hurt from the blows Ifan had given him for daring to open his mouth against him earlier. His Mam was now in safe hands, that small advantage emboldened him, what was it they said in the Boy Scouts group Henry and Ronnie proudly belonged to? 'Always be prepared?' They had told him… Then he would prepare himself mentally at least so as not to be caught again by Ifan's physical brute strength against which he had no chance at all. As he made his way along the darkened street it came to him, he needed reinforcements, he needed the Gassy Arabs! Changing directions, he crossed the road and set off towards the council estate where Henry and Ronnie lived. Huw knew that they were intending to go to the town drill hall tonight where their scout group had been invited to meet with some of the American officers, not for anything the Yanks had to say, but they always brought treasures with them to hand out to their audiences, Henry and Ronnie would not miss out on such a free beano from the Yanks.

Huw made his way to the council terraces where Henry lived, the snow was falling thickly now his footprints leaving a trail behind him. His urgent knocking on the back door of Henry's home brought his mother wiping her hands on a towel in answer, 'If you want Henry, Huw, he's just finished his tea…,' she disappeared inside with Henry appearing a moment later. Henry listened as Huw outlined his needs. 'Alright Huw, I'll come, it sounds a bit dangerous, I don't wanna get no trouble with the cops though, we'd better pick Ronnie up 'fore he goes to the Yanks Do, I'll get my coat.'

A shouted warning came from inside, from his mother, 'No later than ten o'clock, yer Dad's on night shift so don't be late or I'll send him after yer! Henry looked heavenwards, 'I got two hours then Huw, c'mon. Let's go to Ron's house.'

Ronnie took a little more persuading, after some minutes standing outside his back door he agreed, but only if Huw shared the next jobs the Yanks gave him fairly, he too needed the pocket money. Huw could only but agree, there was strength in numbers he had remembered from history lessons, the Gassy Arab army was not exactly a battalion. As the three them trudged along, Huw was reminded that he hadn't eaten since the morning, his tummy rumbled loudly and suddenly he felt desperately hungry, he said, 'Any of you got anything to eat?' As his two companions plodded at his side, their shoulders hunched, hands in pockets as neither of them had brought gloves, Huw didn't possess any such luxury. Ronnie thought about this for a moment before having a brainwave. 'I got an idea; we were supposed to be goin' to the Yank's 'do' right? They will have started by now and the church hall is just up the road…!' They walked on to the next turning, where the church hall stood on the corner. 'Right, watch this…' Ronnie skipped of round the back of the church hall. There were two jeeps outside and a khaki painted car in the gateway. Huw and Henry looked at each other, 'Where's he gone now, I'm not standing out here all night!' Said Henry rubbing his hands together and blowing on them. A minute later Ronnie reappeared proudly carrying a brown paper bag, 'Look what got…' He announced, 'Provisions right…!' He thrust the bag at Huw.

Huw peered inside the large brown bag, sandwiches, some kind of cake and an orange the size of a tennis ball! 'You'll get in trouble if you've thieved these,' he said to Ronnie, we'll all catch it now…!'

'Nah.' Ronnie replied with mischief in his voice, 'I told their sergeant that me brother was sick and couldn't come so he put these in a bag for me to take home, so I didn't 'thieve them,' I was given them… see…!'

Huw took out the orange, it filled his first, he took a bite out of it, chewed for a moment then spit it out, 'Tastes awful…,' he said wiping his mouth with the back of his hand.

'Idiot,' said a jubilant Ronnie, you're supposed to peel it first, here, I'll show you.' Grabbing the orange from Huw's hand and expertly removing the peel, 'Now try.'

Huw had another go and found it much improved without the peel. The turning to the sandwiches, sniffed suspiciously at the contents, 'What they got in 'em…?' He enquired of the still laughing Ronnie.

'It's Spam, go on try it, tastes ok honest…'

'Spam…? Huw peered at the pink material as he curled back the edge of the sandwich, 'What's Spam clever clogs…?'

'You don't know nuffin' do you, and you a friend of the Yanks,' Ronnie inhaled ready, to give his well-rehearsed answer, 'It's *Scientifically Processed American Meat,* that's what's in it. *SPAM!*' He stood back waiting for the prize to follow this pearl of wisdom.

'Gizz one then,' Henry muttered and grabbed a sandwich, 'Hmm, not bad,' he said through a full mouth.

Huw was converted, taking a sandwich he munched on his as they continued walking up through the town. Much better now that he had something inside him though he was still a bit unsure about the filling. The snow was still falling, settling on their heads.

Henry then had a brainwave and said, 'Right, we've all got these haven't we,' producing from his pocket a knitted black wool school balaclava, 'if we put them on, we'll look like commandos… Yeah…!' The three of them brought out their home produced knit wear usually consigned to their pockets as soon as they were safely away from their mothers' watchful eyes. Donning the balaclavas so that they left only the slits for their eyes, they admired each other's new spy like image. Like something out of a Dickens novel, the three of them trudged their way across town chatting as they went, then up the steep winding road leading to where the cluster of houses sat on a wide ledge on the side of the mountain looking down on the town two hundred feet below.

The boys soon found themselves near the big stone built house where the brothers Martin lived, Huw pointing out the clearly visible date, even in the snow, '1880' above the door of detached old stone building with the big barn like garage set on the flat land alongside. The big wooden double doors were open, inside the illumination from an oil lamp cast shadows on the walls as the men inside appeared to be working a lorry at the back of the garage building. The three moved a little closer hiding behind the wall that separated the garage by a few yards from the road outside house. 'That's their Morris Commercial.' Huw said knowledgeably, 'it's got a two and a half litre engine…!'

'How'd you know, it might be a Bedford truck? Said Henry immediately challenging him, 'Bedford's are better.'

'Cos, Ifan told me, I seen it before when them come to pick him up, it's a Morris…' Huw said confidently, it's got Morris on the front so there.'

'I'm cold,' sniffled Ronnie put in rubbing his hands and blowing on them, 'Don't see the difference, still a lorry isn't it, what are we goin' to do now?

'Wait and see what they'd do an' where they go, when they leave it's for something important and I wanna see what it is…'

'Why, it's freezing, we could have gone to the Yanks do instead of this, bet we missed cakes and them sweets the Yanks got…' Ronnie moaned petulantly.

'Because I got a score to settle with Ifan,' he nearly shouted. 'HE murdered my Dad…!' Huw almost given them away, 'And he's got away with it 'til now, that's chuffin' why…!'

The other two boys looked at each other in dismay, didn't know what to say as the enormity of Huw's accusation seemed ridiculous, impossible to believe even of a swine like Ifan sank in. Huw was shaking, it wasn't with the cold, his nose had bled again, a trickle he wiped away with the back of his hand. Not wanting to argue, in silence they turned back to watch the three men in the garage.

Inside the garage, the brothers Reg and Bill Martin were in deep conversation with Ifan. The taller of the two, Reg, dressed like his younger brother dressed in workmen's blue overalls stood near the door and was making a point very clear to Ifan, 'I told you, you get paid when the job is done, not before…! You wanted to be part of this, now, are you in or not?' Both brothers were big heavily built men, well used to intimidating anyone fool enough to stand against them, cruel enough to enforce their will with their fists if they didn't get their way by talking to lesser mortals like Ifan.

Ifan was desperate, he wouldn't go back home now, he was banking everything on the promised one-way trip to Liverpool to deliver goods with Reg Martin, his new start. Martin had told him when they had spoken about the job in whispers in the corner of the pub, there was a lot of money to be had for his help in this deal they were putting together, a hundred pounds if it went well…! Maybe a bonus on top if he worked hard. This would be his bankroll. More money than he had ever seen or had in his whole life, a fortune to start anew away from this place with a miserable wife and her snivelling kids. Liverpool, where he had a brother, there were always openings to be had there and money in his pocket.

'Sorry, Reg, just needed some pin money, I'll do whatever you say.' Ifan cowed by the thought of losing his chance, backed down before the matter became an issue, he had too much to lose now.

'Right, then climb up on the back and give Bill a hand.' Reg shouted to his brother working in the back of the lorry, 'Bill, have you tanked her up?'

Ifan climbed into the back of the lorry beside Bill Martin who was stacking five-gallon jerry cans against the back of the cab under the canvass cover, 'Yeah, both tanks are full and I've another six drums up here to take down to the yard later, we'll make a fair sum from them needing petrol…' Ifan helped him stack and tie down the load. The jerry cans were American service issue, the petrol inside was not, it was from a dealer with whom the Martin's traded regularly for goods that couldn't be obtained legally, it was Black Market fuel, worth its weight in gold…

'Right, start her up, we've an appointment to keep and I want to be early to look at our clients, we can retire after tonight if the deal is as good as I think it's going to be. I might just up the prices a bit for services rendered to our associates, they won't find another service like ours tonight, we can call the shots, they won't be able to negotiate with nowhere else to go…' Both brothers snorted with laughter. Ifan, who was about to take out a cigarette to ease his nerves, when he remembered the petrol…

The Morris Commercial thirty hundredweight, pulled out of the garage onto the apron cutting fresh tyre tracks in the snow. Closing and securing the garage doors, Reg jumped in beside his brother and Ifan in the cab. They ground their way out in first gear and onto the road towards the summit of the headland, the wheels slipping wherever the snow had lain deeply. It took twenty minutes of skilful driving on Bill's part before, engine roaring, they crested the top of the narrow road to where the going was flatter and the approach to the summit began.

Huw and his two friends ducked beneath the wall, watched them go, waiting until the lorry was grinding its way over the top of the hill before setting off to follow the tyre tracks. Easy, thought Huw as nothing else was moving, the snow had allowed a silence to fall as it deepened. They walked on sliding as the slope increased toward the top, 'What are we going to do when we catch them Huw, they're all bigger than us and we got no weapons to fight with if Ifan turns nasty again...?' Ronnie was genuinely frightened; he had seen the damage that had been regularly inflicted on Huw's face and body.

'Yes, we have...!' Henry said unbuttoning his coat to reveal his scouts uniform underneath, 'Look, you got yours too Ron...' he pulled out the boy scout knife from its sheath and waved at Huw, 'We got these if he turns nasty with us him being a murderer...' Henry brandished the six-inch bladed knife in the air making blood curdling red Indian noises, stamping then dancing, hopping from one foot to another.

Suddenly Ronnie gulped and shaking his head announced that he had had enough, 'I'm going home Huw, I'm freezing, can't feel me fingers and I don't want anything to do with fighting Ifan with knives, he might take them off us and stick us with them...!' Ronnie put his hands in his pockets and despite Henry's shouts of, 'Chicken, chicken Ronnie's a chicken...!' He turned and hurried back down the slope slipping and sliding as he went.

Huw reluctantly watched him go, a dark silhouette disappearing back down the hill, 'There's only two us now...' he voiced quietly,' you can go too if you want Henry...'

Henry shook his head vigorously, 'Nah, chuffing 'ell Huw, I'm sticking with you, you might get into trouble by yourself then your Mum will blame me like she always does... Come on Huw, you can share my knife if you want...'

The two resumed their upward plod, walking between the tyre tracks in the virgin snow. As they crested the brow of the hill, the road now leading onto the first flat snow covered pasture land stretching before them, Henry peering into the distance said, 'We better mind out Huw, there's a guard house when we get to the road leading up to the summit, they'll stop us there won't they…?'

Huw thought about this, he knew these fields and the surrounding land well, excellent places to snare rabbits, there was indeed a guard house of sorts with a barrier gate across the road half a mile ahead. But then if the Martin brothers had business up there then there was no way Huw and Henry would be allowed in, unless they sneaked across land over the fields. There wouldn't be patrols around the perimeter fence surrounding the summit funny concrete building in this weather, or would there? Huw chewed on this then coming to a halt said to Henry, 'Think you're right, they'd see us miles off, but look,' he pointed down at the Martin's tyre tracks, 'nothing else has gone up here tonight, there's no tracks see? If the Martins have got to the top, then they'll be back down in a bit. There's the sheep pen up ahead beside the road, we'll hide in there and watch the road for a bit in the shelter Henry,' They resumed their plodding through the snow, the blustery wind had abated, then had died away suddenly and now large feathery snowflakes were falling, their boot squeaking as they clumped onwards in the half light on the top of the long bleak headland of the snow encrusted Wurm.

Half a mile away, Huw and Henry reached the sheep pen, both were cold, Huw had hitched up his well darned woollen socks using the turn down two inches up to cover his knees, the knotted pieces of second hand knicker elastic his mother had made for 'hold ups' he tightened over the knees. Both of the boys stood in the dark watching the road, nothing was moving. After a while Henry said, 'What time do you think it might be Huw…? Neither boy having a watch.

Huw screwed up his face and did some mental arithmetic, he had left home about seven o'clock as near as he could guess, that's when Jonesey was coming to pick up Peggy for their date, then the trip across town, picking up Henry then Ronnie, then the climb up to the Martins, to now… 'I think it must be about ten or half past Henry, why…?'

Henry looked pained as he answered, 'I got to go home Huw, there'll be hell to pay when my Dad comes of shift, my Mam said I had to be in by ten… You heard her…'

Huw knew Henry was right, although Henry's father was nothing compared to Ifan, he wasn't to be messed about with and would take his belt to Henry if he thought it necessary. 'Go on Henry, you go, nothing happening here, I think I might have got it wrong, You go and I will follow you in a bit, I just gotta wait a bit longer before I go back…'

'Thanks Huw… Think you'd better take this…!' He reached under his coat and brought out the scout knife, 'You have it Huw, you can give it me back tomorrow…'

Huw accepted the gift of Henry's precious knife, placing it in the waist band of his trousers under the snake shaped belt buckle. 'Thanks Henry, hope you don't get a hiding from your Dad.' He said meaningfully.

Henry pulled his balaclava down, put his hands deep in his pockets and began the slog back down the track, their tracks they had made on the way up almost obliterated by the snow now.

Huw leaned against the cold wall of the sheep pen. What could he do next, he was now alone, somewhere up ahead in the snow were Ifan and the Martins. Then, emboldened by thought of Henry's scout knife as a weapon, he decided to go on. Setting out back on the road he trudged his way along until he came to the fork in the road, straight ahead lay the route to the summit but the snow was undisturbed. To the right, the path that led down to the grave yard and church, there were visible traces of the tyre tracks, he took that path thinking as he plodded on, my Dad is in that churchyard, it was a small but significant omen in Huw's mind, that this way led to where his father William, had been buried those years before. Huw had visited the grave many times and the ghosts held no fears for him, at least one would be his friend. The way sloped downwards until the stone wall of the churchyard came into view, there, in front of the lynch gate stood the Martin's lorry.

10

Back down the mountain outside the gate to the Bryn Morfa cottages, Jonesey had just pulled up in the jeep intending to pick up Peggy as arranged for the evening dance date. He saw and heard a commotion outside the Owen's home, got out to investigate switching off the engine before making his way up the path.

Peggy saw him and ran towards him, 'Jonesey, thank God that you've come, Huw's had a battering from Ifan and he's ran off, his mother's beside herself with fear for the boy, if he has gone to follow Ifan he'll kill him this time…'

'Right, get a coat Peggy it's gonna be cold, c'mon, we'll find him don't worry, the jeep's pretty good in snow and we'll be a lot faster on four wheels.

'Hey, I'm coming too…!' Gunner Bob had overheard and was buttoning his great coat as he walked towards them, 'Where you think he's gone Peggy?'

'He said he was going for his mates, that'll be Henry and little Ronnie, they live over near the gas works in the council terraces. He'll go there first, then, if he's planning on following Ifan, the Martin's house up on the Wurm, he told his mother that he was following Ifan there, if you drive back towards town Jonesey I'll tell you where to go…' Peggy went back to tell Mrs Thomas what they were going to do, then came back climbed into the passenger seat with Gunner Bob getting into the back of the jeep through the opposite open side.

'Ok,' yelled Jonesey as he gunned the engine, 'here we go…!' The jeep cut new tracks in the snow as they drove back along the wide road into town passing the dance hall they had intended to visit before things had taken this twist, the 'Winter Gardens Palace Peggy,' he pointed across, 'Would have rather been in there tonight Peggy, I'm told they were putting the heating on to mark the occasion…!'

The jeep with its three occupants took the shore road then taking a right turned inland towards the gasworks and the small built up area where most of the town's working families lived. Pulling the jeep up outside the house where Peggy knew Henry lived, she hurried up the short path and banged on the door. Henry's mother appeared, told her that the boys had left earlier, that as far as she knew they were going to the scout meeting with the Americans at the church hall, was there anything wrong she had asked?

'No, just Huw had been upset when he left home,' Peggy said diplomatically.

'Aah, it's that Ifan again isn't it?' Henry's mother added not looking surprised, 'he's a bad lot is Ifan, they will have gone to pick up Ronnie, you know where he lives, when you catch up with them remind our Henry he's got to be back here for ten o'clock, his Dad's on night shift and I don't want him wandering in late again…!'

It was the same story at Ronnie's home, his mother told them that the boys were in their scout uniforms and were on their way for treats with the GIs nodding over to where Jonesey sat with the jeep's engine running. Peggy thanked her and climbed back aboard. Jonesey drove the jeep back through town, it was silent, nothing moving no people about. Along the main road through the main street, white now under the cover of snow, then up to where the end of town rose into the last shops and buildings at the bottom of the long narrow drive up onto the mountain. Taking them through the quiet road junction at the bottom of hill, Jonesey pointed the jeep towards a rise and they began to climb the first zig zags taking them up onto the mountain road. Then after leaving the main road and began the drive up the steep incline to the bottom of the mountain, engaging low gear, Jonesey took her up, jockeying the jeep weaving from side to side to gain traction in the snow, the engine labouring with blue exhaust smoke trailing behind them as they climbed gaining a yard at a time in the deepening snow.

Jonesey was guided by Peggy as they navigated twists and bends until eventually, they arrived at the road junction which led off to the left to where the Martins place was. He pulled the jeep up outside and the three of them went up to the door and Peggy knocked, her heart in her mouth as she prepared for the confrontation with Ifan which was inevitable. The house was in silence as with all other buildings the black-out curtains were in place, it was a foreboding dark and dismal looking place. Jonesey went around the back, there was no sign of life, then crossing over to the barn like garage called Peggy and Bob over.

'Hey look here, there's been some activity and very recently,' he pointed at the tyre tracks and footprints alongside.

'Yes and look at these!' Bob was standing by the wall to the road. On the ground were a number of flattened footprints in the snow, 'Look at the size of these, they are all smaller than those by the garage, these are the lads' footprints Peggy?'

It was abundantly clear that the prints had been made when the boys had crouched by the wall, Jonesey followed them out into the road where they fell in between the tyre tracks of the lorry. 'This is where they went, they're following the tyre tracks, where does this go Peggy?'

Peggy stood looking up toward the hill said, 'But there's nowhere to go up there, only the installation on the summit and that's out of bounds for everyone, there's nothing else on the mountain only a church, with grave yard on the lower slope with only sheep and goats. Could it be the sheep, they could be stealing those but they're in lamb now, rustling you call it, the flocks of sheep to sell, they would stoop so low as to do if there's money to be made, that I know...?'

Jonesey followed her gaze up the mountain side, in the short time that he had been here there had never been any inclination to explore the slopes in the bad weather, though Peggy had told him of its beauty in the Summer months.

'Then there's only one way to find out, climb aboard, we'll go and see, they've left tracks a blind man could follow...!'

Jonesey gauge the slope, then backed up outside the Martin's house, 'Hold on, this is going to be fun...!' He slipped the clutch taking a run at the slope to gather speed with Peggy clinging onto her seat and Bob bouncing about in the back of the jeep. Again, weaving from side to side the vehicle growled up the steepest part of the slope. As they reached the crest a small figure came into view.

'Huw!' shouted Peggy, 'it's Huw...!'

'No it's not, this one's too small, is it one of the other boys...?'

The jeep pulled up on the near flat surface, towards them came Ronnie, hands in pockets and his pinched face a picture of guilt. 'I told 'em I was going home, it's nothing to do with me, honest...!' He was almost in tears and Peggy got out to put an arm round him.

'What is Ron, what are they doing up here?' Peggy asked the boy feeling him shivering under his coat.

'I dunno, Huw's mad about his Dad and Ifan, if they find him there's going to be trouble, that's why I'm going home…'

'Can you make your way back down to town on your own Ron?' She asked him, worried about the boy's plight and the cold.

'I'm thirteen Peggy, I'll be fine, I just wanna go now…' Ronnie looked a picture of misery, clearly anxious to get away before any more questions were asked of him.

The three adults stood beside the jeep, Bob saying, 'If we take him with us, he'll freeze, it's better if he keeps moving.' A quick decision was made, it was best to let him go, checking on him on the way back to make sure he arrived safe at home.

Jonesey pulled back his cuff, looked at his watch, 'It's near ten thirty, we've wasted too much time, get back in let's see where the boys have got to never mind the idiots Huw's chasing, they've obviously got something going down up here somewhere, we need to make sure young Huw and his buddy don't come to any harm, get in…'

The Ford Willys engine took a moment to start then growled into life, it faltered then picked up again as Jonesey pressed down on the accelerator. They bumped and slid their way along the narrow track the margins of which were now becoming blurred by the deepening covering of snow.

11

The Irish Sea off the Welsh Coast

22.15hrs

The Lady Patricia plunged again into another trough, then righted seeming to shrug off the water from her deck as she laboured ponderously with her screw steadily churning the water under her stern. Lewis had taken her for nearly five hours on these necessary back and forth tacking dog leg courses against the wind to make headway against the oncoming tide. With a glance at the compass and checking against the clock he turned to Finn and said, 'It's half past the midnight hour' Lewis announced. 'We're as near to the mark as I can make out, we need to keep the revolutions down now, just to be holding our position, or we'll creep back if this water pushes us. Is it all ready below Finn?' The big built crewman Finn nodded and shouted back, 'It is that, the boy is looking after the engine and we've stacked what loose cargo there is with ropes holding it so nothing will move. It'll be difficult though when it comes time to bring anything on deck Boss. It's as slippery as hell down there!' He referred to the forward hold area under the large deck hatch where normally the catch would be stored when it came aboard from the nets with water pouring from the catch as it was man handled below. The residue of so many fishing trips was coating the wooden deck and the access ladder to the hold, fish scales, the spillage of marine diesel which now slopped about with the single pump working hard to control the foul smelling mixture at level where it wouldn't swamp the small engine room. Neither man liked to think about the dire consequences of a flooded engine in such a hostile sea so far from any help and the friendly waters of home. Long minutes dragged passed then Mick shouted again to Finn, 'There's a lull coming on, we must be near the centre of the storm, the sea is not as rough and we have crossed the point where two strong tides merge; there's calmer water ahead I'm sure.' Then, Mick eyes, struggled for seconds to focus in the darkness off the bows, to make sense of what he thought he had seen. 'There, off the starboard bow, see that Finn?' Both men directed their stare to a point off in the darkness and searched the horizon. 'There, there it is again!' Mick pointed to where a white light shone for less than a second before disappearing, then a moment later it returned, then again.

Finn's eyes took some time to adjust his vision and to realise that what they were looking at was not at sea level at all, it was hundreds of feet above the water and unlike any vessel there was a steady light when it came on, flashed then went off, clearer now as this was controlled illumination repeating over and over. 'It's a lighthouse Mick…!' 'Aye, it is that. We need to come about smartly to port and begin to steer parallel to those cliffs, make sure the boy knows, we've arrived!' He replied pulling a large-scale ordinance survey map out of the chart drawer and laying it on top of the nautical chart on the small fold down table jabbed a finger at it. 'Now look, here is our present location and heading.' He pointed to the long French loaf like irregular shaped headland jutting out northwards into the Irish Sea from the North of Wales, which was according to the map, the coast of the county of Caernarvonshire. With his index finger he traced a line across the water from the isle of Anglesey eastwards then to the upper most point of the headland, 'That's the light we've seen,' pointing it out on the map then gesturing with his head over his shoulder to the disappearing beam from the light house to their stern, 'we're now running south west towards this feature' he said pointing again to the map. Mick tapped an outline on the map that resembled the middle fingers of a giant hand with each of the digits poking out nearly two hundred feet into the Liverpool Bay. Between the fingers, lay long channels separating each of the promontories. 'This is where we're heading Finn,' Mick indicated the eastern channel where he had marked with a cross a point close into the deepest penetration landward, 'These cliffs above are nearly three hundred feet and sheer, but there is a path I'm told, this is our destination this night!' Finn quickly gazed across the water across the starboard bow, now he could make out the sound of waves crashing against the base of the cliffs a mile off, and did he imagine or was it real, could he see the faint luminescence of the spume and spray thrown up by the force of the inbound waves? 'It's your boat Mick,' he rolled the words out seriously, 'Will the lee there give us shelter enough to unload I'm thinking?' Mick Lewis, pulled at his beard and shook his head, 'At this moment Finn, I know as much as you. The map and the drawing I have shows a ledge of limestone running half way out from the base towards the mouth at around eight to ten feet above sea level at high tide, we need to anchor off there with about twelve feet of water safely under our keel. There are supposed to be iron mooring points and a sea ladder set in the wall at the end of the inlet, that's all I know, and God help us if they're not there.'

With her engine chugging turning over at slow revolutions, the Lady Patricia cautiously made her way in, rising and falling with the swell as she coasted landward to within a hundred yards of the cliff face until Mick had nursed her bows gently into the mouth of the second inlet. Oddly there had been enough dim light with which to make out the jagged rocks forming the entrance, with Finn standing on the prow poling with an oar to ward them off ward off the teeth like rocks. Easing against the wall of the natural harbour, Finn had flung the old tyre roped to the Lady Pat's sides between the vessel and the rock wall, secured and made fast the lines to the bow and the stern to the stout iron rings protruding from the rock face. With the rubber tyre on lashing ropes now hanging over the sides they were acting as cushions between the vessel and the rock wall. Although the Lady Patricia still rose and fell with the swell, they were made fast at a safe anchorage. The water was eerily calm given that they had just left the rolling waves only yards behind them, the waves lost power as they surged in, their momentum tempered by the angle of the onto the sea. The remaining swell slopped against the walls of their lime-stone haven. Ahead towards the looming mass of the headland, it was just possible in the twilight conditions to make out that the inlet continued inwards and opened into a voluminous cavern which appeared to stretch well under the mountain into the darkness beyond, while above the roof was faintly discernible a good hundred feet above them. Across the breadth of the inlet there was at least a clear hundred feet from where the Lady Patricia lay and the parallel far wall. The wave actions of the millions of tides over hundreds of thousands of years had burrowed, eaten their way into the lime stone of the mountain creating a deep and wide inlet then further back a cave where there was room to hide a leviathan sized sea monster from the folk stories of old. Mick shut the engine down, young Gerry came up from below, despite the rigours of the past hours he still looked fresh and remarkably undaunted, 'Ready below Dah,' he shouted to his father. Mick had tousled the boy's thick unruly hair patted the stubble growth of an emerging beard and said to his son, 'When this is over Me lad, I'll see that you'll have earned enough from this trip to buy your own boat, so help me!' It was a genuine sentiment, the boy had given his all and Mick knew that, was grateful for the skill of the boy's hands and the natural seamanship he appeared to be innately endowed with, perhaps it was in the blood his grandfather and great-grandfather had too spent their entire lives at sea, as men and boys from a very early age. First, they needed to explore their immediate surroundings, Mick sending Gerry and Finn up the iron ladder set in the wall onto the ledge above. There were torrents of water cascading down from the cliff above mixing with the falling snow, but there was little to report back other that there was what seemed a goat or sheep track rather than the expected path, which ran raising diagonally across the face of the cliff upwards. This fragile ascending route appearing to turn back on itself zig-zagging upwards until it was lost out of sight in the darkness. There had been no sign of life or any obvious recent activity visible other than a battered lobster pot which had been thrown up at some time, no prominent features other than that of a wide stone shelf which continued well back under the over-hanging cliff stretching into the yawning recesses of the cave behind. Finn had taken an oil lamp and shielding it from the seaward side had made his way with Gerry deeper into the cave, the yellow beams from the lamp casting shadows as they edged along the shelf deeper under the mountain. Although slippery with seawater and the detritus thrown up by the waves there was little of note other than the echoes of the pounding waves resonating from the rear of the cave in the all-consuming darkness around them. Mick had called up, from the rising and falling deck below, 'Anything to see up there lads?' Receiving negative shouts from both Finn and Gerry, he called them back down, returning in their wet sea coats to the comparative warmth of the Lady Patricia's wheelhouse.

As Finn and Gerry made their way back down onto the deck, Mick leaned out over the side casting a look forward in the direction of the far reaches of the vast yawning cavern, the sound of surf on shingle, the tide was turning, the water level would begin to drop now very soon. Finn took depth soundings over the bow and stern with a hand line, announcing surprisingly that there was a good thirty feet of water under their keel. The depth of the inlet was much deeper than either had anticipated, the tide actions had gouged out a trench along the bottom from the mouth of the inlet inwards back under the mountain. Above they were hidden from any opportune prying eyes by the jutting overhang of the cliffs, only to seawards astern was the Lady Patricia even remotely visible to the naked eye. They were snugly tucked into a safe secure mooring, for the moment at least were concealed from detection. While Finn was pouring them each a generous toddy from the remains of his whiskey bottle, Mick had brought out the radio set in its case and raised the two-yard long whip antennae feeding it through the small side window. He turned the set on and watched the lights as they glowed into life. It whistled and crackled as he turned the knob 'till he found the wavelength he had been given to tune in to. Now, 'we wait,' he thought to himself reasonable satisfied with their progress thus far. Taking out his pipe and with some due care not to spill any of the precious mixture filled the bowl, tamping the tobacco down he struck a match cupping it in his hands facing away from the stern of the boat lit his pipe. Then, once the tobacco had caught well, sipping gently at the fiery fluid in his mug, Mick, taking a deep pull of smoke gazed backwards out at the snow now falling steadily beyond the glass of the wheelhouse and settled down with the rise and fall of the boat, to wait for the signal…

It came, at 23.48hrs, in English, 'RAGNAR,' repeat, 'RAGNAR…!'

Lewis, in an almost whispered voice, answered with, 'LOKI…' 'LOKI…!'

It was done, there was nothing he could do to stop the thing now, he reached for his pipe again at the same time asked Finn if there was anything left in the bottle, 'Hung for the sheep or the lamb, it made no difference,' he told himself with a long drawn out sigh.

12

On the Bridge of the Armed Trawler
HMS Juniper
20.50hrs

Both officers and the two ratings manning the wings of the open bridge were tired cold and frankly bored. Another leg of the daily patrols across the Liverpool Bay, basically keeping the land to their starboard side on the outward leg, to port on their return. From their base station near the port of Holyhead across to Hoylake off the Wirral near the estuary of the Mersey. They had routinely crisscrossed for days and nights on a sweeping patrols pattern covering set courses within the AM92 to AM93 grids of the Irish Sea. Nothing of note was entered into the log except the turning points and compass bearings, apart from sightings of the merchants shipping and their Royal Naval escorts crossing the sea lanes into the Liverpool Bay it was proving to be the usual dull and tedious tour of service. This night was no different, leaving the port then rounding the point where the South Stack light house's sweeping beam falling across the heavy seas was left behind them, then out onto a northerly course into the Irish Sea then south easterly they had steamed on into the relatively calmer waters off the east coast of the island of Anglesey on a heading following the coastline to return again to the Hoylake station.

The five-hundred-and-thirty-ton Dance Class, elderly armed trawler, 'Juniper,' she was a fleet auxiliary vessel with a crew of thirty-five, used primarily, as an in-shore patrol craft and sometime training vessel. At a little over forty-eight metres in length with a shallow draft of only two and a half metres, she bobbed on the heavy waves much as a cork and as such much to the discomfort of her crew. The open bridge offered little shelter with the commander and first officer spending their watch huddled in their duffel coats from the penetrating wind and sleet.

Lieutenant Commander Stewart Penrick eased his aching frame in the bridge chair, turning as a rating brought up steaming enamelled mugs of cocoa from the galley below. 'Have you added a little rum Jenkins…?' He growled at the man bad temperedly, then with a little more sympathy for the pinched face of the man struggling to dole out the mugs on the rolling bridge, 'Thanks, need something to keep out the cold up here, give the men an issue too when you go below.' The younger officer, half his age, standing beside him said, 'Another foul night Sir, are you holding this course on the usual pattern?' Penrick sipped his cocoa secretly wishing his *'Wavy Navy'* number one would shut instead of insisting on chattering on answered, 'No, I want to bring her on ten points to starboard and close with the shore line, the water is slackening, we may have less of a bumpy ride if we come in closer at the next turning point, hold her steady on this heading for another five minutes then sound of the change of watch there's a good fellow. I'll be down in my cabin if you need me.' The first officer watched as Penrick climbed out of his seat leaving him to take over, then left the bridge descending the ladder with agonising slowness.

'Poor old bugger…!' He thought, this was a young man's war and Penrick by any stretch of the imagination was not young, he had been brought back out of retirement for the duration, a crusty old Sod, but not too bad a CO given he was well over twice the age of any member of the ship's company he thought as he took over the ship's con, opening the voice pipe in front of him he called, 'Below, captain's leaving the bridge, relief officer to station and stand to all hands for change of watch.'

Lieutenant Douglas Porterfield RNVR, raising himself full height before sitting into the captain's chair, proudly looking around the command now under his control, not bad for a Royal Naval Reserve Officer's first posting he mentally congratulated himself, what could possibly go wrong, monotony and boredom were the biggest enemies which he had to endure, yet, with a little luck he may get another posting to a fighting ship, and even a promotion if he could just keep clear of the old man's temper and stick it out through the tedium of pointless patrol duty. With these thoughts he wrapped his gloved hands around the cocoa mug, looking down over the bridge screen at the little pop gun of the four-pounder gun on the fore deck of the trawler, not quite a battleship, but for moment he was the officer in command, he happily stared out looking as manfully responsible as a Royal Naval Officer should, into the sleet now turning into snow, well, he thought somewhat amused, even Nelson had started on the bottom rung of the ladder…!

Below, in his tiny cramped uncomfortable cupboard of a cabin, Penrick shrugged off the heavy coat, hung up his hat and sat down heavily on his bunk. His hands and feet ached, he looked around his dismal surrounding feeling the anger and resentment return, 'A glorified fishing boat, a waste of time coming back to be overlooked in favour of young snotties who had little aptitude or experience at sea. He reached into the locker beside the bunk lifting out a bottle of rum and a glass, poured a large measure then downed it in one. Pausing for a moment then think, 'Oh to hell with them all…!' he poured another downing that one as quickly as the first with the same recklessness, he filled the glass for the third time feeling better, 'Routine, routine that's all it is,' he murmured to himself in a melancholic tone, 'Nothings going to happen that the young snot can't deal with, he can earn his pay for once, see if I care a dam…!' Within minutes his head had fallen forward his chin sagging onto his chest, he had fallen asleep slumped across the bunk with his legs stretched out in front of him.

When a little over five minutes had elapsed, Porterfield rang down the order to alter course, the Juniper turning her blunt prow in through the flurries of snow toward the distant invisible Welsh coastline ten miles ahead off her starboard bow in the darkness. As her captain had guessed the sea had calmed, the eye of the storm was passing overhead had allowed them some respite from the worst of the unpredictable moods of the seas for at least a short while until it gathered its ferocity upon them once again.

The Juniper gathered way surging ahead at her stately ten knots heading into the calmer coastal waters of the Welsh bay, her first officer elated, her commander however, obliviously quite dead to the world.

13

Five Miles Off the Northern Welsh Coast
January 8th 22.30hrs

Reinecke and Leiter, on the near awash bridge of U-367 gazed up at the menacing cliff face looming out of the blackness to meet them, visible now even a deeper black mass in the darkness. This mass before them rose up, like some monstrous leviathan of the deep, the open maw of which emerged to take on malignant shape at the bottom of the cliff, like a gigantic hideous mouth flecked with the spume and saliva of the sea. Reinecke thought it looked like the entrance to the underworld, to the beckoning vision of the 'Hell' of Orpheus…!

'Surface the boat,' he called down, 'slow ahead both, depth sounding please, and crews close up for docking stations…?' The answers came back immediately, three knots with an ascending shelf under their keel, twenty metres of undulating seabed lay beneath them. The boat raised herself out of the water another two metres, the waves washing over her steel decks now with the muffled roar of the diesel exhausts grumbling in their wake. Reinecke could make out the three fingers of the rock promontories reaching out towards him, he made a minute alteration of course to port, the submarine was now aligned with the left hand opening to which they were closing with by the minute. A brief torch light flickered from deep inside the inlet, winked on and off, a Morse signal for the word 'LOKI,' then repeated 'LOKI'… He gave an answering series of flashes on the bridge shuttered Aldis lamp. Leiter turning his head said to Reinecke, 'Who thought of that one, it's a little dramatic…'

Reinecke smiled saying aloud, 'It would be for us if that was seen by anybody else, fool of an Englander…! It's actually very appropriate Leiter, Ragnar was a Viking, a curse to the Saxons, he raided this coast in the ninth century. Loki, lord of the underworld in Norse mythology, and that lying ahead, looks like the gateway to Hell…!' 'Crew to the bridge, docking party on deck…' As the bow of the U-367 drew abreast of the rocks guarding the entrance to the inlet, the six-man deck crew on the fore deck stood ready to fend off as they made the final approach. Reinecke's eyes strained in the dark, what worried him were the bow diving planes either side of the bows, these were controlled by chain drives, any damage would be catastrophic to the vessels ability to dive and surface. 'All stop, slow astern both…!' The boat's progress slowed then began vibrating as the engines braked her forward motion allowing her to continue forward with the remaining momentum. Gliding into the calmer water of the natural harbour the U-367's nose entered the inlet like a giant grey sea snake. 'Stop all…! Docking crew on deck… Standby to secure lines. Oblt Leiter, take over the con,' advise our guests below that we've arrived, their reception committee is here…!'

As the U-boat came to a rest, drawing slowly alongside the Lady Patricia as her long nose was now probing well into the dark recess of the cavern, as the conning tower and bridge drew abreast the wheel house of the other vessel Reinecke ordered, 'Finish with engines, secure the boat…' then sensed rather than felt, the forward keel gently touch gravel on the floor of the subterranean harbour. He shouted the orders to the deck crew who had climbed up out of the conning tower and down onto the fore deck, supervised their readying for the securing of lines to the other vessel. Immediately overhead of the conning tower the cliff rose above them, the remainder of the U-367 lay outside the shelter of the cave, exposed where the snow fell steadily onto to the wet after deck and the band stand AA mount at the back of the bridge. There was very little light, only a storm lantern giving off a weak pale circle of light around the fishing boat's deck area, shielded from the seaward side by a piece of canvass draped over the side of the wheelhouse. The captain of which was energetically putting tyres over the side between the two vessels aided by two more men who appeared to be his deck hands. Both vessels rose and fell gently in unison on the water. Reinecke looked down upon the three men standing on the deck of what was obviously a fishing boat, they were dressed pretty much the same in seaman's clothing, none had the bearing of service personnel he noted. 'Greetings Loki…!' He said in English, picking out the older man with the cap who been placing the tyre cushions, who seemed to be the captain, 'Lines coming across… I hope we haven't kept you waiting, the sea was rough here yes…?' The other took off his cap revealing ahead of bushy grey hair and a beard and waved up at him.

14

Mick Lewis had watched the submarine loom up out of the darkness, it was a pretty frightening monster sliding in then filling the space beside them like a knife in its sheaf. He greeted the officer who stood above him on the submarine's bridge, he looked competent enough, then over at the six crew who had tumbled out and were working on the fore deck. Finn, threw them lines fore and aft to secure their boat, Mick himself placing the rubber fenders over the side between the two vessels. He thanked God for the blessing of a sea now becalmed, this manoeuvre would have been impossible if the waves and storm had persisted.

Over on the submarine, the officer with the white crowned naval cap climbed down the outside short ladder on the outside of the conning tower and made his way over, nimbly jumping the closing gap between the boats. The other took off his cap and put out his hand smiling, as he spoke in passable English, 'Bruno Reinecke, of the Deutche Kriegsmarine… Good to see you captain, are you ready for us?'

Mick Lewis, grabbed the hand, 'We are that, you're welcome I'm sure, it's a pretty sight you make coming in out of the dark like that, could frighten the children with a big thing like your boat. Aye, we're ready for you and I will be glad to get done with this night, this place and set sail for friendlier waters, I tell you that Mr Kriegsmarine…!' He took in the single cross medal on the left breast of Reinecke's sea jacket, apart from the white cover to his hat there was no other insignia or decoration marking him as an officer, Lewis had expected gold braid at least with silver buttons…!

Reinecke agreed with Lewis's remark, 'Then the sooner we get our business finished here then we can both be on our way Herr Captain, my men will begin passing over the cargo now, you will need to speak with Herr Breitfeld and Herr Schumann, they are the ones responsible for the load we bring you, I am just the means of transport, here they come now…!'

Down from the conning tower onto the fore deck climbed Breitfeld and Schumann, both looking relieved to be out of the confines of the U-boat. Both men stretched their legs, looked up at the white flakes of snow drifting down from above in eddies above the deck. They made their way to the fore hatch and Leiter consulted his notebook, whilst Schumann gingerly crossed to join Reinecke on the Lay Patricia's deck.

They could hear Breitfeld beginning to reel off orders, 'Boxes one to eight to be brought up first, in numerical order, don't get this wrong…! You, you and you…,' he ordered three of the deck crew, begin to unload numbers one to four up onto the land first, leave the others on the deck of this tub, clear…?'

The men looked across to their captain questioningly, Reinecke yelled over to them, 'Herr Breitfeld is in charge now, obey his orders lads…!'

The crewman began to heave the box up through the torpedo hatch onto the deck, the first four appeared, seemingly quite light and easy to move.

'Forgive me captain, I need to re-join my men, this is a crucial moment.' Reinecke hopped back onto the U-boats port pressure hull and back upon the fore deck. Up with the men working on the deck of the U-boat Reinecke stood to appraise progress, it was23.15hrs, he wanted to be clear all being well by 23.30 if they get Breitfeld and Schumann to get a move on, 'Now…,' Reinecke said to himself and to the deck crew, 'We unload the rest without delay, once our 'guests are off the boat we're finished here, then, we set course for home boys…! All hands look lively, open up the forward torpedo tube hatch, let's get to work.' The crew bustled about their stations and the square loading hatch was cranked open to reveal the circular torpedo loading opening with its securing wheel now exposed. Reinecke look up catching sight of his first officer, Georg Leiter's troubled face gazing down upon him from the U-boat's bridge. He waved up at him, 'Not long now Georg, keep them working below, tell Remischke to start to plot our course home…!' There was something about Leiter's empty face that worried him, he would speak with him later, now to get on with the job…

Leiter watched the activity going on below, saw the open torpedo hatch way with the boxes coming up with agonising slowness, he felt himself begin to sweat despite the cold. If they were caught here, a hundred metres in from the sea, if they were spotted from above, God knows what lay up above their heads, they would be trapped, there would be no way out… Leiter' heart was beginning to beat painfully in his chest. Reinecke did not seem to be bothered…!

Below on the decks. The first six boxes had been carefully manhandled onto the submarine's steel deck then across over that of the fishing vessel, then in stages up the iron rungs of the ladder onto the shelf above, two more lay ready to be moved. The first four now lay in a group at the foot of the cliff lit by another shielded lamp, this sited near the pathway leading upwards, Leiter stood beside these organising their numbers. Two more were being passed across the deck of the Lady Patricia when a voice called out from above…

'Hail the boat below…!' The disembodied voice called out of the darkness somewhere close above. It came again…

Breitfeld, standing at the foot of the pathway yelled up in flawless English, 'Show yourself and be recognised…!' He was joined by Lewis with Schumann making his way over to join the other two now peering expectantly upwards. Reinecke note that a pistol had magically appeared in Breitfeld's hand, he held it behind his back as he waited for the owner of the voice to show themselves. This, he thought to himself, is where this show really gets under way, if the Irish were already here, the next to come must be the fabled Welsh conspirators…!

He did not have to wait long, another shout and then two men came into view making their way down the pathway from above. The first, a biggish burly individual appeared to be the leader, the second, a more insignificant individual, clearly and underling. The bigger man squared up to Breitfeld, 'Are you Lewis the Irishman then. I'm Reg Martin, the boss here?' He grunted pushing his flat cap back from his forehead then placing both his hands on his hips in an assumption arrogant authority then continued nonchalantly. 'I'm in charge here, your business is with me, nothing moves without my say so.' Reg Martin grinned in the manner of the one who holds the whip hand, 'So you do exactly as I say, is that clear…?'

'No, I am your contact and it's my orders which must be followed, this however, is Lewis whom I believe to be Irish, if that is of any consequence…!' Breitfeld clearly was not amused. 'Now, we need to get things moving quickly, where are your men…?' He looked towards the path expecting another set of feet to appear.

'There's just us and my brother up aloft, you'll need the help of your sailors there to get this load to the top, it's a hell of climb in the dark with this snow,' he gestured towards the crew working on the U-boat who were already carrying the next load of boxes across the Lady

Patricia's deck.

Reinecke felt it was time to introduce himself and make it clear that the sailors were under his command. 'Reinecke, Kriegsmarine, those are my men, they have nothing to do with your arrangement, once unloaded we sail, what you do here is your business Herr Martin…!'

'Herr Martin is it…? Well let me tell you nothing moves until we have an agreement, now do we get your men or not?'

Lewis entered the discussion, 'Look, we have our cargo on board now, we want to be away before the tide changes, but we can't leave tied up to that thing!' He pointed at the shape of the U-367. So, maybe we should cooperate. Hey! Finn, Gerry, get up here and land a hand, the quicker we do this then we can be gone…'

Martin hesitated for a moment, 'Alright, you' he said pointing at Gerry, take the first box with the big fella,' he nodded at Finn, 'you two take the next,' he jabbed his finger at an amazed Schumann, then Ifan, who was looking well out of his depth in understanding the fearful implications of the precarious situation he found himself now involved, 'Treason,' in his naïve thinking he remembered vaguely, 'was a hanging offence…!' He licked his wet lips, merely nodded at Reg Martin, the avaricious thought of the money was enough to empower his weakened courage onwards once more.

Breitfeld had no room to argue, his anxiety grew as the minutes were ticking by with no movement, 'Get on with it then…!' Inwardly he was seething. 'You have a strange way of demonstrating your patriotism Mr Martin…!'

'Then you're no judge of character, the only 'cause I serve is my own, this is business, nothing more…'

The first two of the numbered boxes, were lifted with a man at each end on the rope handles, then grunting under their loads they disappeared slowly upward. It was near to fifteen minutes before the four men were to reappear ready for the next load.

Breitfeld was beside himself with frustration, there were still four more of the heavier boxes on board waiting to be brought up through the torpedo hatch, the few which had now arrived and been stacked at the foot of the cliff were the heaviest, the crewmen struggling to lift their weight. Six now to move…

Lewis had returned to his boat; four crates had been manhandled down the hatch into the hold. They were ready to go… He pulled the hatch cover across and made fast the tarpaulin cover.

Reinecke shouted across to Leiter on the bridge, 'This is going too slow, I'm going to lend a hand, keep a watchful eye astern Leiter.'

Leiter couldn't believe his ears, 'Herr Kaleu, you cannot leave the boat…!'

'Easy Leiter, this won't take long, get the men back on board, tell Hartmann to get the engines ready, we leave as soon as I get back.'

'But Herr Kaleu…!'

'No Leiter, it's an order, prepare to get under way, clear…!'

Reinecke didn't wait for a reply, unless this was moved on and quickly, then they all ran the risk of detection, beneath him was enemy territory, Breitfeld didn't appear to appreciate that. He grabbed hold of a box and gestures Leiter to take the other hand, 'Now, c'mon get on with it…!'If the other man was about to argue, he changed his mind, as the four prepared to lift the next load between them. Being fresher, Reinecke and Breitfeld went first feeling their way up the slippery narrow pathway as it snaked upwards. In places the snow had settled, and it was dangerous under foot carrying the weight of the box between them. Behind them, Ifan and Schumann struggled with the heaviest load yet, they could barely lift its weight tottering forward with both men gritting their teeth as they began to climb, a string of invectives coming from each man in their own language growing louder with each step.

The going wasn't quite as difficult as Reinecke had imagined; the steepest part was just before the top where the path cross to the right then abruptly turned inwards for the last six metres onto flat land. They were met by Reg Martin, 'Bring it this way he indicated to where a lorry stood parked up outside what was obviously the lynch gate set in a two-metre-high wall to a church. The snow-covered apron in front of the gate extended some twenty to thirty metres square where the hearses once would have had room to turn their horses. Beyond, the roadway such as it was, drifted up a slope and out of sight. Reinecke fought to remember the details from the maps he and Leibnitz had worked on, this was the nine hundred-year-old church of St. Mary on the Mount… From what he could remember it covered the flat area right above the coves below. The path leading down they had just climbed had been made by smugglers two centuries before… 'History,' he thought, the wrong time to pick such flowers, the next boxes were coming up now…!

Finn appeared with Gerry, carrying a box between them, then Reg Martin, of Ifan and Schumann there was no sign yet.

Bill Martin supervised the loading onto the back of the truck the five boxes under the canvass awning now heavily laden with snow, neatly stacking and tying these near the wall of the driver's cab. Another three to come, Reinecke counted. He sought out Finn and Gerry, 'Your work is done here, get yourselves away as quickly as you can, as soon as the next boxes come up I'll be joining you below…'

The two Irishmen looked at each other then turned to leave, over his shoulder Finn shouted, 'Your God go with you Reinecke…!' With that they both made their way back down the rocky path meeting Ifan and Schumann struggling up with their heavy box still thirty metres short of the top. Finn and Gerry carefully made their way past them where the pathway turned the last corner before the final stretch to the top step.

On the bridge of the U-boat, Leiter made a decision, 'Close the forward hatch, secure the deck.' The on the voice tube to the command room below, 'How many boxes are left on board?' The answer came back from Remischke, 'Four, still in the forward torpedo room Oblt Leiter…'

'Then secure them again where they are, prepare the boat for sea. As soon as the Herr Kaleu comes aboard, we sail…!'

Remischke was not at all comfortable with this, he, isolated in the confines of the command room could only imagine what was going on up top, but then Leiter must be aware of what was happening and be in communication with Reinecke. 'Your orders Oblt Leiter,' turning to the men standing around him waiting for news he said, 'prepare the boat for sea, secure the cargo forward, no more to be unloaded. Secure internal and external loading hatches… Now…!' He reasoned, if there was any come back, then he had just obeyed a direct order from the senior officer on the boat… Around him men began to take up their stations, he called through to Hartmann's engine room and ordered him to warm up the engines and prepare for sea. He did not think however, of adjusting the trim to compensate for the weight of the cargo they had just unloaded…

15

Reinecke's apprehension grew by the minute, Breitfeld had wanted to climb into the truck to double check the box numbers, Reinecke had noted that what they had loaded on so far was all of the lighter boxes, it didn't make sense, surely the heavier ones should go on first? Martin pushed Breitfeld hard in the chest with the flat of his hand, Breitfeld stumbled in the snow on the ground had been trodden into mush at the back of the truck. Breitfeld was a scientist, a biologist, he was no soldier, he sat on his backside in the snow looking up at martin with murder in his eyes, helpless to do anything more.

Reg Martin now started in earnest, 'Now, Mr 'I'm in Charge,' or whatever your real name is, we've got a bit of a problem here, me and my brother Bill, I think given all of our efforts on your behalf that we need to renegotiate the terms of our contract… come with me, I want a word with you in private…' Breitfeld looked to Reinecke and saw no support, so getting to his feet brushing himself down seething followed Reg Martin through the lynch gate into the churchyard then the few steps to the door of the ancient church. Turning the large iron handle in the oak door, it creaked open. Martin stepped into the gloom of the interior and struck a match. 'Ah, that'll do.' He reached for a brass candle stick on a table beside the entrance, held the match against the candle. It caught with in a fragile flicker of yellow light.

Reg Martin's face looked positively devil like as the candle threw shadows upwards lighting his glowering face. 'Now, as payment, I see that our fee should be in proportion to the risks we have taken, you and your mate, expect us to take you and this load on, to Liverpool no less. So, the price has gone up, two thousand pounds in cash…!

Breitfeld was beside himself with rage, the man's greed was obvious, yet he was in a difficult position to bargain at this stage. 'You've had your money, we paid you well in advance… And, I don't carry any funds with me, so you'll have to stick to your deal my cheating friend…!'

'Or what, you going to go home, take your goods with you? I don't think so, if you don't have the ready cash, then we'll take one of your precious boxes instead, I think I know what's in them and there's plenty to share so you won't miss one box of 'fivers' will you,' he tapped the side of his nose for emphasis, 'there's your deal, take it or leave it...?'

Breitfeld could feel the whole operation coming to pieces, all because of this man holding all of the cards, his anger began to boil over. 'You swine, you planned this, don't you realise what's at stake if we don't get the whole shipment to where it must be, we only have hours God damn you Martin...!'

'I do, so that's why you're going to play ball with us, one box will be left with us in fair payment...'

A sudden noise broke the stand-off, the grating of wood on the tiled floor, Martin lifted the candle stick higher, 'Who's there, show yourself!'

A boy stood up from behind the wooden pew where he had been hiding, pale faced thin youth with a look of terror on his face. Huw Henryd stood, paralyzed like a rabbit caught in headlights. 'I didn't mean anything mister.' He started to say when Breitfeld produced the Walther pistol from his pocket and pointed it at Huw's face.

At that moment Reinecke entered and stepped down the step into the church where the characters were frozen like a wax works cameo. 'What's going on?' He demanded.

Breitfeld's face was screwed up with rage and frustration, 'We have an interloper and a thief, both are about to get what they deserve...!

A yard away, Reg Martin stepped back at the sight of the weapon in Breitfeld's hand, 'I want no part of this, count me out...!'

'No, you don't understand do you cheating pig, you are the thief and when I dealt with this trash, you are next!' He turned the pistol and levelled the barrel at Huw's face... Sorry, but you are in the way fool.' His finger tightened on the trigger.

Then, a number of things happened simultaneously, Reinecke had moved swiftly between the boy and Breitfeld, as he passed Martin he desperately lunged out slamming the flat of his hand on top of the candle. A load explosion deafened all of them in the confined space, Reinecke felt the bullet nick his cheek as it passed between him and the boy, less than a second later a second explosion, much louder than the first, the scene for an instant illuminated in the flash from the muzzle of a second weapon.

A second passed and with a scaping of a match Martin reignited the candle. As the candlelight flared, the acrid smell of cordite filled the nostrils as a haze of blue smoke hung in the air. On the floor, Breitfeld body was splayed out, the back of his head blown away. 'Jesus,' said Martin, 'You've killed him…!'

'No, but I have…!' Framed in the doorway of the church stood Mick Lewis, the smoking barrel of the big colt pistol still held steady in his hand, his face set in a grim rictus of stone. 'He, was going to kill an innocent child, I've met his kind before and this is overdue, for me… Now, you,' he pointed the gun at Martin, 'clear out before I rid the world of more filth, so help me I will…'

Martin needed no further encouragement, he turned in a panic to get out of the door, ran towards the gate calling for his brother, 'There's murder here, c'mon we're not facing the rope for this, get in the cab… Leave everything NOW…!' Bill Martin had the engine running as his brother lumbered over and climbed in.

'What happened Reg… I heard shooting…?'

'You did, now put your foot down, there's going to be hell to pay and we don't want any part of it… Drive for God's sake…!' The truck lumbered up the slop, Bill Marten frantically pumping the accelerator as the wheels sought purchase in the snow causing the rear to fish tail back and forth.

In the church, the candle had been dropped by Martin in his haste to leave, Reinecke set it back on the table where it belonged, and the flame gave off a glow to the three faces. Mick Lewis looked at Huw, still standing frozen in a state of shock, 'Are you alright son, it's a terrible thing you've seen this night…?' The boy still stood immobile, his mouth working to get words out. 'We need to get away Reinecke,' tis a mess we're in now that's for sure, and that man there, we need a grave and here we are in a churchyard full of them…!' Suddenly Lewis heard again to himself, the Devil chuckle in a corner. He laughed aloud frightening Huw, 'Now what do yer say about that my friend?'

'I know where there's a grave, there's one by my Dad…' Huw spoke quietly.

'What's that, how do you know Junge…?' Reinecke said gently, looking as kindly as he could at the waif, frozen, frightened like a little mouse.

Lewis took off his hat scratching his head, 'Let the boy be Reinecke, he's had enough, just look at him…' Deep inside he felt the memories of the fate of his two young sons' surface, this boy was no different, he was an innocent.

'I do know,' Huw became animated, 'I fell in it outside when I was climbing the wall, I could show you…' Without saying more, Huw led the way back into the snow-covered graveyard.

When Huw had spotted the Martin's truck as he approached the church, he had turned to his left crossing the slope to the wall running at right angles to the where the truck was parked. Climbing over the stone wall he had dropped into the graveyard beyond close to where his father's grave lay. He had been this way many times in the past, usually in daylight. Tonight, he found his father' marker covered in snow, then had started to edge towards the church door when suddenly the ground had given way beneath his feet. Huw had stumbled on the tarpaulin covering and open grave. He scrambled out, his hair standing on end as he peered into the deep pit below him. He hadn't waited, made his way to the church door and gained the relative shelter of the inside, shivering in the dark, when he had heard voices approaching and sank quickly between the wooden pews out of sight.

Huw led Reinecke and Lewis over to where the open grave was part covered by the tarpaulin cover the grave diggers had left. There was even a spade still laid on the mound of earth beside the hole. 'There, I told you there was one, didn't I, that's my Dad over there too…'

Lewis said to Reinecke, 'We need to leave no traces, we can put the fellow in here, all tucked up, he'll have conquered his piece of Britain, so he won't be minding now I'm thinking…?'

Reinecke looked heavenward. What more could possibly go wrong? he asked himself, a mad Irishman, two Welsh swindlers and a dead member of the SS intelligence service? Blood trickled down his aching cheek from the bullet nick, snowflakes fell from above and a small boy looking on like something from the English Christmas Carol story…! If he had been religious, then this would be time for a prayer.

Lewis saw the look on his face, 'All in God's good time Reinecke, the boy's right, if we lay him in here then cover him with an inch or two of that soil, there's a chance no one will notice when they put the proper owner in on top?'

They set to work immediately, carrying Breitfeld's dead weight over to the open grave and laying him at the bottom. Lewis crossed himself reverently as they laid Breitfeld down. Reinecke felt inside Breitfeld's inner pockets, taking out his note book and his letter with his orders, they must not be found even if the body was, he shovelled the earth down until the bottom looked fairly even as far as they could tell in the poor light. Placing shovel back and the tarpaulin in place, in a matter of hours it would be covered again with fresh snow. 'Where's the boy...? Lewis was looking around, there was no sign of Huw.

As they round the corner of the church and onto where the truck had been, the sky out to sea suddenly lit up, followed seconds later by an echoing loud bang. They both broke into a run, a star shell! It hung for seconds on its parachute about two miles out giving out its incandescent white glaring illumination.

'Holy Mother, that's a warship out there!' Lewis wasted no time saying, our only chance is to get clear before that comes any closer, the winds getting up and the waves too, the eye of the storm has passed he shouted as they ran. At the top of the cliff, Huw was coming up the last steps to the opening in the wall above the path.

'We don't have time son for farewells, so take care o' your self-boy!' Lewis slipped and slid as he hurried downwards.

Reinecke behind him, stopped briefly, 'I don't know how to say in English... Why... you were here, what you were doing in this terrible place, will you be safe Junge...?' He didn't have the time to get the right words out, he did however feel a responsibility for the boy and the air of profound sadness written on his white childish features.

Huw couldn't say anything back at first, he, for some reason now had a look of sheer numbed terror on his pallid face. 'I'll be Ok Mr I can go home now...' The words came out strangled from deep in his throat, a voice he didn't recognise as his own.

Reinecke couldn't spare any more time, he didn't truly understand what the boy had said, his own ears still ringing from the concussion of the shots fired earlier, each moment now precious, he hurried down after Lewis dangerously negotiating the trodden snow on the downward path, scrambling with near reckless speed. The boy Huw, was left entirely alone with his thoughts, motionless, stock still with the strengthening wind now whipping the hair on his exposed head, a state of utter shock and exhaustion beginning to set in.

16

On the bridge of the Juniper, Porterfield was exuberant, congratulating himself on his good fortune his seamanship. What a stroke of luck had fallen into his lap! The fates had taken a hand, capriciously offered him fame and a victory so early in his career, it was literally a gift from the gods and he certainly wasn't going to waste it.

The rating responsible for the sonar had picked up an echo again, faint then it had mysteriously disappeared close into the Welsh coast. Despite numerous sweeps he didn't manage to find it again. Porterfield had rung down for the captain, there had been no answer, three more times Penrick failed to answer, he could send a rating to the old man's cabin? He decided no, so he had taken on himself the responsibility for the next course of action. He rang down to alter course to follow the coast at a distance of two miles running parallel to the shoreline. This they had done covering some fifteen nautical miles in an hour without any further contacts or sighting of even a seagull to break the monotony. The glass was falling rapidly now, visibility closing back in, the seas increasing with the waves rearing up again, his moment was slipping away…! Then he had a brainwave, a star shell. Illuminate the waters ahead of the ship. He shouted down the voice pipe to have the four-inch gun crew muster at their station and pressed the alarm bell for action stations. The first of the flashes of lightning began to flicker and light the sky heralding the arrival of the tail of the storm.

The gun crew had closed up, then their senior rating had signalled that they were ready. 'Shoot…!' Porterfield had dramatically given the order and the resulting bang from the explosion shook the vessel. Below, in his cabin, Penrick had been shaken out of his stupor by the sudden report from the four-inch.

'What the Hell is that…? He tried to get up from his bunk, stumbled and fell, then rising without pulling on his duffle coat made for the bridge ladder swearing as he went. It took him some serious concentration to climb up to the bridge and was met by the white light in the sky forward of his command. 'What the Hell do you think you're doing, you idiot…!' He shouted, furious at his number one's folly. Pushing Porter out of the way he grasped the forward edge of the bridge and seethed with rage as the light shell extinguished and fell into the sea. 'You'd better have a bloody good explanation boy, or I'll see you cashiered for this…!'

'Look there Sir, look at that, I've ordered full speed ahead, we're making just under sixteen knots… Look at that will you…!' Porterfield's excitement got the better of him.

Penrick, put his anger on hold for a moment as he grabbed Porterfield's binoculars, swinging them to scan the sea ahead of the Juniper. He stared in amazement. 'Oh my God!' Was all that came out of his mouth as for a full minute he took in what lay before them. A submarine on the surface, a gift from the gods! Then Penrick's heart gave out, he fell forward clutching at his chest, collapsing in on himself onto the deck of his own bridge of his command. Penrick's numb unfeeling body slumped to the deck in an undignified heap. His last conscious thoughts were that his last command now lay in the hands of a completely incompetent fool… Then with his eyes still staring, was lost into an eternal merciful oblivion…

17

On the bridge of the U-367, several things happened in quick succession, Leiter could see that the two crew of the fishing boat had returned at a run, he had shouted over to them demanding to know what was going on? They shouted back that there had been a foul up top, that things had gone wrong with the shore party. Where was Reinecke? He shouted again, his nerves now beginning to cause him to tremble violently... Then, a thunderous bang out to sea behind him, Leiter spun around to see a brilliant white light suspended in the air, its eerie brilliance lighting the waves about mile offshore...!

Leiter's nerve broke completely, he screamed into the voice pipe, 'Bridge, sound... *ALARM*...! Astern one third both, *NOW*...!' Then to the two rating at his side, 'Cast off those lines.' Frantically pointing to the cleats holding the ropes securing them to the Lady Patricia. The klaxon sound echoed through the boat and out under the cavern, U-367 coming alive with the hull vibrating as gradually she got under way, her screws bit rapidly churning the foaming water under her stern. Below chaos reigned as the shouted orders came down from the bridge, the navigation officer looked to the other members of the crew in the command room, 'Somethings happened up top, we're leaving station fast, close all water tight doors, secure for action as we go astern. I hope Leiter can get out of this one... All hands to *action stations*...!' On the bridge, before Leiter could even begin to think clearly, an oblong missile whistled from above striking the port side of the anti-aircraft bandstand with the resonating clang of a cathedral bell, bursting with the impact force intensity of a small bomb. One of the crates from above had impacted, exploded onto the steel structure sending sharp jagged wood splinters in all directions, some hitting his deck crew, at the same time the afterdeck and that of the fishing boat were being showered by a cascade of bright yellow coins which metallically rattled, whirled and clattered onto the metal and wooden deck surfaces of both of the vessels.

All eyes turned skywards, as a high pitched blood curdling scream rent the air, growing in crescendo until it was cut short abruptly as the human body hit the stern deck plates head first near the rear edge of the conning tower, it bust into jellied fragments as it smashed into the steel of the deck in a welter of blood, viscera and body parts… Leiter nearly screamed in alarm, his already frayed nerves in tatters, the arcing spray of blood had reached him and the bridge spattering him and the others with droplets of gore. He retched as he wiped the red spots from his face with the back of his trembling hand.

In the diesel engine room, Hartmann coaxed his engines into life and the boat reverberated, was beginning to move.

On the right hand side of the U-boat's bridge Leiter turned to look at the entrance to the inlet, he had no men on the after deck to ward off the stern off the rocks, it would have to be just good judgement that they would slide out as easily as they had come in. A cry came from forward of the bridge, the two ratings struggling with the lines as they tautened as the boat moved backwards shouted up to Leiter, 'We can't loosen them Herr Oblt, we're pulling the other boat with us…!'

The man was right, on the deck of the Lady Patricia, Finn and Gerry watched with growing concern as the U-boat appeared to be casting off to get under way then the forward and stern springs began to tighten and the Lady Patricia was being dragged after her bumping their hull against the rock as she went.

Finn raced into the fishing boat's wheelhouse, coming out with the fireman's axe from its bracket on the wall, he hacked at the lines now endangering the vessel. The first came away with a loud twang as it lashed back under torsion. The second was even more taut, when it severed the rope hissed back lashing the crewmen on the U-boat's fore deck with such force that one man had his right arm taken off cleanly at the elbow. The man screamed long and loud, his ship mates dragged him clear back toward the conning tower. The twin diesel exhausts now rumbled and echoed through the cavern with filling the air with wreaths of blue smoke.

Finn and Gerry made their way hurriedly back onto the rock shelf to be met by a hysterical Schumann who, seeing the U-boat's movement back towards the exit from the inlet galvanised himself into a desperate race alongside and in parallel on the rock shelf until he was metres above the moving fore deck before launching himself into space. Schumann landed heavily on the steel deck plates, staggering on to his knees with the force of his leap of faith for the safety of the boat. On landing, miraculously appearing unharmed, he rose swaying, then staggered for the bridge external ladder rungs above which Leiter was looking down at him horrified, 'Where's the Kapitän, what's happening above…?' He screamed out to Schumann…

Schumann was already in a state of exhaustion, near to breaking point himself, he shouted back hysterically at the bridge crew, 'Their all dead, there was shooting, everything is lost, we need to get away… Now Leiter, you saw the light out there, it's a warship…!'

If Leiter had any misgivings about taking the action to get the boat under way without Reinecke's approval, he now felt completely absolved. 'Below, get these men down as quickly as you can, stand by for diving stations as soon as we reach deeper water,' He leaned over the bridge coaming to the remaining three men on deck, 'See us clear of the rocks as we go, use your feet if you've nothing else…' U-367 crept backwards into her true environment, as she neared the entrance, there was a grinding squeal of metal and a buckling of plates as her starboard stern tail fin touched the rocks, then they were clear moving out into the open sea. 'Hard a starboard, port engine to ahead one third, starboard astern standard…!' As the boat withdrew from the inlet she began to turn stern first around the rocks guarding the entrance, as she cleared, a hundred and fifty metres out her bows slowly swung around to point seawards, 'Ahead standard, bring her round eighty degrees on port heading…!' The remaining deck crew climbed the conning tower leaving the bridge to Leiter and his three man watch. The U-367 slipped out to sea gathering momentum as she turned onto the new heading. The lightning, intensifying now threw jagged forks across the mountains of storm cloud, the 'twilight of the God's' Leiter's brain registered a distant memory from Wagner.

Reinecke arrived back on the rock shelf shortly after Lewis, the two of them stopped short as they took in the disappearing prow of the U-boat with the men climbing up the conning tower ladder. 'My God, Reinecke, there goes your boat and yer passage home boy, what are you going to do…?'

Reinecke dropped slowly to his knees feeling completely beaten, he couldn't find any words in answer, Lewis hadn't asked a question, he had made a statement, he was abandoned, caused by his own stupidity…

'Dah,' It was Gerry shouting to his father from the Lady Patricia's deck, you'd better come and look at this…!'

Lewis climbed down heavily onto the wooden deck, 'What is it son, are we holed or damaged too?'

'No Dah, there's no damage done, but this is interesting so help me…'

Lewis went across to the fore deck over the hold hatch cover to where his son and Finn stood in mixed emotions of despair and amazement. There were literally hundreds upon hundreds of gold coins littering the deck. Lewis bent to pick one up, it was a British gold sovereign, the face of queen Victoria stared back at him. 'Well isn't that a thing now…' he said taking off his hat, 'A case of the pennies from heaven then…?' He raised his gaze again to where Finn was pointing to something in the water, 'What do you see Finn…?' He asked really slowly with the realisation of the thing he saw forming in his mind.

'It's a man Mick, I thinks it's the one they called *'Ivan,'* he dropped from above and now, what's left of him's out over there.'

They watched as the torso and body parts floated out among the shattered pieces of wooden crate, bobbing towards the mouth of the inlet pulled along by the wake of the U-boat. Lewis turned his attention back to the figure of Reinecke, still on his knees as he watched the U-367 drift beyond their vision around the point into the increasing flurries of snow and the rising green waves. 'My guess is your in-Hell lad…,' He muttered beneath his breath, 'God help you now son, for no one else will…!'

Reinecke regained some of his self-control, and called down to Lewis, 'Have you got any glasses, any binoculars captain?'

Lewis hurriedly brought forth the small pair from the wheelhouse and tossed them to Finn who in turn threw them up to Reinecke. He carried these quickly picking his way over the shelf then out towards the extreme right point of the promontory, standing feet planted akimbo on the rocks he put the glasses to his eyes and searched in the darkness for sight of his boat. A brief flash of forked lightning lit up the surface sea, for one second there was a reflection of the agony of the two vessels at the moment they struck, then the darkness consumed them. It was minutes before Reinecke returned to the Lady Patricia, Lewis and his men had cleared all evidence of their activities on the shelf and were now stood upon the deck with their boat' engine ticking over.

'You'd better come aboard,' Lewis called up, 'There's nothing for you here boy, come down we've got to get under way now, this is no place to be caught…!'

With some reluctance Reinecke joined him on the deck of the Lady Patricia, 'If you've a mind to sail with us, you may want to get rid of that now…' Lewis was pointing to the iron cross on Reinecke's sea jacket, 'You may pass for a deck hand if you're lucky but not with that and your hat, here, try this…' Lewis passed over a seaman's knitted skull cap, 'Try that on…'

Reinecke finger the cross on his chest, then plucking his award from the jacket, looked at it for long second, then threw it over the side, a minute splash and it was gone, sinking down into the silt at the bottom of the inlet coming to rest under the Lady Pat' keel. The hat followed after he had torn off the Kriegsmarine badge and cockade wreath from the front, with Reinecke donning the cap Lewis had provided him with. The Lady Patricia moved astern, then manoeuvred across the inlet till her stern came close to the opposite wall, Lewis took her ahead and they turned towards the mouth of the cove and open sea beyond. Gerry went back to his beloved engine, on deck, Finn busied himself picking up the pieces of their windfall in a heavy sack.

18

On the bridge of the Juniper, Lt Douglas Porterfield lately an employee of Benson's 'Famed' Car Showrooms in Portsmouth, knelt down to where Penrick lay on the deck, the two ratings stood alarmed aside waiting for orders, 'What do we do now Sir...?' Jenkins the rating begged an answer as the ship ploughing into another green mountain of water.

Porter stood up back to leading edge of the bridge to face forward, there, in the distance he could just make out the low silhouette of the U-boat against surf still at least a mile off starboard bows. They were beginning to close the distance rapidly, he needed to think and act quickly he told himself, 'Close up the depth charge hands, tell them to set charges for shallow detonation, say at forty feet. Tell the sick berth attendant to get up here on the double, he can take care of the captain, we're going ahead!

Jenkins, to his left on the bridge wing shouted over through the spray, 'Aye, aye Sir, but are you sure Sir, that's shallow water?' He frantically asked before he relayed the orders below.

'Of course, I know what I'm doing, now get on with it... Gun crew, load with armour piercing, engage as soon as the target comes to bear!' Porterfield, despite the chaos caused by his actions and the commander's sudden collapse was exhilarated, his chance had come at last and he was going for it with everything that he had. On the open platform of the four-pounder, the three men crew ducked as the spray crashed over them, 'Proper little hero we got there!' One of the crew swore as the order came down to engage, 'Bugger thinks he's on the Rodney...' Another added contemptuously.

On either side of the waist of the boat the senior ratings began setting the four depth charges on the shallow setting ordered, these would be rolled overboard when the order came, the Juniper didn't sport the depth charge launchers of larger vessels. The senior rated shouted across to his opposite number on the port side, 'You heard him say forty feet didn't you Nobby? Well, I'm telling you the depth setting, you follow me, I'll take the stick for it later...!' The other dipped his head in agreement.

A voice yelled out, 'These'll blow us out of the water if we drop then too soon…!' Another anxious young seaman had added his bitter observation. 'Nah, the young Jimmy knows what he's doing, so get on with it…!' The senior rating shouted, as he carefully set his depth charge with the hand tool.

'Depth charges set and ready Sir!' He shouted in cupped hands to the bridge above. The Juniper surged on heading deep into the next waves, her crew at full action stations, her commander, the veteran of Jutland lay below on his bunk once again, beyond all earthly care.

19

High on the cliff above, the figure of Huw Henryd stood forlornly in the gap in the wall at the top of the steepest part of the snow-covered pathway leading up from the cove. Below him the slope upward rose for some five or six yards at an angle approaching forty-five degrees, at the bottom of the incline it turned a sharp right corner to the next section of track, at this point beyond the turn there was nothing, the sheer cliff dropped away to the rocks far below. The snow was now beginning to cover the tracks of the men who had so recently laboured up with their loads.

Schumann had been stumbling backwards up the last yards to the gap with Ifan on the other end. Both men were physically exhausted, although fit Schumann's muscles failed him, his breath coming in wheezes like old leather bellows. Facing him, Ifan was no better, he was doing the main lifting, the bulk of the weight at his end, despite there now only being only a few steps left to go, his strength gave out. At exactly the same millisecond Schumann's face was lit up with unearthly brilliance, then an ear shattering bang from behind Ifan out to sea. Schumann fell backwards shrieking with the shock dropping his end of the box onto the snow filled rocky path. Ifan was caught mid half step forward, the weight of the box dropped forward thrust him back towards the precipice at his back. The box started to slide towards him, his feet finding no grip on the slope he was being driven steadily towards the edge. It baked for a moment, Ifan's felt his legs behind him dangling into empty space, his right hand still clutched the rope handle of the box whilst with his left he clawed at the rock edge trying to find a grip for his fingers, the box nudged forward and six inches and Ifan screamed long and loud. The before his eyes, framed by the white of the snow a terrifying apparition appeared above him out of the darkness, it stood glowering down at him, a wraith from Hell itself filled his vision...!

Huw watched from the gap in the wall as the two men had struggled up towards him, then he recognised the face of Ifan, he wanted to cry out. Suddenly there was a blinding light followed by an almighty bang, the man with his back to him had jerked backwards letting go his load and falling flat onto his back on the path recoiling from the ghostly light,

Ifan slithered backwards toward the yawning abyss at his rear. Huw, make no conscious decision, he felt himself carried forward by his hatred of this thing of utter horror, an '*it*' demon that had tortured and terrified his family. He stepped over the prostrate form of the man lying on the ground and stood above Ifan, the wind now moaning as the full force came howling in at him from the sea blowing the balaclava back from his numb face.

'Please, please help me for God's sake…!' Ifan screamed, then he recognised the figure, 'Huw, it's me, your Dah, Huw, help me give me a hand…!' Huw gazed down at the snivelling face of his tormentor, then out into the darkness behind him. 'You murdered my Dad, go back to Hell where you belong…!' He drew back his right leg, all the hate, all of the tortures, the torment and the cruelty were focused in the kick he aimed at Ifan's face, the heavy leather toe cap with some force connected with Ifan's nose shattering the bone and splintering the teeth below it. Ifan screamed and reactively clutched both hands to his face, his body arched out backwards into the void a long scream coming from his lungs as he turned cart-wheeling over in the air his arms flailing, windmilling against empty air. Huw watched him disappear, heard the scream go on an on then stop. One moment Ifan had been there, now he had gone. Huw stepped away from the edge, coming up against the box, 'And you can take this with you!' He did not recognise his own voice as he pushed the box with all of his might, it slid then gathered speed shooting out into the darkness, a second or two later he heard a hollow sounding 'boom' from somewhere far below.

The second man got to his feet as Huw turned back, at first it seemed he may push Huw to follow Ifan, then he opened his mouth and shouted words Huw didn't understand. He man's face was screwed up in rage, Huw recognised that with no need of an interpreter, 'Get out of my way…!' It was not a request as the man pushed at Huw as he headed downwards. Huw, was unsteady but kept his balance, he climbed back up to the two steps to the gap in the wall. This was where he was still standing when Reinecke and Lewis arrived minutes later.

20

Meanwhile, earlier on the top of the Wurm, another drama had acted itself out, the participants the victims of the whims of fate. Jonesey had steered the jeep bucking and bouncing along the track in the deteriorating weather, the snow flurries collected on the narrow wind screen the wipers inefficiently incapable of clearing the snow driving directly into them. Jonesey had to concentrate with all of his senses to pick out the covered twisting rout ahead, the jeep's engine stuttering and jerking, their progress becoming slower as they gained height. Jonesey and his passengers missed the turn off to the church and carried on ahead trying to keep momentum up to prevent them grinding to a halt. The jeep's traction in the slippery conditions was good but it was still a fight to keep her firmly on the path. They had also missed the figure of Henry, who had crouched at the sight of the oncoming dimmed headlights, he had no intention of being stopped and questioned by anyone, was anxious to avoid any delay in his run for home and the trouble he already faced. Jonesey's driving brought them a mile later to where the ground rose in the last stretch leading to the summit. Ahead appeared a closed barrier with the large words HALT written in red letters. It blocked the road with a guard hut either side and another small building just inside. As Jonesey drew the jeep to a stop in front of the barrier, two armed guards came out with levelled rifles, both men had steel helmets on and capes covering their shoulders, 'RAF military police…! Bob cautiously advised, 'Don't make any sudden moves Jonesey, they're probably nervous…'

The first soldier came to the left side of the jeep with a torch, his companion covering them with the muzzle of the rifle pointing at Jonesey, he took in the jeep insignia and Jonesey's uniform, 'Engine off, state your business…' He barked loudly, his helmet dipped low over his eyes trying to keep the snow from his face.

'Have you had a lorry up here this evening Sergeant, we're looking for a young lad who may be with them…?' Turning off the ignition Jonesey fumbled in his pocket for his military ID pass. Apart from the wind it was eerily silent without the sound of the jeep's engine.

The Sergeant examined the pass stating, 'This is a restricted area, no personnel military or otherwise without a permit, this is not a permit…!'

'We don't want access, we're only looking for this lad who may be in danger, have you seen anything?'

The Sergeant looked them over taking in Peggy huddled in the passenger seat, 'Is he your boy Miss?' His tone softened a little.

'No, but he's my neighbour's child, Oh please help if you've seen him.'

'No, nothings been up here since earlier today, anyway, if you stopped for a minute you might have noticed there's no tyre tracks, no foot prints either and anything or anyone that comes up this road has to pass by us. Sorry Miss, but your boy's not here…!'

Peggy tugged at Jonesey's arm, 'He's right, look the snow hasn't been disturbed Jonesey, that only leaves one place left, the church, the Martin's have gone down to the church, they must be after the sheep…'

Bob cut in from the back seat, 'I think we passed the turn off about a mile back, it was hard to see but I'm sure there was a sign-post back there…'

'Bob's right, that's the sign for St Mary's, oh quick Jonesy, he must be frozen by now…' Peggy herself was cold and shivering, the wind had now risen once again, and the chill factor cut through her clothing.

'Ok Serg, thanks for your help, sorry to have troubled you guys…' Jonesey started the engine, it caught then faltered again before picking up. He reversed the jeep then headed back down the path they had come gingerly nursing her round the bends on the downward slope. They had gone about half a mile reaching the point where they had started the last ascent when the engine cut completely without warning, they rolled to a halt in silence. Even the poor lighting had died, there was nothing when Jonesey tried the starter again. He climbed out reaching in his pocket for the small angled flashlight he carried, it was weak but better than nothing. Unclipping the two clasps across the hood, he lifted it and peered inside. Jonesey, although a 'technical sergeant,' had little knowledge of what made engines go, he only drove the jeeps, he didn't fix them when they went wrong, that was for the motor pool boys.

For twenty minutes he fiddled with the carburettor then the points, getting back into the jeep each time to try to start her. Nothing…! Bob climbed out of the back, he went round to the front and bent beside

Jonesey, 'What do you reckon, is she flooded?'

'Nope, the carb is ok, there's just no life buddy…'

I'm no mechanic Jonesey but I had a motor bike once, sounds more like the electrics, let's have a look at the plugs?'

Minutes passed as both men examined the flat four little engine, nothing appeared to be amiss, however much they checked they could find nothing wrong, there was just no spark in her.

'Sparks, that what it may be,' said Bob, 'We haven't checked the battery connections, with all the hammering that she's had they may have worked loose.'

Jonesey checked the battery terminals, at first, they appeared to be tight, as he tried the positive terminal where it connected to the top of the battery however, it came away in his hand. 'Here's our problem folks…!' He announced, spending some minutes tightening the circular link around the terminal, 'Now let's try her again…'

They climbed back in, with a deep breath Jonesey pressed the starter, the engine fired and roared into life. Without any more ado they resumed the downward journey until they reached the sign post, ready for it this time, Jonesey swung the wheel and the jeep nestled into the hidden ruts under the snow following the tracks of the Morris Commercial.

21

In the cab of their truck, the Martin brothers were panicking, Reg had shouted at his brother saying they need to get away as quickly as possible, they didn't need to be mixed up in any murders. They had sped off from the church following the road back from where they had come earlier, the deeper snow now made this difficult as the back axle span the rear wheels as they tried to get a grip on the surface of the road, Reg had tried to turn onto the grass hidden under the snow, al that had achieved was that the wheels sank in almost half way up their hubs. Reg, whilst wrestling with the heavy steering, jinked the lorry from side to side to try to find purchase. His brother, Bill, now unnerved sitting in the passenger seat brought out his packet of cigarettes and attempt to light one in the bouncing cab. 'Must you, we've got to get this load under wraps in the garage, there's no telling what's happening back there but I don't fancy Ifan's chances with that lot, the kid too, they're going to kill both of them, they won't leave any witnesses, we was lucky to get away when we did. We'll lie low for a few weeks, keep our noses clean then we'll sell whatever we've got from them, we'll still make a few bob out of this.'

Bill didn't care, he just wanted to get home where it was safe, put the stuff in the garage secret cellar where it wouldn't be found, that'll be enough for one day.

Reg, was virtually blinded by the snow, the ancient windscreen wipers were useless and as soon as one sweep cleared the glass it was covered again. The lights, the regulation slit lamps, were precious little use barely showing the road ten feet ahead of them and now the lorry was covering that in seconds as the speed picked up. Off to the extreme right, a fork of lightning lit the slopes, for a second Reg picked out another vehicle on a converging path, it was a jeep. The military and they would be caught with this load. 'Hang on…' he snarled at his brother, 'well try to cut over the fields, we can't be caught with this lot, it's all German stuff…!' Reg spun the wheel over working it through his hands, they bumped down onto flatter ground and Reg floored the accelerator, the lorry shot forward with Reg trying to make out the hollows in the ground before them…

'No Reg, turn, turn now the quarries start here…!' Bill screamed at the top of his voice in terror as the lip of the 'Druid's Pit' passed under the front wheels of the lorry which, carried by the forward momentum sailed into space the engine roaring with Reg pumping the brakes as they dropped like a stone onto the rocks below.

The so-called Druid's Pit was a long disused limestone quarry, at this point the drop to the bottom was just over a hundred feet, the Morris Commercial hit the ground nose first, the contents of the load in the back smashing their way through the cab killing both of the brothers instantly. It was completely silent, the pinging of the cooling metal of the engine audible, then, the cigarette which Bill had lit, had been in his mouth when his head went through the windscreen ignited the petrol washing over his crushed remains. The sound, the WHUMP of exploding fuel was like the angry ball of a thunderbolt, the belching oily smoke billowing up into the atmosphere above. The combination of fuel, paper and wood produced an inferno in seconds with the heat at its core near whitening the steel, melting the shattered glass of the phials at the same time cremating and vapourising their contents. The two full fuel tanks burst forward from their mounts on impact spewing their loads of petrol into the compressed wreckage of the cab, behind which six five-gallon Jerry cans of fuel, subjected to fierce heat exploded adding their liquid contents to the inferno. Compacted with the thrust of the other five long boxes loaded behind which shattering into splintered wood, with the thousands of packed paper notes on top of the broken ten glass pint-sized phials which had erupted out from two of the boxes all mixed into the centre of what was inferno pit. Within minutes the bodies of both men were reduced in this furnace to barely recognisable white bones the flesh seared away, these in turn, now little more than ash as the intensity of the fire continued to rage. As the quarry was virtually a deep sunken circle, the flames reaching the surface were limited after the first tongues of fire, these throwing little light on the surroundings above ground level.

***

Jonesey steering the jeep towards where Peggy had said the church lay, had caught the oncoming headlights, which for some reason then swung madly off the road careered on for a couple of hundred yards then vanished. Seconds later a ball of flame soared into the air…! He pulled the jeep up, the engine ticking over, 'Bob, if I pull off the road again I'm likely to get stuck, could you have a look at that while I turn the jeep round, Peggy says the church is just ahead…?' Jonesey was acutely aware of the possibility of Huw being in that vehicle, there could be no other up here and they had seen no other tyre tracks but the one.

'Let me have your flashlight Jonesey, I'll take a look, but don't want to fall in any holes…' Bob knew instinctively what Jonesey was thinking and would spare Peggy that realisation for as long as they could. He hopped out of the back and began to step carefully through the drifting snow toward the red glow.

Jonesey, put the jeep in gear and began to pull forward, 'How far Peggy?' He asked, then noticed Peggy pressing her face to the windscreen, then leaning outside the jeep peering to their front…

'Oh look Jonesey, look…' Peggy pointed ahead and Jonesey brought the jeep to a halt. A figure stood in the road in the throw of the headlights. Although dressed all in black, the snow had covered the head and shoulders so the image was that of a snowman.

'God, Peggy, it' the boy…' He gunned the jeep another twenty feet and stopped. Peggy was out and in front of the figure. A frozen, deeply traumatised Huw was before then, barely recognisable, then he lost consciousness and fell onto his face in the snow.

Bob came back at a run, finding Jonesey and Peggy kneeling over Huw, 'Here,' he said, 'take this and cover him…' Taking off his greatcoat.

'Enough, we need to get him to hospital fast, help me put him in the jeep.'

Once on board they wrapped Huw in the greatcoat with Peggy cradling his head in the back whilst Bob and Jonesey took the jeep back down the mountain, it was a tricky ride but once at ground level Peggy directed them to where the little town cottage hospital lay, not far from the gas works. Behind them, the Martins pyre would burn intensely for hours, despite the fury of the blaze, in the storm conditions no one other the occupants of the jeep were aware of the fate which had befallen them.

22

The U-367 had now completed her turn and was heading for the open sea when Lodz, the sonar operator's voice came through the bridge speaking tube, 'Loud contact bearing three hundred and fifteen, warship closing fast at one thousand metres approx. Herr Leutnant…'

Leiter grabbed hold of the rim of the bridge for support, the reoccurring nightmare he had dreamed so often was coming true, viewing the bridge binnacle compass meant the sighting was off to their port side. 'ALARM, crash dive, clear the bridge…!' As he frantically scrambled with the three watchmen for the conning tower hatch behind the sky periscope. Leiter thought of the loaded bow torpedo tubes, if they could get into position in time there was a chance to hit the Tommy ship before she opened fire on them. The U-367 was juddering, as her stern began to submerge her prow instead of pointing beneath the waves was still stubbornly holding high, there was a problem…!

Remischke shouted a warning, 'We're in shallow water, twenty metres beneath the keel descending, she not diving, we're still on the surface Sir…!'

'Close all water-tight doors, flood the forward ballast tanks, flank speed both engines…!' The U-boat's engine not changed as Hartmann threw the lever over onto their electric motors. The juddering increased with the forward motion and the boat keeled over onto her starboard side, the damaged starboard aft dive plane, its asymmetric buckled surface thrusting the boat through the water at an angle.

***

Porterfield couldn't believe his luck; the U-boat was now at an odd angle broad side on to the Juniper only three hundred yards ahead of them. 'Open fire, shoot! He called to the gun crew.

'Can't depress the barrel any further Sir, their straight ahead of our prow, we can't get them over open sights…!' The senior rating shouted, cut off as a wall of water burst over the deck swamping the gun platform'

'Stand by to ram, engine room give me everything you've got…' The

Juniper's single screw tore at the water and another knot was wrung from her engine by her engineer. Now only a hundred yards separated boat and submarine. Jenkins on the port bridge wing shouted at the top of his voice, 'She can't take it Sir, if we strike the bows will cave in, take her to starboard, we can open up with the deck gun...'

Porterfield was committed, he wasn't going to argue with the rating, the sub could slide beneath the waves and they would have their work cut out to find her again. 'Hold your course helmsman, stand by all hands for collision...!'

Jenkins, now desperate shouted across, 'Permission to order sparks to send a signal saying we're engaging the enemy and our position, Sir...?'

'No, not now, hold the course we'll kill this beast then let the Admiralty know... Steady, all hands brace for impact...' Porterfield and those crew who had visual sight of the impending collision grabbed whatever they could for support and held their breath as the U-boat rolled before then only yards away waves breaking over her as she strove to dive from the doom that stalked her.

In the command room on board the U-367, Leiter and his NCOs gathered clinging onto piping and any convenient surface against the angle of the boat. Hartmann called they were taking on water in the aft bilges, Remischke that they were only partially submerged when disaster struck with an iron fist.

Porterfield's senses were overwhelmed when they struck, the sound of the collision filled their ears with a tearing of steel on steel, the bows rose up as first the prow and then the keel rode over the submarine causing it to roll under them. Everyman was shaken by the ferocity of the hammer blow as the Juniper's five hundred and thirty tons cut into then crushed the port pressure hull of the U-boat just behind her conning tower. The screeching of metal on metal went on as the Juniper's weed covered keel sawed into her victim, then bows began to drop back to the sea, a wrenching squeal of sound coming from below decks. The Juniper with creaks of metal came free of the U-boat, but was losing way as her engine room flooded, she began to settle lower, immobile, dead in the water.

***

Porterfield couldn't comprehend what had happened, they'd sunk the U-boat, now his own ship was foundering under him. Jenkins climbed back to his feet from where he had been thrown by the force of the collision, 'Her back's broken Sir, the old girl's keels gone when she raised over the sub, too much weight on the bows... Permission to get off a signal, now... Sir?'

Porterfield was stunned by the realisation, the boat was going to sink, he came to his senses, 'Yes... I plain language, May Day, give our position and that we've engaged and destroyed an enemy sub... Damage control report...?'

Jenkins had only managed to relay part of the order to the wireless ops when the Juniper violently listed dramatically to port, began to take on water as her rail went under hastened by another merciless wave of green sea. Before any boats could be got away, she rolled over completely, her barnacle encrusted hull lingered for less than a minute, then in a foam of steam and bubbles plunged beneath the surface. Four primed depth charges preceded her on her way to the sea bed.

Porterfield was still on the bridge as she turned over and sank, with final desperation he held on grimly, locking his grip to the bridge rail as the ship took her revenge for his foolishness. Below decks the crew had little chance, most had succumbed as she had flooded before turning over, those that remained were not wearing their life belts as regulations would have suggested for when they went into action. Sixteen men bobbed to the surface, three already dead, their bodies floating face down in the water. Two of the sailors swam for a single life belt that came up from the wreck sixty feet beneath them, they clung to either side, faces just out of the water then plunging below again as another wave hit them. One, the senior artificer who had been given the task of setting charges only minutes before, grabbed at his friend's clothing, 'Hang on Nobby, we got a message away before she went, they'll come looking for us, just keep your face out of the water c'mon, try there's a good lad.'

His shipmate Nobby broke the surface again choking on the oil that he had ingested, bubbles of it were coming up from the Juniper's ruptured tanks, he vomited water, then managed to get words out, 'The depth charges'll go any second, we'll all going to be gutted...!' It seemed to be the last words of a drowning man. His mate stared across at him in the dark, spitting out water, 'Not with a depth setting of 160 feet me old mate,' he choked, 'That's the least of our troubles.' He forced the circle of the life ring over his mate' head, pulled his arms through so they hung over the sides. The cries of the other men alive in the water grew less and less until, only minutes later he found himself alone, being tossed in the dark rolling waves.

***

A little over four hundred yards away from the Juniper the perforated hull of the U-367 came to rest on the bottom, still upright with a lean of twenty degrees off centre, she had partially righted herself as she settled on the bottom, a stream of air bubbles coming from the punctures in her pressure hull. In the main engine room Hartmann and his men had all died quickly in the first minutes overcome by the inrush of water when the hull was breached the sea flooding the compartment; the secured hatches ensured that no one escaped. In the electric motor room the men's heads were just out of the water faces crammed against the ceiling bulkhead, they were in pitch blackness, all lighting had failed in their compartment.

The protesting noises throughout the boat were heralding the death knell of the U-boat, a series of creaking metallic groans sounded accompanied by the rumbles of escaping air from the ruptured tanks. Leiter stood in darkness for a moment then called for emergency lighting. It came on red bathing the faces of the men in the command room in an unearthly light. Around him the faces shone in the ghostly illumination cast by the light, they numbered fourteen crammed into the confined space. From forward there came banging behind the bulkhead hatch where Janeschitz and the men of the torpedo room and the crew quarters struggled in rising water.

'Damage control...?' Leiter croaked.

'The rear compartments are open to the sea; the forward compartments are not answering...' Came the reply from Haenel the senior steuermann...

'Conning tower hatch is jammed closed by the water pressure, it won't move...' Came from a sweating Remischke on the upper rungs tugging at the hatch wheel with both hands, 'The upper control room is flooded, there's no one answering above...'

Schumann, sickly, pale as death, found his voice, 'You must do something Leiter, get us up, get us up now...!'

With a look of final ironic resolution Leiter ordered, 'Blow all ballast, we'll bring her up and take our chances.' Leiter's order was followed by the sound of ballast being blown from the tanks, some of which were already ruptured, the rumble of water being forced out was accompanied by the boat rising a metre or two, then settling back to rest on even keel on the sandy bottom. 'Try again, blow all…!' The second attempt only caused a minor movement in the boat, then, the ominous silence coming back broken only by the sound of the bubbles of escaping the pressure hull, the metallic groans of the hull as it was settling this time permanently on the sea bed.

23

The Lady Patricia's bows lifted as she left the cove coasting into the rising waves of the open sea. Lewis, gripping the wheel peered into the darkness, the never-ending snow whipping in gusts onto the wheelhouse windows within visibility down to mere yards. 'Going to be a rough passage,' he said to Reinecke at his side, 'Ask one of the lads to give you a spare oilskin, it'll keep the worst of the weather off you.' Lewis, his pipe clenched between his teeth wrestled his boat over the first of the big incoming waves, 'It's going to get easier if we can get out beyond the tidal rip, just hang on, give the lads a hand with securing the gear below decks if you've a mind?'

Reinecke sat with the piece of cotton waste soaked in iodine Lewis had given him held to his injured cheek, suddenly felt very tired, his eyes crusted with lack of sleep and the tension of the past hours, 'Where will you make for?' He asked Lewis as he looked down at the wheelhouse compass.

'For *Na Clocha Liatha*, the English call it Greystones captain, we're going home…!' Lewis replied, his face set with determination, 'And an end to this madness, yer welcome to come with us boyo, you can take yer chances in the Republic, there's still shipping to neutral countries from our ports to be had if you can stay out of the hands of the Garda.'

Reinecke could not yet think further than the next minutes, the sea was already rising in green mountains, the coast of Ireland somewhere out there beyond the vastness of an unfriendly and hostile deadly stretch of water, with still the likelihood of enemy surface vessels ever present. 'I'll come with you Lewis, I have nowhere left to go…'

The Lady Patricia chugged on into the murk, Reinecke went forward to the prow where Finn was gazing warily at each wave as it broke over them. It was not possible to speak, the sea and the wind meant keeping one's mouth and nose covered by the buttoned sea coats and the woollen caps pulled down tight over their ears. The cliffs and coast behind them now swallowed up in the closing darkness once more.

Finn staring ahead leaned over the bow, uncovering his mouth he shouted at Reinecke, 'Can you make that out…?' He pointed into the grey waves ahead.

Reinecke could see nothing, he wiped the sea water from his eyes and stared again in the direction Finn had indicated. Then he saw it, a momentary glimpse of something lighter than the sea, it disappeared from view only to reappear with the rise of the next wave. A lifebelt, with a cluster of figures? He waited as they drew closer then saw more clearly, men in the water...! He quickly made his way back to the wheelhouse and alerted Lewis, 'There are men in the water ahead of us, we must stop and help, these are my crew...!'

Lewis stared calmly at him in the dim light of the wheelhouse, 'We can't stop in this, if we lose way, we could breach and the seas will swamp up, we have to keep our head into the wind, we have no choice. Any men out there are dead men Reinecke...'

'No, we cannot leave them, slow your boat, just enough to keep her moving, give Finn and me a chance to do what we can, please...?'

Lewis saw the pleading look on the exhausted man's face, he weighed up the risks, they could lose all for this mistake. 'I can give you one pass, I'll ease her back but when we've passed them we cannot turn back, these waves will turn us over and we'll join them Reinecke.' Wasting no time Reinecke grabbed a coil of rope and went forward again to Finn, Lewis altering course a fraction to bring them alongside the men in the water. They bumped as the bow of the Lady Patricia nosed into them, there were three men seemingly tied to the single life belt. Finn reached down as they began to drift along the starboard deck rail, grabbing at the lines on the life belt while Reinecke tried to stop them from moving further aft. It was impossible to enlist any help from the three men, they didn't move as their clothes were gripped and each drawn quickly aboard, Finn's bulk and strength lifted them, Reinecke held the life raft steady until the third man was brought over the rail.

Finn and Reinecke were gasping for breath at the sheer effort the moving of three dead weights had taken, Reinecke waved to Lewis and the Lady Pat' got under way again just in time to meet the next wave. They laid the three men out on the deck and checked for signs of life, one was clearly past all help, the second's eyes flickered open then closed again whilst the third retched water and mucus from his mouth. Then Finn patted Reinecke on the shoulder, Look here at this...,' his hand touching the first man's collar, these are not Germans, these are English sailors.' He was right, the three men were dressed alike in the uniforms of the Royal Navy, very different from his own Kriegsmarine, these were Tommy sailors, but where from and how had they come to be in the water, the British warship was the only other vessel that had been sighted, that one had killed the U-367...?

With this puzzle aching in his mind, he and Finn lifted the bodies of the two living men carefully below into the shelter of the forward hold. There they stripped away the sodden out clothing, cleared the men's mouths of the oil filth and tried to get some warmth into their bodies. One man's eyes flickered open, he blinked at stared at his rescuers. Reinecke asked him gently, 'What happened to you, where's your boat my friend?'

The man starred up through wide eyes, 'We hit a mine, she's gone, they've all gone...!' He began retching up salt water flecked with spots of oil again. Reinecke rose and stared down at the pathetic men, they were not his men, but they were sailors therefore had the common bond of all seamen despite their differing uniforms.

Reinecke made his way back to the wheelhouse to acquaint Lewis with the situation. 'We've a dead man and two just barely alive Lewis, what are you going to do?'

Lewis stared out into the night, then said, 'We can't take them back with us, too many questions if we make it safely to our own harbour, the dead man could go over the side, but the others...?'

Reinecke cut him short, 'They won't live long enough for you to make home port Lewis, you know that as well as I, they'll die, it's a miracle we found them when we did, an odd coincidence perhaps but that is the sea. They're British sailors Lewis, these are not my men...'

Lewis regarded him with raised eyebrows, 'It's a strange man you are for sure captain, a few hours ago and you would have been doing your utmost to drown these men, sink their boat, and now you're having a fit of conscience...? What in the name of the Holy Mother do you want me to do, put them over the side perhaps, let the sea finish the job for you, they are your enemy are they not...?'

'No Lewis, the sea is the common enemy, they have survived the sinking of their ship, they deserve a chance to live, there have been too many lives lost this night, these two could be saved, if we take a chance...?' Reinecke's mind went back to the memory of his own command, the U-367, launched at the Blohm und Voss works in Hamburg in 1941, repaired only once at Krupp's Germania shipyard in

1942, he knew her well, every bolt and plate, her history and her crew in intimate detail, now she lay somewhere on the bottom along with her forty sailors, close to where he now stood. He was aware that the men now lying in the hold were part of the ship's company who had put her there. 'It rests with you Lewis, this is your boat, these are your men on board, the decision is yours to make, thank God, not mine…'

Lewis laughed aloud shaking his head, 'Oh it's a wicked thing the fates do play on a man. Your right Reinecke, even in this upside-down world there's a time a man must look into his own soul and decide what manner of man he wants to be remembered for being. Now I've an idea we might just tempt the gods, brazen it out. You and I know what faces us out there at sea, there are heavy odds against us getting across the Irish sea at all in this weather, we've already pushed our luck. Now, I'm going to put this before Finn and Gerry, their lives too are in the balance here Reinecke, then, if they agree, we'll try for a fishing port on this coast. If we can get by the questions, we may be able to say we were driven in off course by the storm, we seek refuge from the storm, off load our poor boys below so they can have your 'chance at life,' then we get under way for home as soon as the seas have died down and our chances improve…'

Thirty minutes later the Lady Patricia passed under the beam of the lighthouse they had seen from afar only the day before. With her navigation lights lit the fishing boat cruised around the point off the Wurm's headland into the furthest reaches of the estuary to the river mouth at Conaway. Finn again on the prow signalled to Lewis they had company up ahead. A fast patrol vessel was approaching them at speed, her bows throwing up a whitewash of water as she closed with the Lady Patricia, coasting alongside the officer on the bridge called to them through his loud hailer. 'Who are you and where are you from?' The patrol craft's powerful Vosper diesels rumbling as she held way in the water.

'Lady Patricia, out of Na Clocha Liatha, we've injured men on board, there's been a ship in distress out there, we've picked up these survivors, have you a medic on board captain…?'

'Aye, we know the ship out there, that's where we're heading, a message was picked up from a warship saying she was sinking, we're on our way to help, there's a flotilla of fishing boats coming along behind us with the same mission. No, we don't have a medic, you need to put into to Conaway immediately, you'll find help there. We've got to get under way, there'll be other men in the water, thanks for your help…!' The sleek craft's engines picked up and with a lift in her bows she sped off in the direction of the Wurm headland. The Lady Patricia laboured on, shortly after three fishing boats crossed off their starboard quarter, as the nearest swung past the deck crew shouted across, 'Keep to the channel, the buoys are lit and you'll hear the bells, keep clear of the beaches…!' Then they too disappeared astern of Mick Lewis and his crew.

They entered the mouth of the river, a high swell running, holding well clear of the marker buoys and the trolling of the bells at their little mast heads. Lewis cut the speed and they puttered through the narrows into the basin of the town of Conaway. Ahead of them the ancient suspension bridge over the river rose up above them, to their right a quayside loomed up out of the darkness, there was activity on the top area where men could be seen above the three boats tied up alongside. Lewis brought the Lady Pat around parallel to quay to lie in the water beside the nearest fishing boat. A lamp shone a voice shouted, 'Send a line across, you can tie up with the men on the boat closest to you…' Finn cast a line over which was caught by one of the figures who drew then in closer, then another line secured the stern. Lewis shut down the wheelhouse calling down to Gerry to stop the engine. They were resting alongside a similar vessel to their own, both gently rising and falling in unison on the tidal water.

More lamps and a deck light now illuminated them as well as the snow dusting on the boat alongside, men in fishermen's garb climbed across onto the Lady Patricia's deck and with Finn leading went below to bring up the two survivors, they were carried across boats and up onto the quayside, the last being the body of the dead man lying on the deck covered with a tarpaulin, then he too, just as carefully was transferred to the quay. Lewis, Finn and Gerry followed, climbing the steel rungs set into the stone wall, up to where a number of men, all clearly fishermen, young and some very old were clustered around the two men on the cobbled quayside…

One of the older men came over to Lewis and grabbed his hand shaking it vigorously, 'It's a wonderful thing that you did, these lads might make it thanks to you, who are you and where are you from?'

Lewis took off his cap and ran his fingers through his hair, he knew he needed to be economical with the information he gave away, whatever was to happen next depended on not just what he said but how he said it. 'Mick Lewis, my boat's the Lady Patricia out of Na Clocha Liatha, these are my lads,' said gesturing to Finn and Gerry.

'Well you've done well Mick, pleased to meet you, where again did you say you're from?'

'Na Clocha Liatha, I think you know it as Greystones, on the coast across the water, we're from the Republic of Eire…!'

'Well bless us I'm sure, then Croeso i Gymru, a Welcome to Wales, you're amongst friends here Mick…!' The other was wearing a similar fisherman's cap to Mick's own, he pushed it onto the back of head and called to his fellows, 'This is Mick and his lads, they're Irish and heroes…' The other men gathered around each taking it in turns to pump Mick's, Finn's then and Gerry's hands. One announced that an ambulance was on its way would be arriving any minutes. As if on cue, the ringing of bells drew their attention to the bridge two hundred yards away, the lights of the vehicle could be seen racing across accompanied by the sound of the furiously clanging bell.

The ambulance threaded its way through the silent streets of the town and down through the medieval arch onto the wet cobbles of the quayside, within minutes the two casualties were being loaded onto stretchers, then into the back of the ambulance, the doors closed and the vehicle set off again with the loud ringing of the bell preceding its journey through the streets and back across the bridge.

'Where'll they be taking them?' Mick asked.

'To the new hospital over in the Bay, they'll be well taken care of, but this other lad…' He nodded at the body under the tarpaulin, the gently falling snow settling between the folds in the canvass, 'They'll need to come back for him, but I don't there's any great hurry in his case.'

While they were talking another helmeted figure approached under the arch who strode purposefully towards them. Lewis blanched having quickly returned his master's cap to his head as he noted the uniform of the police, the bearing of policemen everywhere. The man had a sergeant's stripes on his sleeve.

'Good morning Hughes,' he nodded to the man with whom Lewis had been speaking, 'All under control then I see?'

'Aye it is,' Hughes deferred to the man's obvious authority, this Mr Lewis, master of the fishing boat the Lady Patricia, they've just come in bring lads they've saved from this storm.

Another figure rushed up to the group, hurriedly trying to button his coat over what appeared to be blue pyjamas, 'Right lads, we were expecting you, had a radio message from the harbour boat saying you had casualties on board, I rang ahead for the ambulance before I came down.'

The first fisherman waved around to the newcomers, 'This is sergeant Roberts from our Conaway police, this is Mr Hughes our harbour master and I'm William Hughes master of the Orion, the vessel you've just come over!'

Lewis looked confused, 'Hughes, are you related to him then?'

Hughes number one laughed, 'No, but amongst us here are another three Hughes lads, it's a popular Welsh name in Conaway, I'm Hughes of the Orion, over there's Hughes off the Glendower and there's two more in the group over there.'

The police offer walked across to the edge of the quay and looked across to where the figure of Reinecke stood watching from the deck of the Lady Patricia, 'And who's your other man?' He asked taking out his notebook, 'I'll need the detail for my report.'

Lewis's brain raced for the appropriate answers, 'I'm Mick Lewis master of yon boat, this is my son, Gerald Lewis, my mate, Kieran Finn and that' my deck hand, Mack O'Riordan.' Lewis watched as the sergeant screwed up his eyes under the light of the lantern scribbling the notes down…

'Now, to more important things,' it was the harbour master, 'Lewis, you'll need to take your boat out mid-stream and anchor off, the other boats will be back and each has its own berth here alongside. When they come in we should expect more casualties and clear away here to receive them, I'll need to get back to my office and make contact with the Lieutenant piloting the harbour vessel to see where they are and what they've found, good morning to you gentlemen…' He turned and was gone running back up the slope from where he had appeared earlier.

'Right lads let's get ready as the man said, there may be more to do here, clear away, put this lad at the side, take care of him, there are going to be others this night. Lewis, get your men back aboard before Roberts gets carried away with his moment, not much happens here and he'll want to do everything by the book.' He looked across Lewis, seeing the other man's concern written on his face he continued, 'Lewis, what you and your crew have done is a wonderful thing, but I'm going to tell you this, as of midnight tonight we are under an official lock-down, no vessel will be allowed to come in or go out for five days. There's to be some kind of activity at the river mouth where the admiralty has got something hush, hush, going on, effectively nothing will move on this river. If you and your lads are a mind to get clear before you're stranded here and all the red tape that goes with it, then my earnest advice would be to sail on the early evening tide, there it is, I shouldn't be telling you but you've risked everything to bring those boys in, Roberts will be busy for a while getting his report details down, he seems to be on his way to follow the ambulance, which will mean he'll have to find a car, it'll give you a little time to consider what I've just said my friend…'

Lewis spoke for a few more minutes with his fellow fishermen of Conaway, then with Finn and Gerry climbed down and across to the deck of the Lady Patricia. Reinecke watched them come.

'Cast off fore and aft,' ordered Lewis, 'Take her out into the channel Finn, I want to talk with Reinecke.' He and Reinecke moved to the stern of the boat while Gerry got the engine running and Finn took the wheel. Both men turned to look back at the quay, the first light of the dawn beginning to chase the shadows away. From the town, a bell tolled, eight times. Reinecke looked at his watch, it was morning!

Reinecke sat on the edge of the gunwale, 'It's eight o'clock in the morning, of the Sunday 9th January?'

'It is, and they are a strange breed the Welsh, everywhere else in this country doesn't allow for the sounding of church bells, but here they somehow have got away with it.'

'How do you know?' Reinecke asked.

'Well, it's Sunday morning, I was a mind to ask if they had a Roman church here, it's a funny thing but something in me would have liked to have gone and paid my respects for the close call we have had, Hughes, a lovely man that he is, said they do indeed have a catholic church in the town, the older one that you've just heard however, is their Anglican church, of which they are fiercely proud so I didn't push it…'

Reinecke gazed out towards the river mouth, he listened carefully as Lewis repeated the warning Hughes had given him about the closure of the river to all traffic, then added. 'If the search vessels have found anything in the night off the Wurm, then that would be a miracle, they are now going to be in daylight, the wind had dropped, the conditions for a daylight search are going to be more favourable, I don't expect we will see them before late afternoon, that's when they'll think of giving up as night closes again Lewis, that's going to be the time to leave. If, and it's a likely if, that the policeman comes back, we could be faced with them searching the Lady Pat. What they may find could get you in serious trouble here, at the moment your heroes, that will change if it becomes known what your carrying below, there be no friends then, only an English Court and the rope for each of us!'

'Now I don't know about that,' Lewis began, 'I'm a citizen of the Republic with rights, my boat was driven here in a storm, no fault of ours, We'd claim diplomatic immunity or some such, but I agree for you things could take a different path Reinecke my boy...'

'Then if you get away, I want you to take these with you, keep them safe and away from all eyes. If I can, then I'll find you sometime when things have settled down, you can return them to me.' Reinecke reached inside his jacket and withdrew the Breitfeld note-book and the envelope containing the dead man's sealed orders, 'Keep these safe Mick, they are explosive in content and would damn each of us were they to fall into the hands of the British.'

Lewis took the documents, 'I have just the place,' he said, rest assured they would go over the side in a weighted bag before I let anyone get their hands on them.'

An unspoken mutual understanding passed between the two men as the Lady Patricia halted mid channel and Finn dropped anchor. 'We need to eat,' said Lewis in lighter mood, 'did I tell you about the stew I make Reinecke, it sticks to your back-bone it does that so help me...!' They enjoyed the brief respite of laughter with Lewis afterwards going below to sort out his cooking pots. Each of them bone-tired, each now functioning on automatic reflexes. Lewis was acutely aware of how desperately tired each man was, they must eat if they were to face the night ahead, they must have some rest to recharge their depleted stores of nervous energies, if they were to survive whatever was to come in their attempt to clear the harbour, to be alert to the dangers before authority and fate decided to determine their future. The dawn was coming up and the grey skies began to lose some of their malice as they settled down to wait. Finn and Gerry in the warmth of the tiny engine room, Reinecke, hunched into the corner of the wheelhouse, where in seconds he was soundly asleep. Lewis, wiping the fatigue from his eyes, peeled carrots, potatoes, added a few chunks of the precious mutton from their store to the pot and lastly an onion. Then he too, completely spent, nodded off as the pot began to simmer and bubble.

***

It was four hours later when Reinecke was roused from his slumbers by Lewis tugging on his shoulder, 'Here, get this into you, you need some packing, Finn's making tea so he is, how'd you feel lad?'

Reinecke's body protested as he moved, everything ached, his mouth tasted sour with tiredness still gripping him after the short nightmarish sleep. He eased himself up and thanked Lewis for the bowl he was offering, although it was only stew it was hot and nourishing, the positive effects began as soon as it reached his stomach. The mug of tea was a different matter, milk may have helped or sugar in another world, this however just scalded the tongue and left an after taste he decided not to describe.

Finn called out from the bow, 'There's a boat coming, we've company it seems!' He gestured towards a wooden rowboat heading towards them, two men at the oars, the first Lewis recognised as Hughes, the friendlier man of the early hours. The other he did not, an older man, about fifty the same knitted cap pulled down over wisps of grey hair so clean shaven that his skin shone, a wide smile playing on his ruddy complexioned face. They pulled alongside the Lady Pat and the two came aboard, Lewis welcomed both saying, 'We've gotta a brew of sorts if you'd like gentlemen?'

'No, not this time Mick, we've brought some bits for you, here. A late breakfast,' he handed over a small sack, the contents of which turned out to be a loaf of bread, some cheese, a small bottle of milk and lastly, a half a bottle of 'Lambs Naval Rum,' 'I'm sorry it's not more, but things are a little tight just now. I needed to bring you word of what's happening ashore too, Hughes, the harbour master, he came down to talk to us all half an hour ago, they've found more men out there, none alive unfortunately, looks like the ones you brought in were the only living survivors, the other poor souls they're bringing them back here on the evening tide.

The small group of men, Lewis and crew with their two visitors sat on the gunwales of the Lady Patricia in conversation under the grey sky, the snow had stopped, the incoming swell lifting the boat as Hughes relayed what he had heard from the harbour master. It appeared their arrival was now being over shadowed by the imminent prospect of their own fisherman bringing the bodies into Conaway, the mood was sombre, Hughes said that it had been a naval vessel that had been lost, an armed trawler so there was a fishermen's affinity with the men who had lately served on her. The lieutenant commanding the harbour patrol craft was leading them in, sea conditions off the Wurm headland still atrocious with the likelihood of finding any more now seriously inhibited by the weather and worsening sea conditions.

Lewis lifted the bottle of rum and took a long pull, 'Here's to those lads then, there no more can be done for their mortal souls.' Finn and Gerry took their turns leaving the last for Reinecke who had said nothing during the exchange so far. Reinecke took the bottle, the smell of the strong molasses filled his nose, a mouthful he washed around before swallowing then felt the coursing warmth flow through his body. 'I echo you!' He said sincerely.

Lewis quickly explained to Hughes, 'This lads' from County Mayo, his English nay so good, he's more at home in Gaelic...!'

'Aah, that would explain it, I couldn't place the accent. Now, as I was saying Mick, there's going to be a great deal to do when our lads come back, it might be wise, if you made ready to sail about four as the light is falling, all attention is going to be on the lieutenant, our boats and their pathetic harvest.'

'I believe we'll be doing as you say, I'm grateful for the kindness you've shown us here. Who's your friend, yer not one of our reception committee earlier I don't seem to recall?'

'No, you wouldn't that,' Hughes laughed, 'that's why he hasn't had a turn at the rum, this is Father Liam, you said earlier Mick you thought about going to church, I've brought the church to you...!'

The other man did not have the look of a priest, he wore the blue ubiquitous fishermen's sweater, the knitted blue cap and wore wellington boots. With a deep and friendly laugh, he said, 'Well, God Bless all here. Forgive me, when Brian here told me of your heroic work last night, and that you'd missed the Mass this morning through no fault of your own, I take some pleasure here, when my other duties to the church allow, in watching the boats come and go, the bringing in of the catch and I come down here to make a nuisance of myself with the men at their labours, Brian will tell you how they patiently put up with my annoying presence when not in me cassock...! I therefore was intrigued to hear what you had done, I asked to come and meet with you, understanding you'll sail this evening, I'm Father Liam Heggarty.' His accent was a pleasant blurred brogue hinting of the countryside, 'And your friend here's from Mayo you say,' he raised an eyebrow questioningly,' well he's certainly not from County Kerry that's for sure…!' It didn't need words, the innuendo was there, first Lewis merely grinned and the others followed suit, 'I think we'll keep it that way…!' The mood lightened and the exchange, including Reinecke's was light and convivial.

There was little more to be said, Fr Liam, Hughes made to climb back into their mussel boat, they had said their farewells to Lewis, Finn and Gerry. Reinecke stood and asked. Could you wait for just a minute please, if you don't object, then I'd like to come with you, Mick, I need to speak with you very quickly?' He moved to the other side of the wheelhouse and drew Lewis to him, 'Mick, if you don't mind me call you that, I'm going to stay here and take my chances, at worst, if I'm caught then I will be a prisoner of war. If you are stopped on the sea, if the Lady Patricia searched, you may be able to get rid of the evidence over the side, me, they would arrest you for helping what could be seen as an enemy agent. This way, we both have a slim chance of coming through this. Maybe, one day, when the madness has died away, we can meet up again, in more friendlier times perhaps?'

Lewis could see Reinecke would not be for changing his mind, clearly he had made his decision, 'Then God be with you lad, here, take the bread and cheese with you, it may keep you alive a little longer…!' Lewis passed these over as Reinecke on a nod from Hughes clambered into the narrow mussel boat. They pulled away, Reinecke waved slowly as he watched Finn and Gerry begin their preparations to put to sea. Fr Liam began to chatter away to Reinecke in Gaelic, waving his hands and gesticulating till the boat reached the shingle beach. He then took his leave of Hughes and pulled at Reinecke's arm, 'Come this way lad,' he said in English, 'Let's get you away from the prying eyes.' They walked up along the cobbles through patches of snow through the medieval gateway into the lower town then up the main street, the father nodding and greeting people as he went, Reinecke, his cap pulled over his head with his thick black sea jacket not looking too much out of place as he walked beside the priest, one or two people gave him a second look as they passed. They reached the Catholic church standing back from the town against the medieval walls, Reinecke hesitated, Fr Liam beckoned him to follow him inside. Having made a genuflexion before the altar and crucifix he sat down in a pew of the empty church, 'Take a seat, I'm sorry about the rantings in Gaelic, I thought it would be prudent if people were to allowed to continue to think you were an Irishman. I'm of the mind you may be many things my friend but I don't think you've come from Co Mayo, I don't know where you're from, and I frankly don't care, it seems to me that you may have given away your chance at freedom to bring those boys in last night. Are you of the Faith son?' He asked his head bowed.

Reinecke sat heavily upon the offered pew seat, appraising the other man's appearance and his meanings. Still clad in the ordinary clothes of a fisherman his image belied the questions he put to him, baffling Reinecke's intuitions of that which should be, against the reality of where he was and his immediate surroundings. 'I am padre,' he answered, 'but I haven't seen the inside of a church or given my confession for a long time, forgive me but if you are about to ask, grateful as I am, I'd rather not insult your intelligence by pretending to start again today. I don't think it would help your standing with your flock to welcome a black sheep into your fold father…' Fr Liam pulled off his fisherman's cap to reveal a balding head with a fringe of white hair above his ears, Reinecke was reminded of the image of Friar Tuck from the English Robin Hood legend. He peeled off the Polperro fisherman's sweater under which he wore the black clothes of his calling. These were not the trappings of any priest in his limited experience of men of the cloth. Yet, Reinecke felt no malice coming from the man, only a sense of persistent curiosity.

'I have the feeling you are puzzled, troubled by my interest, it may interest you to know I wasn't always a priest; in my young days I was passionate, I thought I'd found a cause to believe in only to find out too late that I was on the wrong side, we all can make mistakes. Seems to me you've come here a little in the same way, coming in with Mick's boat when you did I get the impression you were bound for somewhere else when the storm came and the fates blew you in here. Are you from one of those lands where freedom is no longer a possibility, a Pole or a Czech perhaps? There are numbers of these people here already, you might find fellow countrymen amongst them' The words were sincere, Fr Liam waited for an answer.

Reinecke's ability for reasoned thinking was slowing, blighted with fatigue and exhaustion, he was struggling with his thoughts in German, then searching for the right words or expressions to translate into words with his stilted broken English, it was becoming harder by the minute. He felt, he knew, he was coming to the end of himself. 'Padre, my name is Bruno Reinecke, I'm a serving German officer, I was picked up at sea by Lewis, I'd never met him before yesterday, there was never any intention of my or his coming here until we came across those men in the water. Now, do with me as you will, if you want to turn me over to the English police, then that is up to your sense of right and wrong, I won't argue with you padre, do as you see fit...'

Fr Liam sat back against the hard pew, then asked in a quiet level voice 'Did you have anything to do with what happened to the sailors you and Lewis brought in last night my son...?'

'I did not padre, what ever happened to them was none of my doing, I was with Lewis when we came across them in the dark, they were in the water when we came upon them, we did what was right as any man would, we tried to save them.' Reinecke felt that he was being as honest as he could without adding the details unnecessary for the priest's ears.

'I believe you my son, but what are you going to do now, if what you say is true, you have no money, no papers and nowhere to go in the land which is at war with your own?'

Reinecke took off the knitted cap, ran his fingers through his matted hair then across the thick growth of beard covering his cheeks and chin. 'I have no plan padre, a week ago I was in France, the things which have happened in the time since I left my friends, my home port I cannot tell you about. Here, my only concern now, is that Lewis and his men who saved me have but a slim chance to reach *their* home harbour, *if*, they are given the time to make good their voyage. The search for more survivors from the British ship, as you have heard, is over, the fishermen, their escorting patrol boat are on their way back, if Lewis had been stopped with me aboard no one would have listened to his explanation for his human kindness shown to me. So padre, I did the only thing that I could, I hope to give them time to get well on their way, only then, I can think about myself and what options are open to me, few as they may be...!'

'Then you must know that you have little chance to slip away, the bridge here is well guarded and is the only way to cross the river for many miles. Close by here there is some major activity beginning tonight which will mean security checks are inevitable on the roads and on the river. Holyhead is the nearest port, there, even if you were to get that far security would not see you board any ship with neither papers nor money. I can give you a few English pounds, it's not much, your welcome to that, but papers and an identity card, without those documents any travel will be impossible, Bruno. And... now I have to prepare myself for my own work this evening, I have a congregation to minister to, a mass to provide for the faithful. If is just time you hope to buy for your friends, then perhaps a place to rest up overnight, there are one or two places where you could keep yourself out of sight. There are the woodlands above the town, take my coat and I can give you water and a little more food if that will help?'

Reinecke got to his feet, it was now dark outside once again, 'This is kind of you padre Liam, I will remember your humanity and words at this time, will you point me in the direction I need to go, then I'll leave you to your duties, hopefully none of this will reflect upon you if I'm caught?'

'I have the privilege of a priest to keep the confidences of anything which is said to me by one of my flock in the strictest of secrecy, rest assured my son, I don't harbour feelings for this war or other conflicts any longer, many people on both sides are suffering unnecessarily, though no fault of their own, I have no interest in the politics, only the suffering caused by men's actions. God go with you Bruno, I hope one day we will be fortunate to meet again!'

Reinecke spent the evening looking for somewhere dry to sleep, it was cold but not snowing, the wind had died away almost completely. As the night began to darken, he headed for the woodland Fr Liam had mentioned, the tops of the trees he had seen earlier beyond and above the town from down at the quayside. After some searching, he found a sheltered spot under ever green trees. The cheese and bread with a bottle of water formed his meal; then settling for the night to try to sleep with his sea jacket collar turned up his hands in the pockets with Fr Liam's old coat as a blanket. By midnight he felt Lewis had now at least a reasonable start, from his vantage point he could see boats had come into the harbour, the Lady Patricia was not among them, with a fair wind and the luck of the Irish, Lewis and his boys should be well on their way, homeward bound.

Morning found him stiff and cold, the hollow on the ground beneath the trees which had served as his bed was unforgiving frosty and hard. He had to blow into his hands, stand and stamp his feet to get some warmth back in his body to get the blood flowing again. The wound to his right cheek now stiffened and sore, ached with the cold. As he waited for the first light of dawn to appear, he took stock of his surroundings and his physical condition. The last of the bread and cheese was gone, he had a half a bottle of left of water, twenty-five marks in German money, some two pounds in English bank notes courtesy of Fr Riordan, his pay book, his identity disc, his wrist watch some fragments of personal paper and that was it… The two English green pound notes given to him by Fr Liam he placed inside his socks then put his sea boots back on. Both were smelly, neither having been off of his feet for a week, though wriggling his toes, was relieved to find that his feet appeared none the worse. Somewhere over in the town the church bell tolled the hour, he checked with his watch, seven o'clock, the morning of what must now be Monday the 10th January, could it be that St Nazaire, was just a week ago he asked himself? Reinecke discarded the fisherman' hat, Fr Riordan's coat he buried under dead leaves, the using the stubby comb from his back pocket attempted to make his hair and beard a little more presentable. Brushing the leaf debris from his debris sea jacket there was little he could do about his appearance, his need for a wash and a change of clothes was a desire without the means of fulfilment, he stank and he knew it. The way back down to the town through the woods was almost pleasant, with some still some drifted snow laying in pockets, there was the occasional morning bird movement in the naked branches of the trees, a crow cawed from high above, through the trees in the grey light of dawn to his left the river appeared, the small craft at anchor, others beached on the muddy shore. The way into the town was through an ancient stone archway set in the walls, there were little signs of life, a dog barked somewhere, he passed a horse and cart laden with crates of milk bottles, the milkman appeared and cheerily said, 'Good morning,' as Reinecke passed, he returned the greeting. Into the main square, he saw the building he had passed the day before with Fr Liam, a tall impressive building of grey granite faced stone, the sign beside the door as he mounted the steps read, 'police station.' The door was open when he tried the frost encrusted brass handle, it let into a square area with a service counter to the right-hand side. Reinecke closed the door behind him feeling the warmth of the inside of the building touch his face. On the counter was a bell, the kind one pushes down and releases to ring, he touched it with his fingertips. There was no one about but he could hear voices coming from somewhere further back in the building. He looked at his watch, eight o'clock, then pressed the bell. A uniformed constable appeared, hatless, carrying what appeared to be a mug of tea…!

'Good morning, can I help you Sir?' The man set down his mug and took in Reinecke's soiled appearance with an enquiring bemused look on his face.

Reinecke took a deep breath, then in his very best English said, 'My name is Kapitänleutnant Bruno Reinecke, I am an officer of the German Kriegsmarine, I wish to surrender to the proper authorities…!'

The policeman took a moment to register what he had just heard, 'An officer of the what? You'll have to hold on a moment while I get my sergeant…' He disappeared for a full minute whilst Reinecke examined the posters pinned to the walls, '*Walls Have Ears,*' '*War Work on the Farms*' and many more papered the walls. Another police officer appeared accompanied by the first, this one had the sergeant's stripes on his arm.

'Now, what's this about German officers Sir?' He said politely.

Reinecke repeated his story, waiting for some activity and perhaps weapons to appear. The sergeant however remained quite placid, 'I see Sir, you'd better come this way,' he opened the folding section of the counter, 'Constable Baldwin will show you to the waiting room, I'll need to contact our superintendent and let him know you're here, Mr…?'

'Reinecke, Kapitänleutnant Bruno Reinecke,' he repeated.

'Mr Reinecke, take a seat for a minute Sir, this shouldn't take too long.'

Reinecke was shown into the waiting room, the first constable came in and took up station by the door. The sergeant before he went to make his telephone call asked, 'Would you like a cuppa while you're waiting Mr Reinecke?'

Another mug of steaming tea appeared which Reinecke greatly appreciated, this time hot with milk and sugar, it tasted like nectar…

An hour later the station officer, a superintendent arrived complete with silver braid on his hat and white gloves. Reinecke repeated his story and asked to use the bathroom if permitted. Again the new policeman disappeared to make another call, in the meantime Reinecke was led back into the cell block, given access to a sink and toilet, he was allowed to wash and dry himself with the luxury of a towel provided. Afterwards Reinecke was almost apologetically shown to a cell, though the door remained open. After another hour had passed, a constable appeared with tray, 'Best we could do mate,' he said, 'Weren't expecting visitors this morning!' On the tray was another mug of the sweet tea and, a neat pile of thick doorstep sandwiches, 'Hope you're ok with bacon, I've put some sauce on them.'

Reinecke ate very, very slowly, the taste of the hot fried bacon and bread melting in his mouth a delight beyond words. He thanked the constable sincerely feeling some strength returning to his limbs.

The superintendent returned a short while after, 'I've made some telephone calls, they say your to stay with us for the time being, the military is going to send a car for you with an escort Mr Reinecke, it may take an hour or so. Have you had something to eat?'

'I have and I am very grateful, thank you.'

'Is there anything else that you need while you're waiting, you know where our facilities are, yes?'

'I do. I am I permitted to smoke here, if so, unfortunately I have none of my own, I would be happy to pay if some could be provided?'

'You are, I'm told to make you as comfortable as is possible under the circumstances, I'll have constable Baldwin fetch cigarettes and matches for you Mr Reinecke, I wouldn't worry about the cost. I'll see you later before you leave.

As was promised, a packet of cigarette appeared and a box of matches. 'Capstan Full Strength,' he read the label and lit one of the aromatic smelling cigarettes, Reinecke coughed and wheezed, they were strong, nothing like he had tasted for a very long time. The constable put the packet on the flat bunk in the cell, apart from the lack of a decent window, it was spartan yet clean, he had food, hot drink, now a supply of cigarettes. For the time being, feeling clean and fed he felt more comfortable than he had been in days.

In the late afternoon, two men arrived in the uniform of the military police, a third appeared introducing himself as Major Roland Thompson, 'We're going to take you to somewhere a little more comfortable Herr Kapitänleutnant Reinecke,' his German flawless without accent, 'if you are ready, we'll set of straight away, it's about an hour's drive from here so please use the toilet before we go, we will not be stopping on route.'

Reinecke managed to quickly pocket the cigarettes and matches, was able briefly to thank the police for their hospitality before being taken down the same steps where he had recently come into the police station, to a large green camouflage military car bearing a pennant on the wing with the driver waiting with an open door. He was seated in the back sandwiched between the two military police, Major Thompson in the front with the driver. The vehicle passed into the main street where a few curious glances were cast at the unfamiliar military car then up into the shadow of the medieval castle where they were halted, the driver passing his authorisation papers to the armed guards on the approach to an old and quaint suspension bridge over the river. As they were waved ahead, Reinecke was able to take in the harbour basin where Lewis's boat had come in the day before, there was an assortment of all manner of craft, mainly fishing boats riding at anchor, at the far reaches near the estuary larger tug type boats were busy towing some big complex structures towards the river mouth, then they were across and Reinecke settled back in his seat to watch the countryside pass, the houses and buildings of small towns passed by, then open countryside where cattle were grazing in fields. An hour later the car entered the driveway to what seemed to be a large and imposing country house, a sentry stopped them for passes and identification then wheels crunching on gravel they drew up to the main doors. Again armed sentries on either side of the door, Major Thompson led his party into the building where Reinecke was placed in a small room with barred windows, here he was told to strip his clothing and pile these on a table, a one piece suit was provided then he was led to a shower room and told to get cleaned up. This was a blissful relief, given a bar of real soap he stood under the hot water for fifteen minutes and allowed the sweat and filth of the past week wash from him. A wooden handled toothbrush with paste completed the luxury. Towelled dry and wearing the overalls supplied he was taken back to where Thompson sat waiting for him in the room where he had undressed. There was now a table with a chair either side.

'Do sit down Herr Katpitanleutnant, we have some necessary paperwork then you'll be fed and shown to somewhere where you can get some rest. Your cigarettes are here' he indicated the packet of Capstans and the matches now resting on the table alongside an ash tray, 'So, let's make a start, this shouldn't take too long if you cooperate.' He had a brief case with him and withdrew a large note pad and placed it on the table, 'Your full name, rank and number and your ship?'

Reinecke took the offered seat, reached for a cigarette and faced Thompson, at the same time he pulled his Kriegsmarine Erkennungsmarke identity disc into view from around his neck with his finger and thumb saying, 'You have my name Herr Major, I'll happily give you my number, more than this I will not, the Geneva convention clearly states I'm only obliged to give you name rank and number and no more…!'

'Quite so, may I?' He held his hand out for the disc, 'It will be returned to you, once we have established that you are who in face you say you are Herr Reinecke, you were found in civilian clothes in a sensitive area, you had English pound notes in your boot sock, why would you have those if you were not expecting to be here? The outlook for you could be bleak if we were to assume that you were an agent of your country, even with the Geneva convention as you have quoted.' Reinecke passed the five-centimetre oval aluminium disc to Thompson, all it bore were the word *'Kriegsmarine,'* a four-digit number followed by a slash, then the numbers 41 and the letter K. 'Thank you, I'll keep this for the time being, you will get it back I promise you, now this, I believe, is your Soldbuch am I correct? He produced Reinecke's pay book obviously taken from his discarded clothing, he thumbed through the twenty-five-page book and rested it on the open title page. 'This is yours?'

Reinecke could see little point in prolonging the debate, 'You have my ID disc, my pay book, I have nothing else to tell you I'm afraid Herr major.'

'An officer of the Kriegsmarine walks into a police station and gives himself up, alone, with a recent injury to his cheek which looks to me as like at having been caused by a bullet! What of your boat and your crew, or did you parachute in perhaps?'

'No, I don't like heights, as I have said, you have the details I am obliged to give, I cannot help you any further. Now major, I would very much like to be sent to a prisoner of war lager as is my right.'

'All in good time Herr Reinecke, I'm afraid that you will have to stay with us here a little while, then when your credentials are confirmed, you may look forward to being transferred to a suitable establishment, for the moment however, I would like to ask you some purely routing questions, for the record of course...' So it went on until late in the evening where Reinecke tired, was shown to a room and allowed to sleep uninterrupted for seven hours. The next morning the questioning began again, Reinecke refused to give anything other than the required information, name rank and number, he stuck firmly to this which didn't seem to frustrate or anger his interrogator. The same process went on the third day broken only by mealtimes and trips to the bathroom, annoyingly an armed guard escorted him whenever he left the room the man refusing to move himself more than a few feet away at any time. At the end of the fourth day Thompson put down his pen and ordered the notes in front of him, 'There was an attack on one of our warships in the Liverpool Bay last week, I have to ask you before we go any further with your case, did you have anything to do with that…?'

Again, Reinecke made it clear that he would offer nothing else, he was adamantly adhering to his rights under the convention. At the end of that day his clothes, having been cleaned, were returned to him and he was moved to another room, this time containing three Luftwaffe prisoners, they asked him friendly seeming questions, Reinecke however, politely remained silent. Then after three more days of the interviewing questioning, Thompson announced, 'We believe that you are who you claim to be Reinecke, you've served with the Weggener 7th U-boot Flotilla based at St Nazaire, of your last allocated U-boat there seems to no mention, almost as if she was purposefully wiped from the lists of U-boats for the active vessels of the 7th Flotilla, no designated number, no history, now why might that be I am asking myself? Though this is not unusual for you is it Reinecke, you have not been either helpful or truthful have you. Also you failed to tell us that in fact you are not German at all are you? No, you are an Austrian, from the town of Österndorf it seems…! However, taking everything into consideration, having given your case a great deal of thought, we are going to move you to be with your fellow prisoner of war officers, I think you will feel a little more comfortable with company of your own kind…'

'Am I permitted to ask where that will be Herr Major?' Reinecke posed the obvious question.

'I see no harm in you knowing Reinecke, you are to be transferred to the Number one prisoner of war camp for officers, it' at a place called Grizdale Hall, near Hawkshead up in Cumbria. Arrangements have been made; you will be leaving in the morning. You won't see me any more Herr Kapitänleutnant, you will be under military escort naturally, so, I wish you a safe journey, till we meet again.' As Thompson rose from his chair to leave, despite Reinecke's wearing no hat, he saluted briefly before turning to go.

And so it was on the following day in March 1944, Reinecke carrying a small canvass bag with his few belongings was transported under armed escort to Grizedale Hall in Cumbria. There his questioning was continued sporadically, he was allowed to mix with his fellow officer prisoners one of whom he shared similar experiences, Werner Lott having commanded the U-35 and had gained respect by the British for his humane treatment of survivors of his U-boat's sinking. Reinecke had access to the German library and spent some time working on the camp farm. Here he spent a reasonable two months before being transferred with others to another, more remote camp in Canada, here he was to see out the end of the war, still obstinately refusing to give any information regarding his service history or to the whereabouts or to the fate of his vessel, the U-367 and that of her crew.

24

Five miles away from the town of Conaway which Reinecke was nearing with Lewis and ultimate captivity, the jeep bearing Huw came back into the reaches of the town near where they had set off. Under Peggy's direction Jonesey steered them along the coast road once more past the gas works then along the virgin snow of the road up to where Peggy said the new hospital stood. They pulled up the drive and came to a halt before the steps leading to the front doors, a porter on duty inside opened up as Bob and Jonesey lifted Huw between them, Peggy holding his head shouted to the porter, 'This boy's hurt, he needs help, can you give us a hand…?' The man threw open the double doors and ran down the steps to help, they carried Huw in through the door into the reception area, a nurse came trotting up the corridor, her large white nurse's head dress bobbing as she briskly walked, her black shoes click clacking on the polished floor.

'Bring him this way,' she said her crisp starched white apron rustling as she bent over Huw, putting on a light which flooded the area dispersing the gloom, 'here, put him on this bed… Oh the poor lad, what's happened to him?' She asked taking in Huw's white face, his frozen lips blue with the cold. The snow on his coat and hair began to melt in the warmth of the examination room. Another nurse appeared, between the two of them they quickly and carefully removed Huw's outer clothing, then his boots and socks. They paused as the scout knife still tucked into his belt came in view, then placing the weapon on one side continued to work on Huw. He was quite still, although he was breathing, it was shallow, his fingers toes and ears had the beginning of frost bite showing. They covered Huw in blankets, the first nurse announced that the most important thing was to get some warmth back into his core temperature, he was in danger of slipping away unless they could bring him back quickly. The second nurse ran off to get the doctor on call, Jonesey, Bob and Peggy were ushered out of the examination room and told to wait outside. Minutes later a white-coated figure arrived and introduced himself at the duty registrar, a middle-aged man with shirt and tie neatly presented as if he had been just out of surgery rather than roused from his bed. He examined Huw thoroughly, lastly sitting holding the boy's hand as he took the weak pulse.

'He's lucky to be alive, if you hadn't found him when you did, he'd be in the morgue now and not in here. This boy's suffering from the effects of exposure, as a result hypothermia his body core temperature is extremely low. We will need to keep a careful watch on him over the next hours, this could be the critical phase for him, does his mother know where he is?'

Jonesey said that he would drive straight over to the Thomas's cottage and let the mother know, at the same time take Bob back with him where he could get some sleep on the Owen's couch before he was due back at his base later in the morning. Peggy agreed to stay with Huw as the nurses arranged to move him now to a ward where his condition could be monitored by the staff who would be shortly ready for their morning hand over. The first light of dawn appeared through the room window.

Two hours later, in the little side ward of the hospital, an hour after they had brought Huw in, Peggy sat beside the boy's bed. He was unconscious, still deathly pale, his head resting on clean starched pillows, a green hospital blanket covering his lower body. The doctor came back into the room, took Huw's temperature and his pulse again. There was no change.

Another hour passed when Huw's mother arrived with Mrs Owen, she spoke quietly to Peggy who was honestly glad to be relieved, she felt so very tired, her mother said that the Thomas children were being looked after by Peggy's sisters, Nora and young Doris, it would be a good welcomed move now if she too were to go home and get some rest. Mrs Thomas listened to what the doctor had to say, then holding her son's hand asked Peggy, 'Where's Ifan Peggy, did you see him up there, did he do this to Huw?'

Peggy answered truthfully that Ifan had been nowhere to be seen, she didn't mention the Martins, however related to Huw's mother how, after some searching, they had found him in the dark frozen and completely alone. Mrs Thomas stared out of the window, then said, 'He did this, it was him, he said that he wasn't coming back, that's when he hit Huw over and over, I was so frightened that if Huw had found him he would have turned on the boy again. Thank you, Peggy, and your big American, you saved my boy's life. If Ifan comes back this time, it'll have to be the police to deal with him. We can't take any more of this, look at my son...!'

Peggy agreed, 'If Ifan does try to come back, then he could face the charge of attempted murder, Mrs Thomas, they know what he's like and being brought to Court is not such a bad idea, he deserves everything he gets...'

Mrs Thomas dabbed at her nose with a handkerchief from in the sleeve of her coat, 'Thank you Peg.' I'll do what you say. Now you get off home, your Mum's going to stay here with me a while...'

In the days to come they took it in turns to keep a vigil at Huw's bedside, Mrs Thomas growing stronger as she began to take control again of her life and those of her children. Peggy returning to work and Jonesey back to his duties. In the long days which followed, Huw drifted in and out of consciousness, the nurses gave him warm soup from a cup with a spout, roused him each morning carefully tending his bodily needs. Peggy had been alarmed one day when she came in to take her turn, to find a bracket fixed to the side of Huw's bed with a tube coming from under his blanket into a glass bottle, it was half full of yellowish brown liquid. The nurse on duty explained the need for Huw's body waste to be hygienically drained from his body, though it looked grim, it was a necessity not to be alarmed about. The same doctor came to see Huw each day, after an examination declared that his body was healing, it was Huw's mind that he was concerned about, 'The boy's suffered a trauma, not just to his body, we have saved that, it's his mind, whatever happened to him may have lasting effects his being so young, all we can do is take it a day at a time, he wakes no and then, but he won't or can't speak, there's a doctor working in London who has some special knowledge with cases like this, a Mr Freud I'll see if I can make contact with him.' Then came the day in early February when Jonesey came to pick up Peggy to walk over to the hospital, the weather had cleared, and the first signs of Spring were just around the corner of the Seasons. As they walked Jonesey held Peggy's hand, then seriously faced her and said, 'Peggy, we've had orders, we're shipping out to somewhere on the south coast, I can't tell you where, you have to understand...'

Peggy's eyes filled, she looked across the fields to where the grey skies hovered over the white waves in the distant estuary.

Peggy had known this day would come, yet it didn't soften the blow when it came. 'When do you go Jonesey, how much time do we have...?'

'Not much Baby Snooks, our gear is going ahead of us, I get the feeling it'll be within the next week, somethings beginning to go down and the staff telephones are burning hot with whatever's about to happen…' There was little Peggy could say, they had so much to say and so little time left. They walked on, her head on his shoulder, arm in arm up the drive to the hospital.

On Jonesey's last day, he and Peggy went to see Huw for what his last visit before his unit would be pulled out the next morning. Huw's eyes were open though they didn't register any recognition as Jonesey, and Peggy came into his room. Jonesey sat on one side of the Peggy on the other.

Jonesey took Huw's hand in his saying, 'Well partner, I guess you aren't going to see me for a while, I'm gonna be kind of busy Huw. Will you take care of Peggy for me while I'm gone Huw…?'

Huw's eyes flickered, resting first on Peggy's face then moving to Jonesey, his lips moved but no sound came out, tears formed in each eye… He tried again, this time concentration showed upon his face till at last, 'I will Jonesey, I will…'

Huw slumped back on his pillow, a milestone had been reached, something about Jonesey's words reached deep into his psyche' and drew Huw back, he repeated, 'I'll look after for you Jonesey, just you see…!' Peggy began to cry, Jonesey, overcome by his own emotions, stood up and hugged the boy.

'You will Huw, I know it…! Look Huw, I don't have any pennies for you this time, but I'd like you to have this…' He reached into him uniform trouser pocket and withdrew a shiny silver coin, he pressed it into Huw's hand, 'It's not worth much Huw, it' a lucky coin though, one I brought with me from the States.'

Huw opened his hand to view the quarter dollar coin in his palm, on one side was an eagle with its wings spread, the words United States of America on the rim, on the obverse a picture of George Washington's head with the legend beside, '*In God We Trust*' with the date 1941. 'Thanks Jonesey, I promise I won't spend it. ever…!'

***

On morning of the same February day when Jonesey was saying goodbye to Huw, high above them in the church yard on the Wurm, the coffin of one Ezra Lloyd-Williams, an eighty-five-year-old bachelor of the parish was being lowered into the ground by two men. To one side a minister, his white hair being blown by the wind coming up from the sea, said the words of committal in Welsh, the driver of the hearse stood his head bowed, hand folded in front of him. The only other person present was the gravedigger, a sack covering his shoulders as a cape leaning on his spade as he waited patiently for the minister to finish his reading over Ezra's coffin from the book of prayer held in his hands. As they walked back from the graveside the minister pulling on his gloves said, 'It was a pity for old Ezra, to be found like that alone, he had no one left at all in the town or so I've been told?'

'Your right, he'd been gone a while before he was found, they said it was his heart gave out at the end. Pleased we're able to get him up here at last, it's where he wanted to be, with his family, he bought this plot up in preparation for when his time came, left his instructions and the payment for his funeral. Though to be honest, it's relief for us too, I don't think we could have kept him much longer, we've had him since before Christmas, but with the snow and all, we had no means of getting him up here...'

As they walked away, the gravedigger got to work filling in the grave, the shovel's full of earth clattering onto the coffin lid covering Ezra Lloyd-Williams, it also was covering the body of the man a laying foot beneath him. In a matter of minutes, the heap of soil stood proud of the earth, the gravedigger patted it flat with the back of the shovel. Satisfied with his work, he then, donning his cap picking up his bicycle with the shovel on shoulder, whistling, began the long walk back down the mountain to town.

PART TWO

25

North Wales
16th June Modern Day

The open topped elderly Landrover bumped over the rough patch of earth and came to rest beside a bulldozer. Erich Barton reached into the rear passenger seat and retrieved his briefcase extracting an large leather bound note pad before climbing out of the car and looking around for his contact. Seeing a lone police officer stood to one side of a bulldozer a few yards away, Barton walked over beyond to where two police vehicles and three other unmarked cars were parked up. Barton hailed him, 'Hi, I'm looking for inspector Strachan, I'm supposed to meet him here, is he around?' The young constable walked over to him and said, 'Mr Barton is it? The D.I. is expecting you sir, take the path over there through the trees, straight on you can't miss them,' about two hundred yards in through the woods.'

Barton, thanking the genial officer, walked casually into the trees purposely taking his time, with the birds singing in the branches above him, a gentle Summery breeze stirring the leaves it was a little like a picture postcard with the hazy blue mountains at his back and the wooded avenue of foliage framing the newly trodden pathway through the undergrowth before him. It was good to get away from the typewriter and the office for an hour or two. He flicked over the pages of his message pad as he walked, it wasn't clear what David Strachan had meant in the short message left on his answer machine, *'Hi Erich it's David Strachan, sorry you weren't home but I'll leave you a message. Meet me at the road works at Gypsy Corner on the Bangor road at 09.00 tomorrow morning if you can Erich, you said you needed a story. I think I may have one for you. You'll owe me a pint if it's any good…'* That's all he had said so this was something of a mystery, yet Barton's long friendship with him over the years had sometimes yielded interesting morsels of information that had led to some good stories for his journalistic talents to exploit. As a freelance, these leads from reliable sources were supplements to his income when he had little work from the local press. And, this was Summer, the beginning of the 'Silly Season' where good stories were few and at a premium.

Ahead Barton could see a number of uniforms come into view through the tangled undergrowth and the mainly varied deciduous trees making up the woodland. Some ash and majestic oaks waved their leaves in the green canopies while in the breeze while below, a mixed group of police officers, two ambulance men what appeared to be three firemen and two men in civilian clothing were clustered around a cleared area between where the trees appeared to be in the most densely grown part of the wood. Ducking under the *'Crime Scene'* tapes fixed to the trees surrounding the sides of what appeared to be the focus of interest, there was an area taped off of about a dozen square yards forming a square around the gather of men, Barton called out, 'Morning David, what have you got for me?' Strachan stepped away from the cluster of men, briefly shook his hand then led Barton to one side, 'Sorry if I've got you out of bed early on a Sunday morning old man, but I thought you would find this an intriguing little mystery Erich. It seems that one of the lads working on the road widening back there got taken short and being a little shy made his way in here to answer his call of nature.' Strachan beamed and indicated towards the centre of the taped off area, 'What he found certainly eased his bowels it seems, come and have a look.' They made their way to where one of the civilians dressed in an old duffle coat wearing a tweed hat with what appeared to be fishing flies attached to it stood talking to one of the ambulancemen, 'Erich, may I introduce Dr Donald MacAngus, he's our resident tame pathologist!' The other turned with a white bearded smile to greet Barton. 'Take no notice of whatever he says lad, I'm nobodies tame anything and I'm no happy at all in missing my breakfast.' The words were spoken gently with the burr of the Scottish Highlands. He, taking a glove off his hand shook Barton's hand firmly enough and directing his attention back to Strachan said, 'It's obviously old, very many years old, but even making a cursory estimate here, there's little I can say conclusively at this stage other than he's male, fairly young judging by the teeth, some evidence of trauma to the head, a broken left leg, obvious as the bone is sticking through' he indicted t the brown jagged piece bone protruding through the material of the material covering the left leg, 'that happened post mortem, and finally… he's dead! Cause of death…? On that I won't be able to give you anything definite until I've had a look at him in the morgue, however my friends, this is nothing that's happened recently, of that I'm certain,' he leaned over the for a moment and sniffed the air, 'The smell of decay has long departed,' taking his hat off, he scratched his white hair, craning his head back peered above up into the trees above, 'this is no juicy corpse this poor man has been here probably for more than thirty years at first guess, anyway,' he said gruffly, replacing his hat and retrieving his leather bag from the ground turned once more with a final note of reflection, 'I'm done here so I'll be in touch later in the usual manner, Good day gentlemen.' With that he waved to the other members of the group then tramped his way whistling an off-key tune through the woodland back to the distant road.

Barton hand thanked MacAngus before he took his leave and watched as the man was making his way through the woods. 'He's a miserable old sod at times, should have retired years ago but he knows his stuff.' He said with some obvious affection waving after the disappearing pathologist's back.

Barton had thought on first impression that the duffle coated figure with its green wellington boots looked more like a country vet than a pathologist, but he had seemed genial enough, or so he had appeared. He raised a quizzical eyebrow to Strachan asking, 'So, what have you in fact got here David, is this going to be a murder scene or what?' He waited some moments before an answer came...

Strachan took on a sincere and thoughtful look, 'No, I think what we may have here is a tragedy that took place a long time ago, here, come and see for yourself, the photographer has finished and the forensic boys have gathered what pieces of evidence there are and have bagged them up. We're really tidying up the site before we remove the body for examination, but the elements, birds and animals appear to have done their worst over time; when we found him he was hanging down from these trees with his feet not touching the ground, about four feet up, I've the feeling that when he first must have come down, the branches would have held him much higher up in the tree.' Strachan pointed above. 'He was held up there by the remaining silk cords from his harness lines 'til they rotted away, from, it seems obvious, what we think may have been a parachute. This is where our lads from the fire service have helped to bring him down in one piece.' Peering up at the branches above where Strachan had pointed, Barton could make out wisps of material still dangling from branches well up into the canopy, of the parachute material itself, little or nothing remained of the original fabric. Strachan guided Barton to where a screen covered what clearly appeared to be a human form laid on its back on the ground. Strachan lifted the covering revealing yellowing skeletal remains, the head, was laid back with the empty eye sockets staring up at Barton, the remains of fragments of leather covering the skull appeared to be some kind of helmet while the lower remains ending in what had been knee high boots the rest of the body encased in a form of what seemed to be a canvass overall or one piece suit. This suit in turn appeared to have a belt still in place while over the shoulders' pieces of harness and fronds of grey materials dangled loosely. 'Poor bugger.' Said Strachan nodding to Barton, 'what do you think?'

Barton knelt beside the frail bony corpse, he couldn't help being struck by a distinct feeling deep sadness as he gazed upon the pathetic remains of the man laid before him on the ground, silent and somehow very alone despite the numbers of living beings who stood talking around him. 'Don't touch anything…!' Barton cautioned quietly; we're still finding bits littered about.'

At close quarters it was evident that decomposition had taken place some time ago, what remained was held together by the rotted discoloured brown material of the clothing and harness. 'I know everyone else has looked at him,' said Barton, but look at this.' He pointed to the upper left arm where some kind of insignia appeared still visible where a faint traces of metallic thread still shone, 'If that's perhaps either a rank or of a unit marking then this man was a may have been a serviceman?' A large black beetle lazily crawled its way out of the mouth cavity, hesitated a second then opened its wings to noisily whir away into the air. 'It looks there are still some other little residents making their home in there! ,' Barton observed wrinkling his nose; with that he stood up to glance at Strachan a yard away. He, looking down at the skeletal figure then added, 'If he's service, then there would usually be an identification disc around the neck, it may be still there inside the bundle of rags lower down? There's certainly a story here David, and I'm more than interested, tell me what happens to him next?'

'Well, we have to inform the District Coroner obviously, the usual procedure so that the death is recorded with as much information as we have so far. But right now, the first step is that we remove him as intact as is possible to the hospital morgue for a detailed forensic examination. Then we can try to get some clues as to his identity, what may have happened to him to end up where he has been found. Next of kin, *if* we can find any, may be difficult if this is a very old case, they will have to be found and informed about the deceased. You may be right about an identity tag, if it is a service issue then it'll make the job much easier. We'll know better when MacAngus has had a close look at him though I don't see that there's any hurry, this is probably a really old cold case, though the usual routine checks will be made for any listed missing persons. Tell you what, come over to my office on Wednesday morning about ten and I'll let you know what we have found. Until then the press will just get that we have found a body, but it' not being recorded as a 'sudden death' not suspicious given the age. Though,' he paused, 'having said that rumours will leak out when the workmen tell the tale of the body in the woods, believe me…'

In fact Barton didn't have to wait that long, on Tuesday he had a call from Strachan with an invitation to join him on Wednesday morning in the examination room attached to the morgue at the main hospital at Bangor, a post mortem was to be carried out with MacAngus in charge.

26

On the bright and sunny Wednesday morning Barton parked the Landrover in the hospital car park and made his way to the morgue office finding Strachan there ahead of him. 'Morning Erich, I've had MacAngus on the telephone, said that he had found some interesting information on our mystery man. Come on, I'll take you through, he's waiting for us!'

MacAngus, clad in a green hospital surgical gown greeted them at the door, 'A good morning to you both, you'll be wanting to know what I've pieced together about the laddie in the other room? Good, follow me…' He led the way into the examination room where the skeleton was arranged on a white cloth on a large table. 'Now here's our boy,' he said with a flourish, let me introduce you to Herr. E. Dorn, late of the German Luftwaffe…!'

Barton and Strachan were ushered around the table to be presented with the neatly laid out remains of the skeleton. Most of it appeared intact apart from the left hand which appeared to be missing. MacAngus, now clearly in his element hurried on. 'What we have is the remains of a young man, probably in his mid-twenties or there about, around five feet nine or ten so relatively quite tall. Now, this is interesting, you've noticed I can see, that the left hand is gone, that was sometime after death, but here are the really important indicators as to what happened in the short time before he died. See here above the right orbit,' he pointed to a narrow fissure running above the eye socket,' this looks like a glancing bullet wound, it wasn't fatal though it would have probably knocked him out. Then, here, look at this,' MacAngus used a pencil from his pocket to touch at the bones of the right shoulder, 'Now this would have seriously incapacitated the man, there are a number of breaks in the scapula and a butterfly fracture to the collar bone, the right upper humerus is quite shattered, whatever did this to him would have been a forceful trauma, possibly at the same time as this.' MacAngus drew their attention to the left femur which was laid in two parts with the ends where they met jagged and sharp. Now this was probably what led to his death, the break appears to have snapped upwards and inwards, rupturing the femoral artery as it went, this would have caused massive bleeding, my guess is that he would have bled to death in a relatively short time. Given that we can deduce from where he was found, that he had dropped by parachute and crashing into the trees as he came down, then that kind of velocity taking him through the branches would account for the fatal injuries. The damage to the skull is a guess but if it was a bullet, then it was travelling upwards, he would have caught it to the front of his face from below in an upward trajectory… grazing from just above the eyebrow to the right temple! Now this last injury, he moved the tip of the pencil to the right leg just above the knee, this is the result of an old fracture, well healed by the time he died, probably ask the result of some trauma when he was quite young, here, you can see how this has been expertly set and the bone with time having ossified over the damage, I have seen similar in skiing injuries…!' Said MacAngus proudly, standing back looking from face to face as if waiting for a round of applause. 'No, well there's more clues for you, come over here.' He led them to a second smaller table set against the wall, 'Now these are all what the laddie had on him when he left this world.'

On the table were laid out a number of objects, a faded non-descript pocket sized booklet, a bent and distorted fountain pen, a number of coins, a small tarnished age blackened silver crucifix on a chain, an intricate metal badge some two inched high displaying a swooping eagle enclosed in a wreath with two lightning bolts in its claws, and finally an oval aluminium identity disc. The latter was badly oxidised but it was possible to make out the letters etched in the metal, 'L.' then 'Flg,' then to the top right the capital letter 'A,' beneath, in the middle, were a series of numbers. MacAngus continued, 'We can safely assume that his branch of service was the German Luftwaffe, that he was aircrew by the *Flg* which is the shortened version of 'flieger,' that his blood group was *A* as stamped in the upper corner, these stamped numbers, his service in the middle will give us more accurate information as to his individual history and posting, then… perhaps his unit or squadron… when it has been carefully cleaned up. So, you see before you over there gentlemen, the remains of one E. Dorn, about twenty-three or four when he died, an aircrew member of Herr. Hitler's Luftwaffe.' MacAngus paused vigorously rubbing his silicon clad hands together with obvious satisfaction, 'Now, as to his name, you're thinking how did I get this… yes?…Well, have a look at this,' he moved the wallet with his latex covered fore finger, 'There were some papers in his uniform pocket but these have suffered badly over time, the wallet was in his back pocket sadly much of it has been eaten by the larvae of insect life. But, here in his top uniform inner pocket I found this.' He indicated the small faded blue green booklet, some of the bottom part has decayed as he must have put it in his pocket upside down fortunately for us, but look at the cover, can you make out '*SOLDBUCH LUFTWAFFE*'? Both men nodded their agreement, 'Now, the import part, if… we very carefully… open this' He did so very slowly, 'On this second page, it reveals a name, '*Ernst Dorn,*' born 1918, it's his pay book! Now gentlemen, bear with me.' MacAngus led them to a third and final table covered with a rubber sheet upon which sat what appeared to be two bundles of rags. 'Now here,' pointing to the canvass overall laid out, 'The conclusive proof, I think that we were right, it's a one piece flying overall, it would have covered him up to the neck, and as noted earlier a rank badge on the left arm. Now this, I've saved the best until last,' beamed MacAngus, 'is what's left of his uniform. Although it would have deteriorated along with the body, most of it was covered by the overalls so a surprising amount of detail has survived.' What was left was a tunic, trousers and a pair of disintegrating flying boots, both uniform pieces in faded mottled blue material, which, despite the holes and damage a good deal of the original Luftwaffe blue colour still lingered. On the collar patches there were matching chevron tabs on what had been a yellow background. On the upper left sleeve, the rank award of a wireless operator/air gunner. MacAngus finished, stood back with folded his arms. 'There gentleman, I think we have made some progress, however until the disc gives up its information, we have a name for the man, evidences? Well, seems to me this places him as probably bomber crew from sometime between 1940 to 1945, he's a relic of the second world war gentlemen…!'

Barton, suitably impressed as was Strachan, before they left the mortuary said to MacAngus, 'I'm so very grateful that you allowed me to share this, it's been a fascinating morning, I don't know how to repay you for your kindness.' MacAngus cut in before he could go any further.

MacAngus, bowed, then replied laconically with a raising of the eyebrow, 'A good Laphroag would do nicely and much appreciated it will be, …now don't let me keep you gentlemen.' Which very much signaled the end of the meeting.

It was a week later when sitting in Strachan's office, Barton had been given a large brown envelope. Strachan pushed it across the desk saying, 'Erich, there's a good deal of sensitive information in there, I've made copies of the things you may find useful, however, for the moment I ask that you keep these confidential. There will be a while before the details can be made public, in the meantime I'm letting you have these documents to examine at your leisure given that you were in at the beginning. It seems our boy was lost in the March of 1940; he was a wireless operator on board a German Heinkel bomber which had taken part in a night raid on Liverpool. His squadron base had been somewhere near St. Omer in northern France, they appear to have taken off with their staffel as seems it was called, then made their way up over the Irish sea before turning in to drop bombs on the docks area. There had apparently been radio silence, so this aircraft wasn't reported missing until the survivors got back to base. There had been however some sortes from a Hurricane squadron based at RAF Sealand who were protecting Liverpool that night. There is one report of a fighter engaging and hitting a bomber over the sea but the kill was never confirmed. We do know however, that one crewman's body was recovered from the sea not too far from here in the Caernarfon Bay,' Strachan paused to look at notes on the desk before him, 'That was one Walter Frick, the bomber's rear gunner, he was buried locally at first but now he's now resting with other German servicemen in their war cemetery at Cannock. The other members of the crew were all listed as missing in action believed to be dead, that was until Dorn turned up this last Spring and we know that he's dead, his family, like the others, had been sent their official thanks from the Luftwaffe's high command and that was an end to it. Our friend, Leutnant Ernst Dorn, will be now joining his comrade Feldwebel Frick, in Cannock shortly courtesy of the War Graves Commission, the preparations are well under way. There's not a great deal more to tell you about Dorn that you don't already know other than he wasn't German, he was Austrian. We were able to trace his family to a village up in the north in the Brixen valley, a place called Österndorf, there's some family members still living there but none directly related to Dorn himself. We have made contact with one of his living nephews, a Leonard Dorn, but the family don't feel disposed to come over for the funeral. It's going to be a lonely affair Erich, then there's his few pathetic belongings, we'll probably post them to Herr. Dorn. You can attend if you feel that you some involvement here Erich, seeing that you've met the man, that'll make at least the two of us at his send off, what do you think?'

Strachan, to emphasise the point reached into his desk drawer and drew out a small package, then placing a sheet of typing paper on the desk he emptied the package contents out onto the paper. The identity disc, the WO badge, the crucifix, the pay book, the wallet, the pen and six coins. 'Not much to leave behind for a short life is it…?' He said wistfully placing the items into a row. 'Yet, there is some small grace in this, his family will at least know that he's no longer missing after all of these years, he's been found and will have a resting place with his countrymen, that's got to be some comfort don't you think Erich…?' He left the words to float in the air like a heavy cloud.

27

So it was in the first week in August Barton found himself high above the English Channel, mid-way on the Monday morning flight out of Manchester bound for Salzburg in Austria. The previous week he had stood at the graveside in the German War Cemetery at Cannock with Strachan, and an official from the German consulate while the coffin was lowered reverently into the ground, the brass plate screwed to the lid giving the legend, 'Obfw. Ernst Friedrich Dorn.' A catholic priest had said the sombre words of the committal service ending with '*Dominus vobiscum*' then the final, '*Requiem aeternam dona eis, Domine. Requiescant in pace.*' They had stood for a few quiet moments reflecting upon the weeks back into May, they had brought Dorn to the end of his journey, a journey which had began before any man at the graveside had been born. Barton looked down at the English Channel thousands of feet below and thought of what it had looked like on that night in the March of 1940, what had been going through the minds of the young crew as they had travelled in the opposite direction on a mission which was designed to bring fire and death from the skies on a people they could never know, men, women and children? Barton shook himself from the reverie of the daydream, the flight would only be a little over two hours, longer than it had taken to drive to the airport, time now to get his thoughts together. He had agree to attend the funeral of Dorn, then at that meeting with Strachan, an idea had formed in his mind, he heard himself say, 'I come, and I'll take his things home for his family too, after all I did say that there was a story here David, maybe in Austria I can put together who Dorn was, what he looked like, the kind of man he had been to his own people. The Austrians are usually straight forward direct speaking people, I know, my mother was Austrian, so I feel some affinity with young Dorn…!'

The Lufthansa aircraft came into land between the steep mountains either side of Salzburg Flughafen. Passing quickly through customs, Barton replaced his passport and documents back into the pockets of his sleeveless canvass safari jacket, making his way out of the airport main building his to the Herz car rental company booth located yards away in the concourse carpark. The attendant politely took Barton's pre booked documents and minutes later with the map open beside him on the passenger seat he was motoring out on to the towards the access road to the main Salzburg to Innsbruck auto route. It was a two-hour drive along the fast autobahn, much of the traffic leaving Barton's hired Volkswagon in their dust as he made his way at a leisurely seventy kilometres an hour through the sunlight early August landscape. The Alps rising majestically to the left with the flat German plains disappearing to the right in the northerly direction. The time passed fairly quickly the kilometres rolling under the wheels on well-maintained road surfaces, a driving pleasure recalling earlier vacations to meet with his mother's family in the Tirol. Barton, tuning in to the regional radio station had first picked up the weather forecast then the local chat show. Coming up the road sign announced he was approaching the town and junction area of Wörgl, here he would need to turn south across the autobahn to enter the lower reaches of the Brixental. Swinging off the autobahn and by passing the town of Wörgl, he began the winding ascent climbing the Brixen valley road towards the regal mountains of the Kitzbühler Alps. Either side of the route the steep banks were covered by densely clad alpine fir in rising battalions rearing their heads gracefully to the peaks of the foothills. As the road became steadily steeper it twisted and turned through a series of switch backs through the forests gaining height with Barton flicking through the gears as the engine laboured. The green alpine scenery ground past with frequent gear changes needed for each tight turn, with only passing three turn offs to mountain villages with the names, Hopfgarten, Itter and Hacha disappearing in the rear mirror at intervals to break the green monotony. After another thirty minutes of hard driving the sign coming up on the right read '*Österndorf 1 km.*' Barton changed down as he negotiated the last bend onto the turn off in the direction of the village. Here, the road narrowed again and rose climbing the side of the mountain in three loops back and forth until it crested onto a plateau above the valley floor. The village of Österndorf came into view through the trees across wide open meadows of cultivated grassland. At the approach to the village he passed a small wooden roofed saint icon set at the side of the road, there were fresh blooms laid at the base. A little further on the road entered into the main area of the village leading in past timbered houses with window boxes full of red or pink geraniums on either side, then giving way as the entrance progressed, onto taller building towards what would be the town centre. What seemed to be the main thorough fare had a few small single storey shops dotted along the way then in the middle, three imposing half-timbered hotel buildings rose above a pretty gardened area with benches sat under the trees lining the pavements. Barton pulled the car up alongside the largest hotel, '*Land Hotel Adlerhof*' its carved wooden letters proclaimed. Getting out of the car and shouldered his bag, Barton looked above the front timbered façade to where the wide apex of the low pitched roof was framed by the cloudless blue sky, beneath the overhang three levels of dark wood balconies ran the length of the building each over flowing with boxes of the typical red and pink blooms at their rails.

Inside it was again equally impressive, decorated with dark antique style wooden furnishings in keeping with the exterior, numerous sets of deer antlers adorned the walls adding to the rustic alpine atmosphere. Barton made his way to the reception desk to be greeted by an attractive looking blond-haired young woman, dressed neatly with a black waistcoat over her white blouse and Tyrolean style dress. 'Grüss Gott,' She said cheerfully, following on again in German with, 'Have you a reservation Mein Herr?' Barton reached into his pocket producing a booking confirmation and his passport. The young woman looked at it briefly asking, 'English, yes?' To which he had nodded then replied in passable German that he had indeed with an advanced booking confirmation for four days. After completing in the register being given his room key, he was shown up creaking timbered stairs to the second floor where his room was situated towards the rear of the hotel. Opening the door, this was found to let into a small entrance hallway leading into a pleasantly surprising, spacious room. High ceilinged large and airy with again the old traditional alpine wooden furnishings. In the main bedroom area, a wide door beside the room-length window opened onto a heavy timbered antique pine balcony. Barton stepped out, stood and admired the views across more green meadow lands which stretched over the floor of the valley to the tree clad foot of the Choralpe mountain sweeping heavenwards high above the valley. To his left appeared the typically styled white and yellow faced village church with its distinctive onion spire rising above the dome, the building surrounded on three sides by a well-tended little graveyard. It was like an image of an old living picture post card he thought to himself with a satisfied grin.

After laying out the few clothes which he had brought, he laid his notebook, the map, his car keys and oversized chunky wooden key fob on the room table. He had intended to travel light, his possessions loaded into an easy to carry back-pack rather than a bulky suitcase or similar luggage holder, after all what could he need for only four days? 'This would do nicely, a shave, a quick shower a change into fresh clothes then down to have a look at the bar before dinner…?' He spoke the words aloud to himself then went to explore the bathroom off the main room. Contemplating the reflected image of himself in the full length mirror he paused for a moment and studied his turn out, slimly built with short cut brown hair greying a little at the temples, an almost clean shaven face with not too many age lines, yet, not bad for a thirty-eight-year-old out of work writer, recently divorced and with a host of bills to pay. He raised an eyebrow, thank God that there were no children, it would have made life even more complicated than it already was. She had got the house and the money in the bank, he had footed the bill, it had been a fifty-fifty arrangement, he earned money, and Judith spent it. 'Ah well, water under the bridge now,' he told his reflection, *"Must try harder"* as his teachers had said picking up his wash bag.

✳✳✳

An hour later seated in the bar area of the small restaurant having dined reasonably well on a pasta dish, ordering a small beer he took stock of his surroundings. There were only a few guests and the ones that he had over-heard were American tourists. Barton didn't feel disposed to getting into conversation about the scenery so taking his beer stepped out onto the forecourt garden area of the hotel to where benches and tables were arranged beside the road. He seated himself where he could watch the comings and goings of the people in the warm evening air, looking at his watch he noted it was just after six, he was due to meet with the Dorn family at seven. When the waitress came to ask if he wanted to order again, Barton asked in German if she could direct him to the house of the Dorn family? The young waitress readily replied, everyone in the village knew everybody locally, theirs' being was but a small rural community, the Haus Dorn was out along the Dorfstrasse about half a kilometre away. Barton thanked her and calculated about a twenty-minute walk rather than take the car such a short distance.

Going back to his room and picking up the package containing Ernst Dorn's belongings which were tucked in his case, he set out through the village in the direction the waitress had given him to look for the two story farm house she had described. The evening sun shone shadows over the grassland as he walked the road up into the tree line. Barton found the farmhouse built into the hillside looking down the valley to the village across the meadow land. He didn't have to knock, as he approached, he saw the figure of a heavily built square framed man sat at a table outside the front door of the home. A tall but well-built individual in shirtsleeves with meaty forearms resting upon the table. Barton guessed him to be in his sixties with close cropped fair hair, he rose to meet him and spoke in surprisingly good but accented English.

'Barton yes? Your late, expected you earlier, I'm Leon Dorn, do you want beer?' The man's introduction was clipped and rather curt, no niceties blunt and directly to the point. 'Here, have a seat,' then shouted hoarsely, 'Ilse… Bring another beer, we have a guest!'

Barton shook hands with Dorn, his own, not small disappearing into the great paw proffered by the burly farmer. Courtesies exchanged he took the offered seat and sat facing his host, 'Good of you to see me Herr Dorn, I'm sorry I was a little late, we have an hours difference in the time in England, my fault for not considering that when I telephoned you…'

'You came all this way about Ernst Dorn, my uncle, why? The words had no intention of rudeness, again it was the direct Tirolean manner of speaking which Barton had encountered with his mother's family, no offence was intended, and none taken. The conversation paused as the beer arrived being brought by a pleasant looking middle-aged woman who Barton assumed would be Dorn's wife. The big farmer continued, 'All of this Herr Barton, was a very long time ago, well before my time, I never knew my Uncle, he had died long before I was born. My father, was Gunter Dorn, Ernst was his oldest brother, there were two others, Wilhelm who was killed on the Eastern front at Stalingrad, and the youngest Johann, who is buried somewhere in Normandy killed in 1944, and, their sister my Aunt Mathilda, who still lives, but who is a little … you know…!' Dorn said very quietly and meaningfully tapping his forehead. 'I moved here when my grandparents died, I'm all that is left of that generation of my family, I had a younger brother, Peter, but he took his own life many years ago. So, Herr Barton, what has brought you to Österndorf so many years after Ernst's death, are the British feeling guilty after all of this time? He laughed at his own joke and waited for Barton to reply.

Barton took a mouthful of the pale lager beer and began his story, leaving nothing out he described in minute detail the events in the Spring when Ernst's body had been found and then recovered from a wood in North Wales, the detective work involved in the tracing his history, his subsequent burial at the German war cemetery in July and the small package of belongings Barton had brought with him to Dorn's home to his family. Leon Dorn listened carefully without interruption to the account Barton which had given, taking in with the nods of his head when Barton laid emphasis on salient parts of his story. Finally, when he had finished, Barton sat back and waited for a response from the big man.

'As said, I didn't know him or my uncles, they talked about him long after the war, he wanted to fly my Grandmother told me, his brothers had been Landsers, soldiers, but of Ernst himself I know very little.' When Barton put the package on the table and invited Dorn to insect them, he didn't appear impressed, 'Trinkets, this was all that was left of him?' He stated rather than enquired, 'Mathilda might find the cross sentimental, that is if she can remember anything at all these days, but these other pieces, maybe my son would appreciate them Herr. Barton. Do you even know what Ernst looked like?'

Barton said that he didn't, although there was much literary detail in the military records, there had been no photograph. 'Then I show you Herr. Barton, come, I'll walk back to the village with you whilst there is still light.' Dorn abruptly stood taking Barton by the shoulder gestured towards the village, 'some answers to your many questions may be found down there…'

Barton had expected the proud production of a family photograph album with faded historical pictures showing the usual individuals and groups, instead Dorn led him down on the path towards the village explaining as they went leading the way, 'We have a small chapel in the grounds of the church Herr Barton, there are the photographs of those who were lost in there, are kept in there as part of our memorial to our honourable dead of those two wars.' He pointed ahead without emotion to where the small stone chapel building could be made out standing in the grounds of the distant graveyard. 'His and my ancestors lie in that graveyard Herr Barton, in the chapel Ernst, and many of his family and his friends are remembered together by their pictures in there.'

They made their way back along the Dorfstrasse, crossing the grass land where two single horses drawing mechanical cutters were being pulled slowly and with care across the short lush grass. As they walked Barton asked Dorn, who leisurely strode along at his side, why they seemed to be cutting so short an already close-cropped pasture? The older man didn't break his stride, 'They're making the last cutting of the year, this will be the best pasture fodder for the Winter feed, the horses are used as they don't flatten the ground like a tractor, we take of the land and the land will give back to us the harvest...' He rumbled from deep in his chest pointing to the manicured meadows sitting either side of the pathway.

They walked on, in step, turned right into the village, skirted the church with Dorn taking them through the church gate to the churchyard beyond, there, opening a smaller ornamental steel gate he showed Barton into a small circular chapel building standing alone in the grounds of the cemetery. Inside, around the walls were arranged literally dozens of photographs of young men in a variety of styles of uniforms dating from both the periods of the first and second world wars. Dorn reverently cross himself and pointed to a group of three young men clustered together on the right of the far wall. 'Here they are Herr Barton, Ernst, Wilhelm and Johann...!'

Barton looked at pictures of the three fine young men in their differing respective uniforms of service, each staring seriously at the camera as the photographs were being taken. His eyes fell upon the first in the line, noting the name beneath the post card sized black and white photograph, it read *'Obfw. Ernst Dorn, Gefallen im Januar 1940. 23 jahren.'* The youthful features were those of a smartly uniformed young man, with his fair hair showing under his service cap, an uplifted chin, a slightly pained smile on his face as he had posed proudly for the photographer, he wore the rank of an Oberfeldwebel of the German Luftwaffe on his lapels. They spent some minutes standing quietly in the almost hut like little chapel, Barton was moved by the silence and peaceful atmosphere, by the many candles that had been lit and were flickering below faces of long dead young men of the village. 'Thank you for showing me this Herr. Dorn, I am very grateful to you... It's a pity though, I had hoped that you may have been able to tell me about Ernst, what he was like and who he really was...' Barton said quietly feeling the notions of a deep and interesting story begin to drift away with the little information Dorn had provided. They made their way back the few steps from the church back through the centre of the village. As they neared the Adler hotel, Barton said, 'Would you let me buy you a drink Herr. Dorn. I'm staying in this hotel?'

The older man didn't take much urging and promptly made his way to the bier garden area at the side of the main hotel building and plonked down on a creaking wooden bench, saying enthusiastically, 'That would be good mein Herr,... a moment please, *Erica*...!' He shouted to one of the serving girls who was busy delivering frothing tall glasses of beer to the next table, 'Zwei Gross bier mein Liebling…' The young woman clearly knowing Dorn, acknowledged with a nod of her head and disappeared into the restaurant. As they waited Barton, taking a seat at the log table looked across at the large burly framed farmer, his ham like fore arms resting on the table before him. A well-built rustic of a man with the powerful neck of a bull, the permanently weathered skin looks of one who has spent most of his life outdoors.

'Your work must be hard here Herr Dorn, do you farm all the year round or are there other tasks waiting for you on the land?' Barton asked conversationally knowing that in the Alps men and their women usually would turn their hands to a variety of forms of work depending upon the seasons.

Dorn rubbed his hands as the beer arrived, 'I do many things to live, Herr. Barton, I have a small number of good cattle in the upper meadows, nearly ready to be brought down to the lower pastures for the Winter at the end of this month, you would see them coming through the village if you are still here. There is always work in the forest all through the year, trees to marked for felling, others to be tended to and the paths kept clear. When the Winter comes, the tourists arrive and they need, and will pay for sledges and horse transport for their excursions. In the Spring and Summer, I take walkers up into the mountains to climb the Brechhorn. Then there are the deer, oh yes very pretty to you, but here they are a pest to be controlled like your English rabbits, unchecked they will eat everything down to the roots, too many and there would be no new shoots in the Spring. At the back of my house, I have a shed my wife calls, "The Death Hut", there I skin the animals, take the meat from the carcasses for the butchers and boil the heads with antlers to make souvenirs for the tourists.' He then became a little wistful before continuing, 'I have two sons, neither will follow me in working the fields and the forest, they both went to university, were spoiled by the city life and now have fine jobs in the big towns. There will be no one to take over from me when my time comes. Like many of my countrymen we will turn our hands to anything to make our living Herr Barton, the old ways are dying away, it's the tourists who now bring the money in, German, British and Americans, that's where our future rest now it seems, sadly…'

'Barton could see the faraway look in the other's eyes, 'Then forgive me for coming here and only adding to your burden, I truly believed that Ernst's memories might bring some comfort to his family, even though so much time has passed. And I must remark Herr. Dorn on your command of English, my spoken German would never have stood up well to the questions I wanted to ask and your kind explanations.' 'It's simple Herr Barton, we had the Russians at the end of the war, then the American troops, then, later the first of the waves of tourists. At our gymnasium schools we learn English as a necessity, it is a tool for life and not a luxury. Good English is a skill to be honed if you want to make a living in the Tirol.'

'Then forgive me, I didn't mean to pry. My reasons for coming here are two fold Herr Dorn, I did feel very deeply that having some close involvement when Ernst's body was being found and then when he was eventually being laid to rest, that I decided I wanted to bring his few belongings home to his family. Secondly, my professional interest, as I am a freelance writer, Ernst's story seemed unfinished, somehow incomplete after so many years after his tragic death and his remains and whereabouts being lost, so I didn't want it to end at his graveside, I felt that there was a history here, his history, maybe I could find out, through his family and friends who would have known him, about the real young man, the real Ernst Dorn who met his end alone in a foreign land... all of those long years ago...' Barton left this hanging in the air to gauge Dorn's reaction.

Dorn looked up at the crystal blue Summer sky for a long minute then said, 'Then I think you will need to speak to old Reinecke,' he said slowly as if arriving at a decision, he knew my uncle from the old days, I believe they even skied together before the war came. Maybe he can tell you more. And now, you have called my uncle by his first name, from now on I am to you just Leon Dorn, friend, you will call me Leon from now on.' It was not a question it was a statement, Barton felt duly honoured, he felt that he had been accepted.

Then with realisation, Barton started back as the meaning of the first of the words that he had just heard from Dorn registered their mark and hit a nerve, 'Reinecke...? Who's Reinecke? You mean there's someone left living here who actually knew Ernst personally before he left and later died, someone here in Austria?' He was aware that these words had tripped much too quickly off of his tongue before he had time to register the impact of turn in meanings from what he had just heard. The glimmer of hope for a worthwhile story was rekindled in his mind where it had been resting as the germ of an idea. There still being the possibility of a newsworthy story here, if it was of sufficiently warm human interest, a saga that began generations ago, to resurface and be told in a style stroking the imagination of the romantic reading public. Then, if crafted sensitively in the appropriate wordsmanship it may capture the interest an editor, or perhaps of one of the quality weekend papers. Barton's thoughts raced at this reprieve for his earlier ambitions. Dorn, however, was not finished, he continued in his deep rumbling baritone voice while looking at Barton straight in the eyes.

'Not in Austria, Herr. Barton,' rumbled Dorn, 'Here… in Österndorf, not a kilometre from where we are sitting on the other side of the valley. However, I must tell you, he's a very old arthritic man now, doesn't like strangers, or come to think of it he just doesn't like people. A bad tempered touchy old man who lives alone with his thoughts and memories with only his housekeeper for company. I will telephone him tonight and ask if he will agree to see you, understand you can't just go up there to the Reinecke Haus, you have to be invited, it might just be that by saying your interest in this has something to do with my late uncle Ernst, may tempt his curiosity. I'll telephone the hotel in the morning when I've talked to him this evening, I'll let you know what the old man thinks, one way another, but don't get your hopes up too high Herr Barton, he's as unpredictable as an old bear…' The words were said with a deep guttural chuckle.

Barton felt growing sense of optimism, the notion began rekindling, to revitalise reaching back again to touch once more the original idea resting in his imagination. There was now a lead, this man Reinecke, could prove to be a valuable source of human details about the life story of Ernst Friedrich, to put some flesh on the bones in the most literal sense of the words. He lifted his beer glass, 'Prost! Leon,' then adding sincerely, 'please, my friends call me Erich, it's less formal than "Herr Barton", now that's wonderful news, I'd dearly like to meet this man. Where's our bar maid? Hey there Fraulein, two more biers over here if you please…!' As Barton downed his glass while Dorn shook his head looking over the rim of his own, 'English… mad…' He mouthed silently.

The evening sun began to set over the valley touching the crests of the mountains with orange and red. Barton had sat with Dorn in easy conversation with Barton outlining his expectations of putting Ernst's story into print. He had been anxious to allay any suspicions Leon may harbour of any thoughts of sensationalism that he may feel Barton was seeking in probing back into a time when their respective countries had been enemies. When they had left the little chapel with its poignant reminders of the village's fallen youth, Dorn had pointed out the white stone carved war memorial set in the far corner of the cemetery. It had been a study of three German uniformed soldiers in a group cameo, one obviously wounded was being tended by another on his knees whilst the third stood protectively above them. Dorn had asked what Barton noticed about them, a minutes scrutiny yielded nothing exceptional other than the sculptor had carved the men' features at a frozen moment of pain and distress, their expressions cut into the stone gazed out across the pastures to the mountain beyond.

Dorn had waited for a reply only to be met with Barton's compliments on the sculptor's work. 'No, my friend, you missed something important, do you notice although they are clearly in some action, two are still wearing their steel helmets, yes? But none of them is bearing arms, we are forbidden now even in death to show our fallen with any weapons in their hands, is it not so...?'

Barton had to agree, it was curious to note Dorn's accuracy, other war memorials he had seen in different parts of Austria and Germany, were devoid of the machinery of war, it just hadn't occurred to him to note this detail before; however he made a mental note to add this to his writing when he was preparing the first draft of Ernst's story.

Dorn finished his beer wiping his lips with the back of his forearm, 'Then I'll see you in the morning Erich, I'll telephone Reinecke when I get home, then speak to you about ten after my morning work. Erich, bring Ernst's belongings with you, especially his identity disc, Reinecke will want to see them.' With that the big man had stood and bade everyone a good night and left.

Barton was left with his thoughts, he decided on a relatively early night after what had been a long and eventful day, so finishing his beer made his way up to his room. It had gone well, in less than a day he had met Ernst's surviving family member, had an idea what he had looked like and the beginnings of an understanding of the world he had lived in. Reinecke, he thought as he prepared for bed, this would be the key, if this man could flesh out the story so that the Ernst in the graveyard could be given life, be seen as a living being with hope, fears aspirations and ambitions all the things which would make him a person once more. The view across the valley in the blue twilight was stunning, he decided to leave the curtains open and the windows ajar for the mountain air. With these thoughts, Barton turned in and immediately fell soundly asleep.

28

The morning dawned with the early daylight streaming in through the windows. Barton showered, shaved and dressed for the day deciding on a stroll through the forest before breakfast as it was only six o'clock. He took the path into the forest near where he had met Dorn the day before, the heavy scent of pine hanging in the air. As he made his way among the trees a female deer followed by a fawn crossed the path a few yards in front of him, it was a magnificent sight and Barton was reminded of Dorn's depiction of the animals as 'pests', it was hard to believe so attractive a creature in these settings could be regarded as a threat to the wellbeing of the fauna and flora of its own habitat. The animal downwind, sniffed the air and scented Barton's presence then delicately bounded away into the undergrowth. He returned to the hotel invigorated and refreshed sitting down with only a few people about to enjoy breakfast in the open on the hotel terrace. Barton was on his third cup of dark aromatic coffee when the waitress came out from the restaurant saying that he had a telephone call.

Dorn had good news, he had, as promised, called old man Reinecke the night before, initially he had been reticent and unwilling to meet with anyone at all let alone a foreigner until Dorn had mentioned the finding and the recovery his uncle, that of the body of Ernst Dorn in far off Wales on mainland Britain. Then, after a lengthy pause had asked questions about Barton, who he was and how had he become involved? Dorn had eventually put aside any hesitancy he had personally harboured regarding Barton's motives convincing the old man of his sincerity. 'He's agreed to meet us both at his home, Haus Reinecke, at four this afternoon, he didn't want any stranger turning up alone, he want me to bring you over to him Erich. What do you think…?'

Barton felt a sense of gratitude for Dorn's diplomacy, if he hadn't been a family member, a relative of Ernst, then Barton was fairly certain that no introduction or interview would have been possible. Now, he felt a growing anticipation at the prospect of meeting the man, the gems of information he may hold in his memory, the seeds to begin to grow the story from the beginning. 'Leon, I thank you, can I then pick you up from your house at around three-thirty, easier if as you say it is about a kilometre to Reinecke's home?'

Dorn had agreed, Barton arriving in the Volkswagen outside the Haus Dorn at three-thirty. Getting into the car, Dorn had struggled into the small vehicle, with the suspension dipping as he fitted his bulk in the passenger seat saying, 'I hope you know what you're doing my friend, if you get this wrong, Reinecke will probably never have anything to do with me again, people tend to have long memories here, any bad feelings for this, then I will put the blame firmly at your door…'

It was only a short drive along the mountain road leading up through the trees, as the gradient steepened, they negotiated a small series of sharp bends until Dorn pointed to the home of Reinecke coming into view between the tall pinewoods. 'There, that's it, turn off the road here.' A well-tended drive led from the road onto a clearing before the wide chalet type dwelling, the building itself being constructed from old blackened timber clearly having some considerable age and time since the years of its original build. Getting out of the car Barton and Dorn approached the wide wooden steps leading up to the front door, to the left side of which was laid a fairly new concrete ramp had been added in visibly more recent times. Above the door frame was fixed a large magnificent set of well weathered stag's antlers, either side wooden troughs of bright red geranium blossoms added a colourful welcoming touch. Hanging at the side of the door, an old steel cow bell hung out from an 'L' shaped bracket suspended by a leather belt, a strap dangling from its internal clapper, Dorn rattled the bell and standing back saying, 'Welcome to the Haus Reinecke, this is going to be interesting my friend…!'

A minute passed and Barton was about to urge Dorn to have another go at the bell when the wide front door opened, a middle aged women dressed in a heavy woollen dress, similar to the Alpine dirndl style greeted them, she had wide generous features, piercing blue eyes with thick fair hair tied back in bunches, 'Grüss Gott, Herr Dorn, und diese mussen ist deinem freund, Herr Barton, nicht wahr…?' The woman began in her sing song German, then, with obvious embarrassment, apologised breaking into good English, 'Forgive me, I have now remembered, Herr Barton is an Englander visitor, welcome to you both, the Herr Ober is expecting you, do come in.' With that she led them into the main part of the house into a large comfortable room with a low beamed ceiling. 'Herr Ober, your guests have arrived, shall I show them in?' She had continued again much to Barton's curiosity in English.

A very large and commodious chair stood with its back to them before a crackling log fire, burning despite the temperature being quite warm. Again, there was a pause before a voice from somewhere in the depths of the chair answered, 'Bring them in Inge, please bring coffee for our ... guests please.' It was a deep and throaty voice, with an audible wheezy asthmatic tone underlying each word spoken. Dorn led Barton around in front of the fire to face the old man slumped in his chair, blankets covering his knees, Herr Reinecke, may I introduce Herr Barton of whom I spoke to you yesterday. Herr Barton, may I present to you Herr Kapitänleutnant Bruno Reinecke…!'

Barton waited in silence for an answer, then took the initiative, 'Honoured to meet you Herr Reinecke, it was indeed very kind of you to agree to see me at such short notice, I trust that you are well Sir?' He had fumbled with the words and regretted not having perhaps bowed or saluted or whatever was expected of someone of Reinecke's standing in his community, but now the die had been cast.

The older man, his shoulders covered with a tartan coloured throw, stirred in his chair raising himself up and stretching his body slowly adjusted his coverings and waved them both to chairs either side of the fire. Barton had his first real glimpse of the man emerging from under the covers. Wispy white hair crowned a head speckled with brown liver spots below which tufty white eyebrows sat above a pair of pale blue rheumy eyes, the line of old white scar ran across the plain of his right cheek. Barton was reminded of an elderly father Christmas in a children's book. He raised a large but bony hand to Barton and said in good English, 'Forgive me if I don't get up, I'm not as fit as I used to be Herr Barton. Dorn, be seated both of you, you look foolish standing there…!' He broke off as a coughing fit overtook him, he reached for a handkerchief to put to his lips before continuing, Sorry, gentlemen, please make yourself comfortable. Now, how can I help you Herr Barton, Dorn tells me that you have had something to do with the sad news that young Ernst has been found after all these years, before I am asked any questions, I would like to hear what happened to him and your interest in this… Ah, here's Inga with our coffee…'

Barton hadn't taken the old man's offered hand due to the obvious distress of the owner at that moment, he did take the offered chair and pulled it up in front of Reinecke. 'Thank you for your kind and considerate courtesy in speaking in English Herr Reinecke, although I would try very hard, even my best would fall short, I don't think you would appreciate the failures in my spoken German. Now, where do you want me to start Herr Reinecke, it's a fairly long and involved story, I really came into it only in these past months since Ernst remains were found in Wales...'

Reinecke looking directly at Barton nodded, 'Ah, don't worry about the English, I was a guest, you could say in your country for a number of years, had plenty of practice,' He smiled as he said, there being a distinct note of humour in his voice; then, growing serious once more continued on, 'In Wales you say...? So I understand, then please begin at the very beginning Herr Barton, leave nothing out, I want to gain a clearer picture in my own mind where there have been so many gaps, I would wish to fill in my own memories of Ernst in those times, we didn't know what had happened to him you know,' he turned briefly to Dorn who nodded back in tacit agreement, 'Then, please begin Herr Barton.' Reinecke settled himself back in his armchair as Inga bustled about pouring the coffee for the three of them.

So, Barton went back to the very beginning, to his first call from David Strachan, to the meetings with MacAngus the pathologist, the forensic findings then to the graveside in Cannock. Retelling the story took nearly an hour, during which Reinecke sat and listened carefully, interrupting only once and asking Barton to repeat and explain in detail when he described the injuries to the skeletal bones of Ernst, nodding very slowly as his understanding increased with the telling, beginning to form pictures in his mind's eye as the graphic verbal descriptions unfolded the chain of events leading to Dorn's death.

Barton's coffee was cold by the time he finished, relating all that he knew, the last thing that he did was to reach into his pocket and produce Ernst's identity disc and the swooping eagle badge, he offered these for Reinecke's inspection. Ignoring the eagle badge Reinecke reached and took the identity disc, turning it over slowly in his hands. 'Erkenunngsmarke, Herr Barton, when everything else goes, then this is all that is left...' The old man sat deep in thought contemplating the aluminium disc in his hand, then raising his eyes said, 'Ernst broke that leg up on the Choralpe in 1935, he had been a little too adventurous, too fast in his downward skiing and hit the trees... I was one of the team that went up to fetch him and bring him in, we carried him through the snow with him gritting his teeth, he must have been in great pain but he never made a sound, he was only about seventeen then. They took him all the way to Salzburg to set his leg as I remember.'

Barton listened to the old man's words then before he went further asked if he could take some notes as they talked? Reinecke had thought for a moment then had agreed saying, 'There are no secrets in what I am about to tell you Herr Barton, the Dorn family, Ernst and his brothers were both my friends and comrades in a very difficult time in our country's history, please note whatever you will find of interest to you.' Barton, taking a reporter's pad from his pocket began to write as Reinecke began his recollections.

An hour passed before the old man came to an end his story. There had been nothing dramatic in his recounting of the early life of Ernst Dorn, nothing remarkable, an ordinary young man who had been popular among his peers, really just beginning his life when the Anschluss came and Hitler's Germany annexed Austria. The feeling at the time was with the promises of a bright and prosperous future ahead of them, to join in the march towards a destiny which shined in the years to come. Like so many of his countrymen, Ernst had answered the call and enlisted in the armed forces of the German Reich, for him it was the Luftwaffe, with a smart uniform and not getting one's feet wet, he hadn't relished the idea of going to war on foot. Many of his fellows from the village were keen to join the Alpine Korps, to become mountain warfare soldiers, for which many of them would later find themselves fighting on the Eastern Front. For Ernst, his love of the idea of flying and a keen interest and understanding of radio had ultimately found him training as a wireless operator. He had been thrilled and very proud when he had been posted to a Geschwader flying the improved Heinkel 111 bomber as Reinecke remembered in some detail, smiling at the memories brought back from the glorious Summer of 1939.

Reinecke called for Inga to bring more coffee, when she arrived with the fresh jug and cups, placed these on the table then before she could turn away, Reinecke said to her. 'Inga, you said there had been a problem with the log store coming unstable, perhaps Leon could have a look whilst he is here, his hands should make an easy job of it. Could I trouble you for this favour Leon...?'

Dorn raised himself from the chair he had sunken into, 'Of course Herr Ober, give me something to do while you two have things to talk about, I've nothing to add to what you have said already and your memory is much better than mine... Your log store at the back then Inga, lead the way...'

Reinecke waited until Dorn and Inga could be heard talking outside at the rear of the house. 'I want to ask you a simple question Herr Barton, I would be grateful if you would be honest and give me a simple answer...?' He reached and filled his coffee cup waving with his fingers for Barton to help himself to the same.

Barton thought hard, the old man was looking expectantly at him over the rim of his cup, though his hands trembled a little he appeared in no great hurry to hear an immediate answer. Barton's brief inner struggle came to an end, he had known this moment had to come, he consciously decided that here, with this elderly man, then perhaps the blunt and honest truth was quite in order as a respect for the older man's age, his intelligence and integrity.

'Of course, Herr Ober, please ask, I will answer as candidly as I can.'

'Then please tell me Herr Barton, why a long dead airman and the recovery of his body has so taken your interest, and why would you, a stranger, have gone to such great trouble to bring his pathetic trinkets home, just a story for your readers, I don't think so...?' Reinecke gestured toward the identity disc and the eagle now laying upon the table beside the coffee jug.

'You are an astute man Herr Reinecke; therefore, I will tell you the 'why' to your question as truthfully as I am able, you deserve to know the facts of my motives. You see when Ernst Dorn's skeletal remains were found in that isolated woodland in Wales it was a coincidence, one that touched a nerve and opened an old personal family scar. My father, like Ernst, had been a flyer, yet in another conflict many years after Dorn's, my father's aeroplane went missing on an operation over the sea in Southern Asia, his body was never found and all my mother had was the visit from the air ministry officials and a typed letter to say that he was posted as 'missing in action'. I was two years of age when my father died, I had no memories of him, no mementoes of his family life apart from the few photographs of a man in uniform who I never knew. My mother for years, had hoped against hope that somehow or other, that he, or whatever may be left of him would be found one day, at least something to be brought home to draw his life story to some closure. It never happened, my mother for the rest of her life waited for that news, it never came. The 'why' for me Herr Reinecke? Then this was my own personal perhaps even sad romantic belief that all men who die in the service of their country, like my father, like Ernst Dorn, deserve a place where they can be laid to rest, a somewhere to be at the end of their existence. When Dorn's remains were found, it was in a very odd and strange way, that as if fate had allowed me to play some part in giving him what my own father had been denied. As a writer there was an opportunity to fit together the missing pieces of a jig-saw puzzle to make the man more than just a body for burial. I know, he was just but one man of so many… I'm not sure if this answers your question with what you expected to hear Herr Reinecke, but that is the reality…'

Reinecke said nothing, he sat back in his chair and for long seconds searched Barton's face, then turned his head to stare in silence out at the blue alpine sky and the trees beyond the window. To Barton he appeared to be a man struggling to come to terms with some inner conflict buried deep in his psyche.'

Under his breath but just audible he said more to himself than anyone who could hear, 'Just one… there are forty more… waiting…'

Barton leaned in towards the older man, 'I'm sorry Herr Reinecke, I didn't hear very clearly the words you just said, did you mean forty more men like Ernst?'

Reinecke roused himself suddenly quite erect in his chair, he turned his head around to engage Barton's eyes with his own, a tear formed and ran down his left cheek, he quickly wiped it away with his left hand, 'No, you heard right, but that is another story and not for today. However, and very importantly for me, what you have told me about your own family history, has helped me to put some things in order for the peace in my own mind and soul Herr Barton, I thank you for your candid and clearly painful answer, and yes, it did satisfy my question, I am content for you to use my ramblings to put together young Ernst story, I wish you well in that work, perhaps you could let me have a copy when you have finished, then I would be grateful to you. Inga will give you the address here and please be so kind as to leave me yours Herr Barton. Now, you must forgive me… I tire very easily these days; I would ask you to leave me to my rest this afternoon. Please be so kind as to call Inga as you leave Herr Barton, I'm going to take a lie down for a while… Good day Herr Barton Aufwiedersehn.' Reinecke rose unsteadily from his chair reaching for a walking stick from the table at his side then walked with shuffling short steps slowly and obviously painfully from the room without looking back. Barton called after him, 'Thank you so much Herr Ober, for your time and your patience…' If Reinecke did hear Barton's final words he had made no sign of acknowledgement.

Barton watched him go, he owned a genuine feeling of kindly

concern for a very old and very tired old gentleman. There had also been something about him beyond description in mere words, a form of dignity, held firmly in the proud lift of his head and the tightened jaw, in pain, held resolutely tightly closed even with the apparent ravages of time to his physical frame. When he had risen stood up, he had striven to stand upright and erect, it was possible to imagine him in the uniform of his youth as an officer, as a leader of men and a U-Boot hero of his time.

Barton collected Dorn from where he was happily stacking logs under Inga's supervision. He spoke with Inga and Dorn saying, 'The Herr Ober has gone for a rest Frau Inga, he has asked me to leave my address so there is a note on the table with the details, Dorn will give me the postal address of the Haus Reinecke though I don't think any postman could fail to know how to find it in this particular home in this valley. Thank you for the coffee, come Leon, we'll leave these people in peace…!'

On the road back Dorn had asked how things had gone with Reinecke? 'I think I have what I came for,' Barton had replied, 'how does Inga fit in with the Herr Ober's story?'

'Now that Erich, is not for your book or story, Fraulein Inga came here as a child of a displaced person, her family arrived in the village about 1948, they had settled in well considering they were from the east a village called Waldmunchen on the Czech border, when the Russians came many people fled before them and never returned to their homes. They were poor people, her father worked on the farms and her mother at the bakery. Inga was born here but when she was eighteen her father wanted to take the family to Israel, which he did, Inga decided to stay on here, she worked hard in the hotels in the village, cleaning, waiting on table in fact anything people admired her hard working nature and resilience.'

'Yet, she was…?' Barton began.

'Fraulein Inga Morgenstern is Austrian…' Dorn said firmly. 'That is all that matters… When old Reinecke eventually came home in the sixties, his place was run down, his parents long dead, no family left alive in the valley, he moved into a tumble-down ruin of a house. He needed a housekeeper and Inga was recommended given her experience with catering and the hotels. Inga worked wonders on the place brought in the right workmen and the Haus Reinecke returned to its former glory. Inga has the top floor as her apartment, her devotion grew over the years for the Herr Ober, she has become like the child he never had, though he would never tell you that.'

Barton's next day was spent busily writing up his scribbled notes in his room, in the evening he was joined again by Dorn in the bar and a pleasant conclusion to the three days in Österndorf were brought to a close. In the early morning Dorn had come to say goodbye, they had agreed when Barton's work was done, that he would return to the village, as a friend and not a visitor. He reached inside his jacket and produced an old and yellowed envelope, it's strange Erich, last night, I went up to say good night to Mathilda, Ernst's Aunty you will remember, she had found this amongst the old things she keeps in a box in her room, if it's of use to you, take it with you. When you have finished Ernst's story, then send it back to me. Barton with great care, opened the envelope, it contained a post card sized photograph, a black and white good quality print showing a Heinkel 111 bomber with her five crew members posed sitting on the grass beneath her nose canopy. They were five smiling young men in their flying gear, one-man Barton instantly recognised from the chapel photograph, as the young Ernst Dorn, in front of him another crew member cradled a Dachshund dog. On the back was a date in faint ink, *Oktober 1939*.

'Of course, I will return this to you. How strange that Mathilda should find this now?'

'I know,' said Leon, 'I think there is more going on in her head then we will ever know, she must have heard us talking about her brother, perhaps tripped some old memory...' He smiled warmly at Barton, 'Then good luck to you Erich, you've done much to finally lay a ghost to rest here...

With a sincere shaking of the hands and pats on the back they had bid one another farewell and Barton drove the road back to Salzburg to catch the late morning flight to Manchester.

29

The homeward journey was uneventful, during the drive then on the aircraft Barton reflected upon the past four days, the speed at which they had passed, the friendship and respect which had grown so quickly with Dorn and his family, the meeting with Reinecke and the pages of notes that he had taken as the old man had spoken of his recollections. The story wasn't going to be a dramatic history, Ernst had been too ordinary, the tragedy of his death and those of his brothers would make the bones of the story. The girl he had left behind in Österndorf in 1939 had been in later life being a grandmother of a tribe of farming lads and girls in the hills around the village, she too now lay in the quiet village churchyard so her story remains untold unless she spoke of her lost handsome young flyer to her children. Barton wondered whether perhaps, had she stolen some moments later in her life to visit the little chapel and gaze again upon the picture of her sweetheart? No, Barton decided, there was more than enough to build the healthy story line without resorting to speculation, it would then remain to be seen if it would be strong and viable enough to publish. His only regret being that he had not had the opportunity to see old Reinecke one more time before he had left Österndorf. Yet he had the telephone numbers and addresses of Dorn and of Reinecke, with these he would keep the remarkable old character, an officer and gentleman, informed of his progress.

***

It was a two weeks later whilst sitting in his small second bedroom converted into an office in the tiny cottage he rented, while busy typing his notes into a draft manuscript format that the telephone insistently rang… Barton was mildly annoyed, he was halfway through an important section but it persisted, so he picked it, 'Hello, please be quick I'm rather busy!' It wasn't a good line, the receiver crackled in his hand, then the voice he recognised as Leon Dorn spoke. Barton listened for some minutes, asked some brief questions then thanked Dorn for the call and put the telephone down on his desk. Reinecke had passed away in his sleep sometime during the night two days ago. There was to be no post-mortem, it was quite straight forward as the old man had planned well in advance for this inevitable eventuality. He was to be laid to rest in the village cemetery with his family, it would be the end of an era. Dorn had added that Inga, was Reinecke's only meaningful person in life, and as such in death he had left her the deeds to the Haus Reinecke with a small inheritance to pay for her upkeep and that of the property.

Barton sat back in his chair gazing vacantly across the valley stretching out beneath the window, the first signs of an early Autumn were appearing in the changing leaves, the hay fields reduced to stubble after the last of the harvesting. On the desk were the identity and breast badge belonging to Ernst Dorn, Leon had insisted that he accept them a small token of the family's gratitude for what he had done on their behalf. His thoughts went back to the brief time he had spent in Österndorf such a short time ago, the village set against the backdrop of the majestic mountains, the meeting with Dorn then the memorable hours spent with the Herr Ober. It seemed so tragically sad that the man's life had come to an abrupt end, his leaving this life alone, with only his adopted Inga to find him cold in the morning, his own life history hinting of a promise of tales of wide and varied adventures in the war years and after. Though Barton's meeting and his knowledge of the old man had been so fleeting, what had occurred between them had left him with a deep respect and enduring impression of this remarkable man.

Two days letter a letter arrived from Frau Inga Morgenstern, hand written in neat readable English, in her cursives script she advised him to expect a parcel, the Herr Ober had left instructions for her to send this on to Barton as something which he may find of use. Although Reinecke had obviously only done this very quickly in the days after Barton's visit, he had made it specifically clear that this package was to be sent only to Barton, but emphatically only when the Herr Ober passed away. Inga had put a foot note that she nor he had realised how soon this event was to happen. His time had come without warning, too quickly.

Barton felt a definite lump in his throat, he had not felt anything the like of since the sudden death of his own mother nearly twenty years before, that too had been without warning, a heart attack the death certificate had read. That too had been a lonely funeral with no family only some friends in attendance. The immediate temptation was to telephone for a flight, to board an aircraft to Austria, to attend the old man's funeral to stand once again at a lonely graveside. Then no, he would serve the old man's memory better by creating something lasting, something good out of the conversation they had had over Dorn. For now, the best thing would be to wait and see whatever it was Reinecke had been so keen at his end to send to him. A vague suspicion began to form of the receipt of a carved wooden piece of Tyrolean sculpture, well, when it came it would have pride of place on the wall…!

✳✳✳

Three days later the postman had knocked at the cottage door, in his hands was a large stout brown paper parcel, about eighteen long by twelve across and a good six inches in depth. The sculpture? I was certainly very heavy, weighing perhaps three- or four-pounds Barton mused as he carried it up to his office come study. He sat down at his desk, shook the parcel, it didn't rattle, no it was quite firm with coarse string tied end to end and across, red sealing wax had been blobbed carefully on the knots. This was going to be a moment to be savoured so he reached for a pipe from the rack at the back of the desk and his leather tobacco pouch, filling the bowl with aromatic tobacco he tamped it down then lit the pipe with a match. After many puffs to get it going, satisfied he turned his attention back to the intriguing package. A letter opener served to sever the knots, then the several sheets of brown paper therein. A layer of linen surrounded the innermost contents, it was a book…!

What lay before Barton was a worn and well-thumbed thick brown leather-bound volume. The flap covering the centre was embossed with a brass lock, finding closed when he tried pressing the catch, he searched among the paper debris for a key. Instead of a key found a small brown envelope addressed to himself in dark blue ink, opening it he unfolded the paper, it was a letter, as he slit the edge open with the paperknife a small brass key fell onto the desk.

The written in English, in a scrawled uneven hand Reinecke's words were in places a little difficult to decipher, he had obviously laboured over his writing painstakingly to get across what he clearly had wanted to say.

My dear Mr Barton,

Enclosed this is my personal journal, the record of my life, of the things I have seen, that I have done and have witnessed since my boyhood, here in these mountains. When you came to see me bearing tidings regarding my friend Ernst, I was transported back for a while to those idyllic days of my youth, when life lay before me as an adventure yet to begin.

Among the many things of which I have written in my journal, you may find one entry in significantly of interest, something which happened a long time ago, back in the year 1944, an incident in which I was to play a major part. This may, for you and your conscientious nature, strike a chord relevant to your peculiar sense of morality and history. It may be that as far as any of the official sources and accounts were concerned at the time or after, either from the British or German sides in that conflict, there was never to be a conclusion or explanation given for a what was a foolhardy failure, a folly which cost many lives unnecessarily with neither gain or ultimate meaning. In recorded history this was an event which never happened Mr Barton...! You may wish to put the records right if you have the time and inclination to do so. This task, to take on, or ignore, as you will, I now am going to pass on into your capable hands and to your fertile mind. This nightmare has troubled me deeply, has been gnawing away in my mind constantly these past years of my life, eventually I no longer had the will power or strength to do what was right. You now have that ponderous decision to make on my behalf. This, then I leave to you in the confidence a conclusion may yet be found. If you are reading this letter Mr Barton, then it is because my time will have come, in the sound knowledge of this I must ask that you do one of two things with my journal, if you read it and decide in your wisdom to do nothing, then you must burn it along with this letter, you must <u>destroy it utterly</u> much in the manner as I had intended to do before our meeting. If, on the other hand you are moved to set in motion an investigation charged to look at the evidences and facts which covered up a long concealed tragedy, then this will give me comfort, some peace for my soul to know that for the peace of 'forty' of which you had asked of me during our talk, there might be some resolution found at last. What finally became of those hapless casualties in those dark days, then if you can put this story together in the public eye, it may be revealed, a memorial for posterity and to the families of those fine young men, to have their rightful place in living memory. This I leave this to you to carry out these my final wishes in my sound belief in your honesty, your persistence and strength of character. In these endeavours, I wish you good fortune. Farewell Mr Barton.

I remain yours in confidence.

Kptnlt. Bruno Reinecke.

Barton reread the letter several times before turning to the diary itself. Placing the key in the lock it opened easily, the pages were yellowed with age all were written in the same neat legible handwriting until the final pages dated fairly recently where the hand writing became decidedly difficult to interpret as seemingly arthritis had probably affected the writer's ability to control his trembling hand as he wrote. The first entries began in the Summer of 1937 and ran through the decades of entries with the final words being written the year before Barton's visit to Österndorf. This was clearly going to be a challenge to his personal stamina, his patience and to test Barton's limited language skills, the ability to translate Reinecke's handwritten German of the text into more a readable format. Before embarking on the work in hand he needed to prepare, his comprehensive Cassell's German dictionary, a large A4 ruled note book and a large quantity of coffee before commencing to read and attempt to comprehend the meanings of the Reinecke diary and the secrets which were hinted to lay hidden within its faded pages.

Barton would adopt a tried and tested approach to the translation process, first to skim read at least three times, then to painstakingly interpret the grammar and nuances to keep as closely to the original meanings as was possible. Counting the pages of the diary he noted they numbered some three hundred and twenty, each page holding forty finely ruled lines of handwritten script. It was going to be an arduous time-consuming task, making notes in the margins as he journeyed through he estimated there would be at least two day's work involved in creating the first working draft.

Barton consciously decided to mentally clear his head from all distractions, the work ahead promised a deep and fascinating look into the life and thinking of a man he had met but once, yet the time spent may pay dividends. Ernst Dorn's story had unlocked a door to another set of linked stories which themselves may prove to be meat for a larger more in-depth saga to explore for the journalistic possibilities. This could evolve into more than a story, this could become the basis of a book, who knows what there was to be discovered in Reinecke's extensive writings? First though, before that, to lay in provisions to feed the man, then to seal himself away for a day or two to begin the work on the translation.

The first skim reading of the diary went well, better than he had anticipated with Barton pleasantly surprised as his ability to translate the text became easier as he progressed, language knowledge and interpretations returning to him as the pages flowed past his eyes. He had halted suddenly, eyebrows raised he read and reread the passages written after the fact of a series of events in early 1944. The impact of these paragraphs written clearly with great pain cause Barton to sit back from the diary in incredulity, this was an unbelievable revelation, he mentally compartmentalised it to come back these words, the enormity of what had been written as both an account and an indictment. Pressing on with the second and final reads in similar fashion making notes on his jotter for reference, the handwritten words began to take on life, to paint an incredible series of pictures in his mind of Reinecke's life's long and eventful story. Beginning with the ambitious young man skiing in the snow-clad mountains of his youth, to the harrowing years of the war. To his time as a prisoner of war and being kept captive in England, his apparent harsh treatment when he had refused to cooperative with his inquisitors which eventually was to lead to his being transported to a POW camp in the wastes of Canada as misfit with dangerous tendencies. His being held in internment until 1947 as he was deemed still unrepentant of his war services as an officer of the Kriegsmarine. His near fatal exploits in the war in Indo China in the 1950s serving as a French Legionnaire. Then with his return to Österndorf ten long years later where his first meeting with Inga Morgenstern took place, the woman who was never his lover but was later to become both loyal devoted housekeeper and only friend to him for the remainder of his years.

Barton was stunned at the detail and by the emotions raised in him by the reading of the Reinecke accounts in war and in peace, yet he was drawn back to the sinister and salient depiction of events in that January of 1944. Here lay the nub of Reinecke's anguish, his private haunting demon, the torment from which was to remain with him for the rest of his life. Although the diary in its entirety was more than enough to merit a book in its own right, the January 1944 entries were clearly those that had surfaced in the old man's mind on that day when he and Barton had spoken so briefly. Barton reflected on the letter, read again Reinecke unconditional instructions with which he came to the conclusion that they were clearly aimed to bring him and this section of the diary together. There was a deep profundity of understanding now beginning to emerge from his thinking, to crystalise developing and magnifying in his mind, the awesome portent, the extent of what would be needed to be done to honour Reinecke's wishes and his memory. The sheer magnitude of these realisations left him both breathless, exhilarated, even excited by the prospect of an adventure to compare with T. Haggard's King Solomon's Mines, yet at the same time a genuine sense of terror at what such revelations, a venture of this kind may, if embarked upon provoke, disturb forgotten ghosts from times long gone, the provocation of such things and people should really, be left buried in the past undisturbed.

Barton shook himself, decided before he did anything else, he needed to establish facts, the diary on its own was only the novel writings of one man, there were a number of the references in the 1944 section which could be verified with a little research with the newspapers printed at the time, the nearest decent library was ten miles distant… this would be the first port of call.

The visit to the local library yielded little information, most of the news in the first weeks of January 1944 had been centred around the havoc the storm damage had caused in the area, in one front page edition of the local paper, an article, which related to the area of headland area referred to by Reinecke, described a tragedy which had occurred, a black and white photograph depicted the burnt out wreckage a vehicle in which two local men, hauliers had been killed when their lorry had crashed and burst into flames. The following week however there was a small note on the second page which read: -

Released yesterday evening from official sources: The Admiralty has announced with regret, the loss of the vessel HMS Juniper of the coast of N. Wales this past weekend in the violent heavy storms in the Bay of Liverpool. The vessel is believed to have foundered in heavy seas with the loss of thirty of her company with her captain Lt Commander Penrick, a heroic veteran of the Jutland action in 1916. Two seamen were recovered from the water alive and are recovering in hospital. The search in the hope for any further survivors has now been abandoned due to the severe weather conditions in the Liverpool Bay.

This Barton decided might have some bearing, the time scale may be just coincidental yet in the same area and under the same conditions? He made a written copy of the article to add to cross reference with his notes.

Back at the cottage after dinner, he began to reread the diary, two paragraphs of faded writing were proving problematic, at some time in their history the writer had returned here to these entries countless times, the page was illegible, worn by touch much more than the rest of the entries for the year of '44. Two sets of words describing that which Reinecke's U-367 had carried with her as "cargo" on her last mission in early January were elusively difficult in their contents, these alone made little sense, there was the description of the loading of boxes in St. Nazaire, twelve of them, then followed by the blurred writing and unfamiliar words, he would have to resort to the dictionary for a translation. First, he tried to copy them out in his own hand, printing the words letter by letter until he had a sequence which began to make sense. *"Der Münzbarren"* he decided in the nearest English was referring to 'bullion', could this literally mean treasure...? The second set of words were more tantalisingly difficult to interpret, Barton used a magnifying glass to enlarge them under his eye, again he laboured until he had a number of readable words, *"Die Pest, Plage Heimsuchung..."* He turned to the dictionary, an uneasy feeling overtaking the elation he had felt only minutes ago... No, there had to be some mistake here, he read again the dictionary interpretation then looked back at his own written translations... *'Pneumonic Plague bacteria...!'*

Barton spent more minutes making sure he had made no mistakes, cultured or cultivated pneumonic plague... He reread his notes yet again, with a growing feeling of unease, a sense of something akin to alarm beginning to take root the longer he spent staring at his own words, in disbelief. If he was right in his attempts at translation, then he had stumbled across entries of something Reinecke had written down a while after the events in nineteen forty-four, a very long ago time in the distant past. Yet given Reinecke had been interned until 1947, these recordings couldn't have been made before his release from the Canadian internment camp. Before that he had been imprisoned up in the Lake District, at a POW camp for German officers, an old country house called Grizedale Hall had been commandeered by the War Department to house difficult prisoners who were considered as high security risks. Whilst there his every movement, and those of his fellow prisoners had been kept under close scrutiny day and night, he couldn't have made journal notes of such an explosive nature under those kind of confinement conditions, he must have related these entries at a much later date when the detection, the highly volatile revelation of these clandestine subversive operations, with the potential of apocalyptic consequences would be kept for his eyes only. He had been alone, writing in isolation with his recollections, free from the threat of detection with the journal secured somewhere safe from prying eyes. Barton could imagine a younger Herr Ober, poring over his journal in the dead of night, safe within his sanctuary in the Haus Reinecke, struggling with his memory to remember the facts the details of all that had happened so many years before. Reinecke was suggesting in his writings, that the U-367 in the January of 1944 had indeed carried a very mixed cargo, of weapons, a lot of money and the gift of one of the deadliest historical diseases known to man... the Yersina Pestis, the plague bacterium...!

Barton pushed his chair away from his desk, were the these the ramblings of an embittered old man, somehow concocting elements of the as he went, or were these the factual accounts of the things he appeared to describe in such detail? Even allowing for false memory syndrome, there was too much detailed description to be purely the workings of a vivid imagination, the description of the numbered crates, their contents and the people who had been involved, from both sides for this to be confabulation. Barton was now convinced, there were truths in these pages, an appalling scheme had been devised, many minds had worked on the logistics and the carrying out of a detailed complex operation, the evidence of its reality lay before him, it had been set in motion in the January of 1944, it had almost succeeded...! This left the burning question, what to do with this information now? This was highly charged sensitive intelligence material. To whom or to which offices would it be destined or divulged? Such knowledge was a power in itself, Barton felt the next round of considerations he must make would be crucial, to ensure whatever he took to which ever authority, must be in the first place reliable factual documentation backed up with some supportive hard evidence. Supposition and fairy stories were not enough. The diary's author was resting in the ground in Österndorf, was no longer available as an eye-witness, the contents of the diary could be challenged as merely the recollections made after the events to which they related.

Barton came to three conclusions for his next actions, the first being that time was not an imperative, the events were already decades old, nothing was pressing to act immediately. Secondly, he decided in the first instance that he would share what he possessed with David Strachan, indirectly if he, David, hadn't made the telephone which had initiated the trip to trace Dorn's family, he would not be sitting looking at the Reinecke diary now, David's contacts with the various authorities might prove to be useful. Thirdly, given that he had now agreed with himself, time was available, to explore another possibility. Gary Johnson, was another old and trusted friend from school days he had a boat in the nearby Conaway harbour, he had run trips for divers out on the wrecks off the coast of Anglesey in the past, he had the equipment and the know how to perform a small scale sea bed search for what Reinecke had inferred was still lying, in twenty fathoms of water...!

With this mental plan of action forming in his mind, Barton began to make notes on how next to proceed. Top of the list was to call on a knowledgeable old and trusted friend, Gary Johnson, to put his madcap scheme before someone who knew what they were doing on sea and on land, to run by him the feasibility of an underwater search of the sea bed off the Wurm's headland...!

30

The next morning, having telephoned Johnson, Barton drove over to Conaway, parking in the road near the quayside where Johnson had a tiny fisherman's cottage not far from the quay in which he carried out his businesses on the water. 'I'm intrigued,' Johnson had said, shaking hands when he opened his front door, 'come in, you've brought the good weather and the kettles on, have a seat Erich, and tell me what's on your mind?' Johnson was an old and well trusted friend, he presented as a forty-year-old physically fit trimly built man in his forties, weather beaten face with cropped grey hair belied his life at sea and on the water. Wearing a baggy old blue fisherman's sweater and faded jeans he certainly looked the part of an old salt.

Barton plumped himself down in a well-used armchair, a seat he had occupied so many times over the years. 'I don't know where to start, and I'm not sure if what I have in mind you will even agree with. However, Gary I have to say, before I begin, that I need your solemn word that what I'm about to tell you stays strictly between the two of us, at least until I'm sure in my own mind of the steps I have to take next. If, and a big if, word of this got out too early, the press may have a field day, if there's nothing in it, then it may just be an embarrassment, but until then my friend, I do need you to keep it under wraps...'

'Fair enough, my curiosities getting the best of me now, what have you got on your mind Erich, you look about to burst, out with it...!' Johnson said chuckling as he poured the mugs of tea for them.

Barton answered slowly choosing his words, 'Some of this you are going to find hard to believe Gary, so bear with me, I need to show you what I have gathered so can I use your table?'

Johnson grunted, 'Help yourself... Here, use the table, what else do you need?'

Barton cleared away space on the wooden dining table, laid the OS maps he had brought, his notebook and the diary down. Spreading the OS maps out, he folded out the parts depicting the Wurm, the bay beyond between the mountain and the Anglesey coast. 'This is the area I want you to look at, particularly this feature here...' Barton's index finger traced the three finger promontories jutting out into the sea on the larger scale map. 'Here, this section of sea, about a square mile off the Wurm in this water.' He indicated the section on the map, then asked, 'Have you got a nautical chart of these waters, Gary?'

'Of course, wait a minute…' Johnson opened a cabinet next to the table and brought out a number of rolled up charts, selecting one, 'Here it is, I'm familiar with the water here, very tidal, its where two tides meet off the head of the Wurm, conditions can change in minutes, these three projections are the 'Merlin's Coves', I've been down there a few times over the years fishing off the rocks from the shelf above the water. What exactly are you looking for Erich…?'

'A wreck,' answered Barton, 'An old wreck, she's been down there a lifetime if she's there at all…'

Johnson mused on this, 'If, as you say, you have a vessel lying on the bottom her, there could be any number of problems, the first is that there are any number of wrecks in this area going back centuries, not all of them marked on any chart. The second I this is fairly shallow water, the seabed changes with every tide, one good storm might see a sand silt up to a depth of six to twelve feet, then a week later it could be gone again. How longs has your wreck been down there Erich…?'

'If, she's there, since the January of 1944, and at the moment all I have to go on is the writings of one eye-witness. I think the time has come to tell you everything that I know up until now, then perhaps you'll understand Gary…' He withdrew from his pocket, Dorn's identity disc and breast eagle laying them carefully on top of the map.

So Barton sat down with his friend and related the whole story from the beginning starting with the telephone call from David Strachan. It took two hours, with Barton referring to the diary and then the maps and chart when appropriate. When he had finished his story, Johnson was intrigued by the implications.

'If you are right Erich, if what the old man, Reinecke, has written are facts and true, then this U-boat, the 367, might still be on the bottom waiting to be found. However, the bottom is, as I have said, strewn with wrecks of all sorts, there are also lobster pots, old fishing nets tangled in the wreckages, these are safety factors we need to keep in mind if you intend for us to dive in this area. We would need to choose our time with care, the period just before the low tide is coming to an end for a short space of time the water runs slack, the visibility clears a little though not very much. Seeing anything on the bottom is a bit hit and miss one day perhaps twenty to thirty feet, the next minute you can't see your hand in front of your face.

Barton had little to contribute, although he was a competent scuba diver and a strong swimmer, he had no experience to compare with Johnson's professional approach. 'Ok Gary, then what do you suggest?'

Johnson looked at the chart once more, 'We could give a try as early as next week Erich if your game, it's a coincidence, but the September tides will be just right for a test dive around mid-week, say a late morning, perhaps Thursday? Though I'll need to double check the tide table and the met office forecast for those days to be sure. It just so happens, I've got nothing planned you lucky man, it's a slack week so would suit me fine, especially as you've now got me hooked with your sunken treasure story…!' Johnson laughed and said, 'And then, I need to introduce you to Megara…!'

31

On the Friday morning Barton received the awaited for expected news, it came in the form of a large manila envelope, the Ernst Dorn story had been accepted for publication, it would be featured in one of the main stream Sunday papers, enclosed with the letter was a generous cheque! For the time being he was solvent and had some little funds to spare at his disposal. He could pay for the fuel and basic hire of Johnson's boat; the pilot search would now become a reality. There was much to do in the meantime, laid out across dis desk were now pages of notes taken from the Reinecke diary, these Barton formed into batches each containing associated information details, the sections on Reinecke's mission, the description of the individuals and the sea conditions were descriptive and highly detailed. Of particular interest were the references to the two passengers the U-367 had carried, Breitfeld and Schumann. These two figures were central to the mission yet Reinecke had only included basic details of their backgrounds and activities, he alluded to documents he seemed to have acquired, a note book and a set of orders for Breitfeld, there was the penned sequence of events on the top of the Wurm where Breitfeld had met his end, his remains being secreted in an open grave, of Schumann there was no clue as to what had happened to him. The major player here was the person of Mick Lewis, the master of the fishing boat the Lady Patricia. Reinecke's last notes in this section were of giving the Breitfeld notes and orders to Lewis, then of the vessel leaving the harbour of Conway homeward bound on the evening of the 9th January 1944. There were no further notes made to either men after this date. Yet, it nagged at Barton, that the diary had been written down much later after Reinecke's release from Canada, how accurate would the man's recollections have been after all that time in incarceration? He needed more information, was there a possibility of Lewis and his crew surviving the voyage home, the son, Gerry or Gerald had been young enough to still be living if he did. Barton took down from a shelf of maps one covering Ireland, searching the East coast he found what he was looking for, the coastal village or town of Greystones fifteen miles from Dublin, in the County of Wicklow in the Republic of Ireland. The home port Lewis had called *Na Clocha Liatha* In Gaelic. With the ferry port at Holyhead only a little over forty miles from where Barton was sitting, this meant it was in easy reaching distance, an hour's drive then the ferry, then perhaps another drive, he could be there in less than a day. Barton pencilled into his note book the need to call the Stena Link ferry terminal, check availability and sailing times for this coming weekend. One could fly, this would mean a drive anyway to either Liverpool or Manchester, whereas Holyhead by car was an easier option to explore. Barton picked up the telephone and put through the call. It was pure luck, there was a morning sailing with bookings available for the next day, Saturday at 08.15 with a return sailing at 22.55 the same night. Barton booked Landrover as vehicle and himself as driver for the return trip. He needed some basic things, his passport, notebook and a map, meals he could pick up on board in both directions.

The following morning Barton stood against the rail of the ferry watching the coast of Ireland come into view. Breakfast had been good and the forty-mile drive to Holyhead had been easy with little holiday traffic. Within the hour the ferry had docked and the Landrover bumped onto the Dun Laoghaire dockside. He was clear of customs in minutes and on the road south in the direction of Greystones. It was a fairly pleasant straight forward drive through the rolling green countryside with the blue haze of the Wicklow mountains off to his right. On entering the outskirts of Greystones he was surprised to find the little town had grown since the village type fishing port he had imagined from Reinecke's writings, it was tourist orientated, gone were any sign of fishing boats, a wide promenade stretched beside the sea line with modern building covering most of the frontage. Barton stopped and asked the way to the church. He had a mind to seek advice from the local priest so armed with the directions he set out for the Holy Rosary church.

There was no one about when he parked and called at the church, a passer-by however pointed him to the nearby house, the presbytery where the resident priest could be found, it was only steps away, Barton walked up the small pathway to the door and rang the bell. An elderly monsignor came to the door, when Barton said that he was looking for information on the family of one Mick Lewis who sailed out the port back in the forties, the elderly father became quite animated.

The elderly priest had a sprinkling of crumbs down the front of his vestment, clearly in the middle of his meal. 'Now there's a thing,' he said jovially brushing the crumbs from his chest, 'I came here back in the sixties as a young man, I do remember though the priest incumbent at the time, the very old Fr Kelly it was then, a lovely man. The monsignor related how his predecessor had spoken of the Lewis's and their family many times, 'Divils and infidels they were to be sure.' You'll need to look in the old Redford cemetery over the other side of town if you want to visit their graves, it's where all the Lewis's have been laid to rest. It's on the R761 road, you must have passed it when you come into town, you can't miss it, there's nothing else out there. Now, for the living relatives, you'll have to visit other establishments than this house my son, now if I were you, I'd try the pubs, the locals there will know more than me.' Barton thanked him for his time, he neither asked questions nor pressed Barton for his reasons, waving to him as he left in the direction of the cemetery as advised. It was only minutes away and Barton found the parking area on the main road beside the entrance to an extensive burial site with the sea in the distance. Parking the Landrover in the space off the road, Barton got out to stretch his legs, strolling down into the graveyard. The sun shone, it was a pleasant Autumnal day, one or two clusters of people were tending graves. He made his way over to where two elderly women were arranging flowers in front of a headstone. Again, Barton repeated his story about looking for the family of Mick Lewis. One of the middle-aged head scarfed women stood up wiping dirt from her hands, 'I don't know of the family, but over there is Mary and her daughter Eileen, they'll know, they've been here forever...' She pointed at two women in what appeared to be the older part of the cemetery, 'Speak to Mary Macquire there, she knows everyone laid here and their families, she's nearly ninety years old so you may have to shout to be heard...' Barton thanked them for their trouble and headed in the direction of the two women they had pointed him to.

Barton walked over to where these two older ladies, similarly clad with scarves about their heads, were engaged in the same tidying of a grave. The older woman was white haired, of a great age yet she stood and cast an enquiring look at Barton as he approached. He once more repeated his request, for knowledge of the family of Mick Lewis? The older woman tilted her head on one side, 'Why would you be asking questions about the Lewis?' She fiddled with a hearing aid in one ear, her voice loud in the silence of the cemetery.

Her companion took her arm, 'Now don't get yourself roused, it's only a poor man looking for the Lewis's, he means no harm mother...' She nodded at Barton, 'It's the arthritis so it is, makes her crotchety.'

The older lady seemed curious now, 'What would you be wanting to know about the old rascal, he's lying just over there, you could go ask him yourself…!' She pointed a gnarled finger at a large granite headstone only yards away.

Barton attempted to explain, that he was researching details for a piece of writing about a time long ago where the Lewis name had come up in his own right, was relevant to the storyline, the trail had led him here to Greystones, he was looking for any relative who may be still living.

The old woman fixed him with steel still evident in her eyes, 'Mick's family were killed mostly back in the days of the troubles, a long, long time ago, his wife, Molly is there beside him, his boy, if that's who you're looking for lives there…' She pointed across the fields to where a farm stood in the middle distance, 'Young Mr Gerry still lives, though he's only young now in name, I remember him when he was a mere lad, he was popular with the girls he was that I can tell you…' She smiled a broad smile showing her few remaining teeth, 'You can tell him I said so too if you see the old fool…!' With a cackling laugh she dismissed Barton and turned back to her daughter, 'I'm tired now so I am, take me home, leave this young fellah to his chasing of the Lewis's…'

Again, Barton thanked both women, then walked over to the headstone old Mary Macquire had indicated as the resting place of Mick Lewis. It was an impressive monolith of grey granite, into which had been cut the names of his family, *'Patrick M. Lewis, his beloved wife Molly departed this life in 1934 aged 38. Of Riordan Lewis died of the Spanish Flu 1919 aged 6 years, of his beloved sons, Duncan aged 6 years and of Rory aged 4 years tragically killed on August 24th, 1921. RIP.'* It gave the date of Mick's own departure from this earth as in the March of 1964. He would have been a grand age Barton thought sadly when his time had finally come, yet how cruel those early years must have been, the loss of three young children and then his wife. He shook his head, the melancholic sadness of the Lewis family story had moved him, what lay behind the words etched into the stone, what suffering and loss, unimaginable heartache these few words conveyed. Staring across the fields, he decided that the best way to reach the farm would be by road, it looked a good half a mile away set on the gentle slopes of a hillside.

Back on the road he followed the road south again until he found a right turning, a little further on an entrance appeared with a five bar gate across the entrance, Barton drove through following a gravel path winding through the fields until ended in the stone flagged courtyard of a modern two storey farm conversion. The farm building itself was large and spaciously constructed, flint clad walls with expensively glazed windows. A man was busy bent over an open bonnet working on a car in what once had been a barn. Now it sported large wooden double doors, the interior containing three expensive looking motor cars, one of which was a Porche. He walked over wiping his hand on a cloth as Barton pulled the Landrover up.

'Can I help you...?' He was aged somewhere in his mid-twenties, wearing an open tweed waistcoat over a broad checked shirt, with the accompanying green moleskin trousers he looked the stereotypical gentleman farmer type. 'Is there something I can do for you...? He repeated as he came up to Barton's driver's door at the same time appraising the Barton's old Landrover with an appreciative eye. 'This is an old one, Series 11A? I'll bet she's not so good being petrol, I'm thinking the diesel's a better proposition with these...!' It was a pleasant observation the younger man seemed genuine enough in his manner.

'I'm so sorry, didn't want to intrude. My name's Erich Barton, I've just come over this morning from North Wales, I'm looking for the family of Mr Mick Lewis, I was told reliably that this is where he lived?' He was taken with the younger man's easy smile and open face, now feeling he was going to have to repeat his story once more, perhaps for last time. The other stood and listened intently, then reached out his hand taking Barton's in a firm grip to shake it then answered.

'I'm Mick Lewis, but I'm not the one you're looking for, he was my great-grandfather and he,' he gestured around, 'he built this place, the family home. This has something to do with the man called Reinecke I'm guessing does it not? I'm thinking it would be my grandad Gerald that you've come to seek?'

Barton could have cried with relief, in such an incredibly short time, more by pure good fortune than design, he was standing before a descendant of Mick Lewis. 'It is indeed Gerry Lewis, I had hoped against hope that I might find him or someone who could tell me about him, yes, it was the man you've correctly named as Reinecke, it was he who started m on this path only weeks ago in Austria...'

'Reinecke is still alive, that's incredible, he must be much older than even my grandfather and he's not young any more...!' The other man raised both eyebrows as he spoke.

'No, sadly he passed away, he left me a trail to follow, with his last wishes to complete, these were written to me in a letter and in a diary he kept many years ago, in which he recounts his adventures with your names sake, your great-grandfather Mick Lewis.'

The other man stood back, gazed across the fields then returning to Barton said, 'The your journey's not been in vain, you'd better come and meet with my grandfather, I think he's been expecting you or someone like you for a very long time. Follow me Mr Barton, by the way, you can call me Mick…!'

He led Barton up the front steps to the main house and into the hallway, 'If you take a seat in there Mr Barton,' gesturing to an open door to the lounge, 'I'll be with you as soon as I've washed the oil from my hands…'

Barton followed the invitation and made his way into a spacious lounge with a low slung oak beamed ceiling, the sunlight streamed through the window lighting a comfortable seating area of matching upholstered couches, he was about to sit down when a door in the far wall opened and a trimly built women dressed in jodhpurs, riding boots wearing a white sweater entered the room. She didn't appear to notice Barton then started when she spotted him about to take a seat.

'Ah, one of Gerry's friends I take it, are you buying or selling one of those tatty cars?' She said this a questioning look with a smile on her face.

Barton feeling slightly embarrassed was about to reply when Gerry followed him into the room.

'Hi Sis,' this is Mr Barton, he's come about Grandad Gerry, Mr Barton this is my big sister, Sheila, Sheila, this is Mr Barton…'

Barton went to shake hands, noting the woman's near waist length long dark brown hair, her poise and bearing were attractively conscious with no hint of arrogance. Her eyes were strikingly attractive, a deep hazel with something of the vulpine charisma of a vixen. 'I'm so sorry, I didn't mean to startle you, I'm afraid I'm neither buying nor selling, I'm here seeking your Grandfather at your brother's invitation just a few moments ago…'

Sheila Lewis laughed, 'Forgive me Mr Barton, we're so used to Gerry's friends popping up, I thought you were one of the regular petrol heads he consorts with…!'

Barton found her immediately appealing, she had the open features of her sibling, appeared a year or two older, perhaps late twenties, taller than her brother she stood around the same height as Barton, about five-nine.

'Do sit down Mr Barton, will you have some refreshment, tea or coffee perhaps?' She seated herself on the long couch and patted the seat beside her.

Barton obediently sat down in the offered seat, her accent had a pleasant almost delicate burr yet was cultured and well spoken. 'Thank you, coffee would be greatly appreciated, erh Miss Lewis?'

She nodded then said, 'That's right. Now Gerry, be a dear, ask Megan if she would bring some coffee and biscuits for us, now Mr Barton, do tell why you've come to visit Grandad Gerry, he'll be pleased to see you, he just loves it when we have visitors.' Her brother disappeared and could be heard calling for 'Megan' somewhere deeper in the house.

So, Barton repeated his story, finishing with having just arrived from North Wales that morning. 'Perhaps I should have written or called ahead, to be perfectly honest, I didn't have the address until I was pointed this way by two ladies in the cemetery across the fields, forgive me if I am imposing on you.'

'The North of Wales, whereabouts or which county have you come from Mr Barton; I think this is going to get interesting?' An amused smile playing about her lips as she spoke.

'Conway area actually, do you know it?' Barton replied returning her smile.

'I do indeed Mr Barton, I'm based over there myself, I work in Bangor at the University, I lecture in Celtic studies for my sins. Like you I only came over on the ferry last night, I'm home for the weekend to catch up with the family. Now, when Gerry junior comes back with the coffee, we'll pop up to see Grandad in all his glory, he'll be in the garden about now I'm sure…' Gerry junior arrived with a laden tray proceeding to pour for the three of them.

'I'm grateful for both the coffee and your time,' he said glancing at his watch, 'Forgive me, I'm a little pushed having booked on the late sailing this evening from Dublin, forgive me, I didn't really plan this well. How is your grandfather, he must certainly be of a good age now, the period which I'm writing about is back in the 1940s, back then I believe he was only about eighteen at the time when the Reinecke story makes a mention of him with your grandfather?'

'You're so right Mr Barton, 'Sheila, answered him, 'Grandad was little more than a boy, yet when he came home from that adventure, he settled down, got married himself two years later in 1946. Our grandmother gave him his first son, our father Sean in nineteen forty-seven, Dad was his first son. Sadly,' She hesitated for a moment. 'Our father lost his life in a road accident back in 1969, a drunk driver hit his car, when we were both quite small, it was our grandparents who brought us up with a little help from great-grandad would you believe. The other Lewis's, Dad's brothers and sisters are spread about all over the world, South Africa, New Zealand and America, however we stayed on here, all that's left here now is the three of us. It's a wonderful place to live though Mr Barton, you can see out to sea from the upstairs rooms.

'It seems your family have had more than their share of tragedies over the years Miss Lewis, I don't know what to say…' Barton was cut short by a loud bang from somewhere near outside, a second later there was another. 'What was that, sounded like gun shots…!' Barton said in genuine alarm.

Sheila Lewis merely laughed again shaking her head in amusement, 'No Mr Barton, it's grandad, I said he was in the garden, he is too, he's taking pot shots at the rabbits or crows with his twelve bore…!'

There were some raised voices outside, the doorway darkened, and a figure bundled in with a folded shotgun under his arm. Young Gerry rose from the couch, 'You're about to meet our grandad Mr Barton.' He said under his breath, 'Hey grandpa, we've got a visitor…!' He called to the stockily built figure who was treading mud into the carpet from his wellingtons as he came.

Barton joined the two younger people and gazed at the figure of the older Gerry Lewis, the man being the central reason for his journey. Given his obvious great age, Gerry Lewis had weathered the years well, he stood tall with no stoop in his demeanour, was broad chested with no sign of surplus fat. He rested the shotgun on the table it's action broken open, 'I got two, another has a sore backside, of that I'm sure, I'm needing a better gun that shoots straight. Now what's going on here,' he gazed around catching sight of Barton, 'is this a party then Sheila, and who's the good-looking fella, have you brought one home at last?'

'Grandad, that'll do…! No, this is Mr Barton, he's come all the way from Wales to see you. Mr Barton, may I introduce our grandfather, this is the Gerry Lewis you've come to find. Sheila Lewis had spoken with a slight annoyance noticeable in her voice tossing her hair over her shoulders.

Taking his flat cap off, the older Gerry Lewis revealed a still thick head of snow white curly hair, features were an aged version of his grandson's, with twinkling blue eyes set in a broad forehead with bushy eyes brows over the weather beaten face suggesting his many years' exposure to the elements of sun and sea.

'Then welcome Mr Barton, you're from Wales Sheila said, how did you come to find me?'

'It's a long story Mr Lewis, but here I was fortunate to meet a lady in the cemetery across the fields there,' He pointed through the still open door, 'a Mrs Mary Macquire, she very kindly said that I would find you here...'

The old man laughed out loud, 'Mary Malone she was when I was but a lad, we tumbled together in the hay once or twice many years ago...' He was cut short.

'Grandad...!' Echoed both Sheila and the younger Gerry.

'Now, now, now...! That was a long time ago, she was one minx, a comely buxom colleen that one... Whatever she's told you is true...! I was a Jack the Lad back then, proud of it too so there it is. Now, what can I do for you Mr Barton?'

Barton took a deep breath, it seemed that he would have to recount his reasons for seeking Gerry Lewis, son of Mick Lewis yet once again, so he did beginning with the finding of the body of Ernst Dorn in a wood in North Wales. Gerry the older seemed to lose some of his joviality, his shoulders slumped a little and he lowered himself onto a large leather chesterfield sofa. His face became serious as he leaned forward to speak to his grandson.

'There's a bottle of vintage Jameson's in the cabinet, bring it and glasses, I've been saving it for this day... Now Mr Barton, I'll fill in the gaps for you, but when I've oiled my throat a little.' He settled himself back into the deep couch drew a deep breath then sighing began, he recounted his version of events back in 1944, piecing together the story from when the Lady Patricia had sailed from Conway leaving Reinecke with the priest and the fisherman, they had set out into the darkness of that evening mindful of the uncertainty of their homeward voyage. The

Lady Patricia had passed the incoming fishing boats and the patrol craft thankfully without incident, nothing short of a miracle as he put it, as the weather had closed in once more Mick Lewis had taken them out into the Liverpool Bay passing well clear of the light house at Holyhead into deeper water, each mile battling the stormy waters of the Irish sea for survival. At one point they were nearly swamped by the incoming head on waves yet in the early morning light of the following day had made a weary landfall in their home harbour at Greystones. Even as they were tying up at their berth, the figures of three men had appeared like ghosts out of the grey light of dawn. Grim and purposeful they had talked with Mick in barely audible whispers on the deck of the Lady Pat' whilst Gerry below, ran checks over the engine with Finn finishing securing her bow and stern lines. The men who had come aboard were taciturn, said little, after a brief terse exchange of words with Mick they had opened the hatch to the cargo hold then had brought up the four crates secured below, taking each of these up onto the quayside before loading them onto a small van. They then proceeded to systematically search the rest of the boat with Mick and Finn looking on before being they were satisfied there was no more to take away with them, as quietly as they came they were gone, leaving as silently with no more discussion or parting words or small talk or thanks, it was purely business. Mick had stood on the deck to watch them go. He had turned to face his son and Finn saying earnestly, 'The debt is paid, we'll not be seeing the likes of them again boys, that I promise, we've been paid off for our trip and there's generous shares all round…' He had shown them a bundle of notes, the payment for their arduous and dangerous work. Finn had waited for long minutes before he said anything, the dawn was breaking with the three now sitting on the deck hatch cover, resting mind and body, relieved the ordeal had finally come to an end. 'Seems to me that we have a small bonus Mick, I took some precautions as we were coming in, now Gerry and me had thought our windfall needed protection so…'He leaned over the leeward side of the boat, reached for the anchor rope and pulled at it, it came up very slowly, 'Give us a hand Gerry, this is heavy…!' He said, with Gerry grabbing the rope beside him they heaved and eventually lifted the hessian sack tied to the end of the rope line. Both men had to struggle to ease the weight down onto the deck. Mick pushed his cap back on his head, 'Now, would you look at that, is it what I'm thinking you pirates?'

Finn had given one of his belly laughs, Gerry joining in, 'It was over the side but well clear of the screw on our way in Mick…' Added Finn.

'It's our pension pot Dah…!' Gerry said undoing the neck of the sack where the morning light caught the glint of metal. 'I don't know how many we picked up Dah, there wasn't time to count with all the hullaballoo back there, Finn reckoned we stopped counting after four thousand…!'

Mick had bent and reached into the sack, he picked two coins, both bearing the regal head of queen Victoria. 'Well, I knew you two had something in mind, but this is the pot and there's no rainbow…' He tried lifting the sack, 'This must weigh near on for a hundred weight…! That's one helluva rainbow if I do say so myself…' In fact, we did try to weigh it later, it totalled a hefty near ninety pounds all together! Gerry continued his story; Mick was careful to ensure their goods were shared out into smaller sacks enough to be a manageable weight to carry the distance on foot home to the cottage. They had made the decision to wait before attempting to realise any of the booty into hard cash, Mick had said if they were foolish any sudden numbers of gold sovereigns appearing on the market would invoke unwanted suspicion, would be better to take the time to drip feed what they had a few at a time, seek out the dealers where the best prices for antique gold coins could be had. This is what had happened over the years which followed, the price of gold escalating in the 1950s, the provision of a steady income; with some well guided investments building up until Mick had enough in his newly created bank account to approach the land agent when this farm had come up for sale. More money was invested in the farm and land as the years passed, to first renovate and improve the buildings till they reached the condition it was in today. None of the family members had been greedy, eventually Finn had decided to go it alone, had bought a small cottage up in the hills away from everyone, there he had seen out his remaining years in a comfort which he had never experienced before, some of that in liquid form probably contributing to his death only two years before. Much more was said with Barton asking the odd question until he had a clear picture in his mind of the beginnings of the new life Mick Lewis had built, the pieces were falling into place in some semblance of order.

Then Gerry the older rose from the chesterfield, 'Now I have something important to pass on to you Mr Barton, something I will be glad to get off my hands at last, I feel there is a curse on what I am going to offer you, yet I am duty bound by my father's wishes to offer you that which Reinecke left with him to be collected at some later date. He won't be making that now as you've told of his passing sadly quite recently you've said. However, he left it to you in good faith to pick up where he had left off.' He rose from the couch and left the room saying as he went, 'I won't be long, bear with me…' The three, Sheila, Gerry the younger with Barton were left sitting in silence.

'Will you be going back to your own family tonight Mr Barton?' Sheila broke the silence, really just for something to fill in the uncomfortable gap before Gerry returned.

'No, I have no family left of my own now, I was married for a while, but we never had children.'

'Then will your wife or someone be waiting for you tonight when you get back home?' Sheila went on, 'It would be a lonely life all alone, especially with the nature of your work?'

'No not at all, I'm divorced, live alone in a twee tiny cottage up in the hills, my bachelor existence suits me, I come and go as I please with no responsibilities only for myself, it seems better that way. How about you and Gerry, do you have families here?'

'No, Gerry is much too vain to get hitched to any girl, I chose my career instead from early on so there hasn't been time for any long lasting relationships, but I have Polly and she's enough to keep me busy…'

'Polly…?' Barton began to make assumptions about past relationships from the inference.

'No Mr Barton,' Sheila patted her jodhpurs, 'Polly is my mare, she's nearly sixteen hands, takes up most of my time when I home, now I'm boring you with trivia, anyway, I think Dad is coming back now…'

Gerry came back into the room carrying a small wooden box, not ornate or decorated, it was plain dark wood around a foot in length, eight across and four deep. It had a small lock at the front, Gerry the older set the box on the coffee table and sat back in his earlier seat. 'I haven't touched this in all the years it has been gathering dust in my desk. I only looked at the contents once, shortly after my Dah died, it made no sense to me, all the writing is in German Mr Barton, yet my Dah said what it contains is pure evil of some kind so I have never been tempted to find out what it means.' He took a small key from his pocket, inserted into the lock, then pushed the box towards Barton. 'And now it is yours my friend, and very welcome you are to it, for my part I will be glad to see it gone. The only instruction my Dah left me, was this was never to fall into anyone's hands other than the person who rightfully came for it, only then, once I was satisfied that the person was either Reinecke himself, or someone given his specific authority, that person I believe is you Mr Barton, the box, with whatever it may contain is yours, here's the key Mr Barton…' Gerry the older sat back on the chesterfield raising his eyes to meet Barton's.

Barton sat quietly for a minute contemplating the box on the table before him, the three others expectantly waiting for his reaction. It had all happened too fast, in such a short space of time he was in possession of much of the other half of the Lewis saga, now what lay before him was a key to the Reinecke enigmatic puzzle. The full portent and magnitude of the possible release of the contents of the box he suspected was beyond anything either Gerry or his younger family members could imagine, he had omitted from his references to the Reinecke diary the deadly implications the mission of the U-367 had housed. The intended release onto an innocent population of a new strain of the plague bacillus pathogen with all of the death and suffering that would accompany such an outbreak of the newly contrived epidemic. Barton knew he must choose his next words with great care, whilst mindful of the alarm his revelations may bring, the awful effect upon the consciences of those with whom he now may be forced to share this knowledge, that he may be in person, the harbinger of the planned doom of many thousands of lives from earlier times; the bringer of a source of unnecessary great distress to old Gerry Lewis, whom already a man of considerable years and at a time when the twilight of his life should be filled with some peace and contentment.

'I am lost for words Mr Lewis, all I can promise you is that I will keep faith with your late father, Mick, I will examine the contents of the box, take into account their bearing on the meanings hinted at in Reinecke's diary. Until I have had enough time examine these in detail any conjecture would serve no purpose at this time. I must however thank you for your trust, your faith in what must appear to you to be a perfect stranger with an interest only in solving this intriguing mystery. The facts are, that it may be much more than that, I am inclined to suspect the contents of this box, what may lay inside, will raise spectres from the past the like of which are the substance of nightmares. Please, I say to each of you sincerely, my name is Erich, I would take it as a kindness were you call me by my first name, to accept me as such, not just an interested party in you and your father's incredible story of survival?'

'Then Erich, you are accepted, here, take a glass of the Jameson's, it'll seal the pact you have made with us at this table. Your good health Erich…!' All three Lewis's raised their glasses in agreement.

'No, Mr Lewis, it cannot be as simple as that I'm afraid, whereas much as I value your honest, comments, your kindness, I would do you no favours were I to only tell you half-truths. There is another part to the story which even Reinecke at that time knew nothing, he couldn't have told you as he was not taken into the confidence of the one man on the mission who held that vital information, Breitfeld, the man your father shot and killed that night…'

There was a visible reaction from both of the younger people, Sheila put her hand to her mouth while young Gerry hunched himself up looking very uncomfortable yet not speaking. The older Gerry spoke for all three in quiet measured tones. 'We have accepted you as a friend Erich, my father did not talk much about what had happened on the mountain that night, he was much too concerned in trying to get us away to safety, even then he took an enormous risk in rescuing those half dead men from the water, taking *them* to safety when he could have got clear himself and no one would have been any the wiser. Now you say it was he who shot and killed the German called Breitfeld, I had always understood it was Reinecke himself who did that, now you've placed the responsibility for his death on my father…?'

'Then can I suggest that you and I continue this conversation without your grandchildren present, I will share with you what I have found thus far, if you then have a mind to make this knowledge known to Sheila and Gerry I will leave it to you when you have heard what I have to say?'

'I have no secrets from my kin, I have kept them informed as they matured over the years to understand about what we did, the bad and black times the family had already gone through, my father's torment till the day he died for the things he had become involved with from his early days. Ireland was at war, with itself for many years, even now we have the left-overs from those times to live with Erich, what could you possibly tell me that may either shock or surprise me after all of these years? No, Gerry here and Sheila are my blood, if you're going to talk about those events, the deeds of their grandfather then they need to hear it, from your lips, warts and all as they say.' The older Gerry did not look angry or even annoyed, if anything he looked saddened, Sheila reached across to hold her grandfather's hand. He continued, 'If either of you wants to leave, you can, otherwise your free to stay and hear what our friend here, Erich Barton… has to say, so speak now, Sheila, Gerry…?' He let the question hang in the air. Neither of his grandchildren got up to leave, 'Then we stay as a family Erich, now tell us what secrets you are hiding from us…!'

Barton looked at each face in turn, the pain in the older Gerry's eyes, shock in Sheila's and the look of incredulity on the face and attitude of Gerry the younger. He felt a deep sense of responsibility for what he was about to do, yet was acutely aware, that at this stage he was still picking up pieces in an attempt to establish a truth, then and only then, when he had all of the facts, the next step, to take all of his findings to the appropriate authority with all that may entail, to unleash with questions and publicity an enquiry. It may bring down the world Mick Lewis had created upon the heads of his living family. This, he decided he would have to risk; first however, he would at least arm them with the factual knowledge to ward off the storm that may lie ahead.

'Does this mean that some investigations may take place if this information is picked up by the authorities Mr Barton? Are not some things best left to lie the way they are after so long, no one really cares now about those ugly, cruel attempts by people long dead these days, most would not like to be reminded, why can't we just let it go?' Gerry the younger spoke with sincerity, his face displaying a deep concern obviously for both the memory of his great-grandfather as well as the welfare of his living grandfather. 'Let the dead rest Mr Barton, for my part I see no benefits in you raking up the past, surely it can serve no one, Reinecke himself is dead, anything he may have wanted to do should be allowed to die with him?' Young Gerry sat back, he looked to his sister and to his grandfather waiting for their support.

The older Gerry answered first. 'I think Mr Barton, or Erich as we may call him now, may have different thoughts on that young Gerry, perhaps we should hear him out…?' The older Gerry swirled the whiskey in his glass and took a sip before continuing. 'We've been sitting on this thing for years, worried that the source of our success be traced back to the coins we brought back on the deck of the Lady Pat,' they literally fell out of the sky landing upon our deck, they were there when we made our bid to brave the storm, to get home; we stole nothing from neither side in that war, with them in later years we have made a comfortable life, I had no regrets or conscience then, I have none now, they came from Germany, we took nothing from the British it was bullion they intended to be used in the war against them, we merely saved it from falling into the sea, diverted it perhaps from the hands of its unrightful owners…!'

Barton shook his head, 'No, this is nothing to do with the gold that you came away with, you wanted to hear what I have to say, then bear with me as there are three crucial elements to my opinion on this matter.'

'Then the floor is yours Erich, I think we all would feel better if we had your straight and honest views on why we should jeopardise our security by resurrecting the events of January 1944?' Gerry the older downed his whiskey and gestured Barton to state his case.

'Then I will do my best as said, it comes in three parts, this is how I see it. First, a fact, we know from Reinecke's notes in his diary, that the U-367 sailed from St Nazaire that first week in January with a cargo of twelve boxes, he noted they were of differing weights, that he was denied any knowledge of the contents from the very outset. Those responsibilities with their ultimate destination lay in the hands of the two agents he carried with them, neither members of his U-boat crew, the first, Breitfeld, is known to have been a biologist, his colleague the man Schumann it would appear was an overseeing official of the Reich Bank. Secondly, the U-367 arrived to rendezvous with you off the Wurm headland, there six of the boxes were unloaded onto the landing point these being taken by the men who met with you to some point above on the cliffs where they were loaded onto a lorry, except one which it would seem was either dropped or fell showering your boat with the contents, gold coin. The other five we have no idea what happened to them next. We do know that Breitfeld met his end on the cliff top, it would seem that he was about to execute a young boy who had appeared quite literally out of nowhere, when your father, Mick intervened and saved his life. Breitfeld clearly had intended there would be no witnesses, this boy, whoever he was, compromised the operation therefore was to be eliminated out of hand. Your father Gerry saved his life, if he had lived he has Mick's quick thinking to thank for averting the murder of an innocent.

Sheila broke in before Barton could continue, 'What happened to this boy you say Grandfather Mick saved? Is he still alive?' She asked with a woman's care in her voice.

'At this stage, truly I don't know, Reinecke's notes said that he had to be left standing on the cliff edge in the dark in a snow storm so his fate at this moment is unknown, that is another trail for me to follow up when I return home later. To continue on with my theory, the whereabouts of those five boxes has yet to be determined, where did they go, what did they contain? The remainder four boxes, you loaded on board which were to reach Greystones in the hold of the Lady Patricia, these were taken by whoever the Republicans were who set you and your father on this mission. This left two which were still aboard the U-367 when she sailed abandoning Reinecke, we can reasonably assume that they were still on board the submarine when she was lost. Thirdly, Reinecke was clearly deeply troubled for the rest of his life over the loss of his submarine and that of his crew, forty men along with the man Schumann, lie somewhere off the Wurm in deeper water, the U-367 is their coffin. Reinecke was taken with my trip to Austria to lay the ghost of another Austrian who died four years before, he was moved that efforts were being made to put that man's story and his body to rest after being missing for so long; my arrival offered an unexpected solution to his dilemma. It was my involvement in researching the Dorn story, process and conclusion to that unsolved mystery which prompted him to arrange with his housekeeper Inga, for his diary to be sent to me after his death, in some way he seemed to believe the resting place of his forty man crew, his friends and shipmates could be located, found from his notes and laid to rest in a similar respectful fashion to that of his countryman Ernst Dorn.' Barton needed to pause for breath then continued. 'Lastly, I would add Reinecke had further noted in his diary, that when Breitfeld was shot, that he, Reinecke, had taken from his pockets his notebook containing details of the manifest along with the details he kept on the contents list of each of the twelve boxes. In addition there was an envelope which contained the sealed orders opened at sea after they had sailed from St Nazaire, these should give an idea as to whom they would be meeting at the rendezvous, to where the consignment of boxes was intended, their primary objective, the purpose and the ultimate destination vector. Those are the documents which I believe are contained in the box which you have just passed into my care. If I'm right, then they will tell of each of those numbered boxes, their contents and for whom they were intended. Here's the most salient piece of information, this I have kept until last. It is highly probable that at least two of these boxes, contained some form of biological weapon in the form of a plague pathogen, it is the fate of those two boxes which is of the most critical importance, we need to know if they are they still in existence, the plague bacillus may still be as deadly now as it was then. The Breitfeld notes may give us a clearer indication of what they may prove to contain, if this proves to be correct, then that is the time to hand the matter over to the appropriate authorities. It is they who will have more informed ideas as to what to do next. The task now is to establish reliable facts before taking this story any further, next week on Thursday, five days from now, myself and a professional friend who is also a diver, are going to make the first of a series of exploratory dives to the sea bed off the Wurm headland. If we can with a little fortune, locate the U-367, then that will comply with part of Reinecke's final wishes, this legacy he has left me will have been carried out to the best of my ability, the debt to him for entrusting me with his diary paid. Between now and Thursday's exploration, I intend to spend time going through the Breitfeld papers, only then can we decided what is to happen next and to whom we turn the matter over to. For my part, I will keep you updated on a daily basis as to the progress and what I may find, then we can, as a group make an informed decision if you are each in agreement…?'

Gerry the older sat thinking for a while before he spoke. 'Your proposition does appear to be the best way forward Erich, you clearly have taken responsibility for now finding yourself the owner of what may be a deadly poison chalice to quote a cliché, do you intend to start immediately looking at the Breitfeld papers?'

'No, with due respect I will need time to attempt to translate them with a dictionary at my elbow, with access to my earlier notes and the diary where I can piece it together at home with your blessing.'

Sheila Lewis patted her grandfather's arm then said in serious tones, 'We have each of listened to this incredible story Erich, the part played by Mick Lewis and our grandad here, in this tale of mystery and intrigue of an event that happened long before even our own father was born. We have an interest, not only in the part our family members played in this, but the outcome the fall out of which could affect us even today. Although the main events in the course of what was happening on that fateful day were centred on plots and the clandestine operations of countries who were at war at that time. Any revelations which indicate involvement by people who were citizens of the Republic, namely my grandfather and great-grandfather, might be viewed by some to have held suspect motives for the part they played, unwittingly or not, if this goes public Erich, then it may attract some toxic responses from certain institutions and individuals who still hold power don't you agree?'

'I can see your point of view on that, however, there are two ways this may be resolved in the very near future. If the submarine is there, if as a result of our search we can state categorically that we have found the U-367 then the admiralty will need to be informed, potentially it represents a historical war gravesite for the men entombed in her. If the documents we have in our possession now indicate a source of threat to the lives of living people today, I can see no choice but to responsibly hand over that information on to those agencies who can deal this possibly lethal eventuality, if we say nothing then we would be guilty of criminal negligence in my opinion. I am a writer Miss Lewis, not a scientist or a politician.' Barton could readily empathise with her position, yet the burden of the Reinecke's warning from the past weighed heavily upon his sense of moral right.

'You say you are only a writer Erich, then writers make their living by telling stories don't they, in reality is this whole thing a story you have stumbled on with the intention of publishing something sensational, something which is going to pay you very well if it sells. What possible interest could you as an individual have in whether long dead men have a known grave like the one Dorn who you have already exploited for publication, you said that yourself, it sold copies in the Sunday papers?' Gerry the younger's face had taken on a defiant look as he got the words out, he had been thinking over and over in his mind.

'Yes, you are so very right Gerry, the story does deeply interest me this is true, I make no apology for that, you are right too about the Dorn publication, I wrote it and I was then paid my fee for the copy. But no, it's not just as a writer, I have the means of putting something to rest that is long overdue, you ask for my motives, then I will tell you, my own father was lost, somewhere over the sea when I was only a little boy, his body was never found, there was never any grave to put flowers on an to say this was my Dad. Across the fields there you have your fitting memorial to Mick Lewis and his family, I have no such place, what I believe I am doing is as much for the memory of my own father as the unspoken promise to old Reinecke, so yes, you are right, I do have a selfish agenda of my own, does that satisfy you?'

Gerry the younger didn't comment though his features lost some of the emotion of a minute before. His sister spoke instead. 'Erich, that's so very sad, obviously we couldn't have known about your father, Gerry is only being protective as I'm sure you will understand. Next week I'm back in Bangor, it's *'Freshers Week'* at the university so I will be welcoming students to my teaching modules, can I call you on Thursday for any news on your dive, perhaps you can give us your update then?'

'Of course, I will happily let you have my telephone number. Gerry, the same goes for you for updates, I have every intention of keeping you well informed, will you be coming over at all in the near future?' Barton felt some easing of the tension.

'No Erich, but thank you for your honesty, I didn't mean to offend, and, you will have to forgive me if I remain the sceptic here. As Sheila returns to her work over in Bangor, I will have my work cut out running the farm, and Grandad has to be watched in case he goes back to his wanton ways. I'm more than happy if you and Sheila keep in contact and let me know what's happening...' Gerry the younger's smile returned, he seemed genuinely relieved to have got things off of his chest.

Barton looked at his watch realising the hours had passed so quickly, 'I'm going to have to take my leave of you Gerry,' he addressed the older,' I won't take the box, only the documents inside, it might be a little difficult if the customs were to ask me to open it when I land back on the mainland if that's alright with you?' He looked to the older Gerry for an answer.

'Whatever you say Erich, the box itself is not important, I understand what you say about the customs, they might be suspicious and want to examine the contents, confiscation at this time would be both embarrassing and uncomfortable, tuck them in your pocket lad, I'll add a page from the pig farmer's weekly for good measure. Now we've got that out of the way will you have a bite to eat before you go...?' The older Gerry's earlier geniality had returned, he chuckled as he made the offer.

A hour later having been treated to a selection of sandwiches care of Megan in the kitchen, Barton prepared to leave saying his good byes to the two Gerry Lewis's. Older Gerry got up from his seat, he looked suddenly very tired, the unexpected visit and the recounting of the story had taken its toll of his stamina, he extended a hand to Barton at the same time speaking in a sincere thoughtful manner his brows knitted in deep furrows.

'I have always known that one day we would have to face the residue of these terrible things which have lain dormant nearly all of my adult life, the awareness of how it would be difficult to contemplate, even painful to have to lay ghosts to rest who should have buried with their hosts these many long years. I will be relieved friend Erich when this is finally at an end. My hope, at this time, is that I live long enough to see the outcome of your work on the Reinecke diary, the Breitfeld documents reach their conclusion, whatever that maybe; I'm far too old a bunny to worry about any consequences for me, I don't think they will put me in prison for my sins,' Gerry laughed at the ridiculous thought he had given words to, 'No, when the time comes for me to close my eyes for the last time, it will give me peace to join my father in the knowledge in that what we were part of harmed no one other than those bent on death and destruction. That young boy… if you are fortunate enough to find him, tell him my father was troubled leaving him there that night, what he had to do did save his life, the man that he killed was a callous, cold murderer who would have taken many lives as well as his if he had not been stopped. Fare well Erich, I, we, look forward to hearing of your research, your progress in the days to come.' He and his grandson stopped at the door as Barton left in the falling dark of the coming evening. Rain was beginning to gently fall as the two stood to watch Barton return to his Landrover.

Barton was accompanied back to the Landrover with Sheila walking beside him with an umbrella sheltering her head from the light rain. 'So much seems to have happened in the few hours you have been here,' she said lightly, 'it would seem life is never dull with you around is it Erich?' She had laughed that infectious laugh again, Barton felt the attraction he had felt when he had first caught sight of her raise itself in his secondary consciousness.

'This is true Professor Lewis, I don't ask for these things to happen, they just come to visit me. Someday I'll tell you about my pet Gremlin, he's called '*Valkon*,' and this mischievous little creature follows me everywhere I go…!'

'It's not professor, I'm only a lecturer so you need to get that right… A gremlin you say, are you taking the Mickey now just because you're in Ireland and have heard of the *Little People*…?' Sheila raised one eyebrow in question.

'No thanks, I've got my own little person, ok, so what do I call you just Miss Lewis or do you have a title?' Barton had to admit he was enjoying these lighter moments now that they had cleared the air with way ahead for the next stage of his research, with all of them understanding how this would be done and the implications for the eventual findings the conversational exchange was relaxed.

'To you just Sheila will do, even my students call me by my first name…' She replied with a mischievous grin on her lips.

'Not like when I was in university then, it was a bit more rigid then, things must have changed…' Barton climbed into the Landrover and started the engine. She sheltered under the umbrella, waved at him then stood back to watch him leave, 'Take good care Sheila, will talk to you next week, fingers crossed it will be good news. Bye…!' He called through the sliding window. Barton returned the wave, was half inclined to either have shaken her hand or perhaps blown a kiss, he dismissed these from his mind as purely juvenile thoughts, releasing the Landover's clutch was already rumbling back down the driveway, then to find the road to Dublin even as the teenage whimsical thinking was dissipating from his immediate thinking. On the return journey he did not see much of the countryside, darkness had fallen, the rain pooled in the road and the drive was mostly made in the light of street lamps, little to distract his thinking until he reached the port at Dublin to catch the 22.50 sailing. The ferry trip back across the Irish sea was uneventful, Barton passed the time in the lounge area of the upper deck conscious of the bulge in his safari jacket pocket next to his passport. At Holyhead, he returned down to the car deck, prepared to disembark. Barton took the Breitfeld documents out from his pocket, spreading them out on the passenger seat beside him along with his map. The manila envelope he put at the bottom of the untidy pile with the Reich stamp on the underside. The leather worn notebook he opened and laid on the top. When his turn came, he drove down the ramp onto the dockside, was directed across to the customs area. The uniformed official approached with the usual question, 'Anything to declare?' Barton answered no, however the officer pointed him to a green lane marked for 'Goods to Declare' so he obediently followed the instruction and turned off the engine and waited to be checked. He was asked to get out of the vehicle, handing over his passport to be examined at the same time. The two officers seemed more interested in the rear of the vehicle inspecting Barton's over-night bag, putting the contents on a table, they were as he had packed them and hadn't been used or opened. They then performed a cursory search of the driving area, prodded the pile of notes and maps on the passenger side appeared satisfied and beckoned him out onto the rain-soaked quayside. He was on the way home, an hour to go to his own front door and bed. It had been a very long and eventful twenty-four-hour day, the thought of a hot shower and a nightcap before turning in he relished with some pleasure as he drove homeward through the early hours of the morning.

32

Sunday morning broke fine and clear, a warm and sunny September morning. A little after ten the telephone rang. To his genuine surprise it was Sheila. 'Just wanted to make sure that you have arrived home safely.' She had begun, 'Grandad Gerry was really taken with you Erich, he doesn't usually have time for anyone other than Gerry and I, in some ways it was thrilling to see him animated, talkative, able to relate to you in the way that he did. Given his great age, we have often been concerned for his health, the possible deterioration in his memory, but with you he was his old self, I'm grateful to you for that, whatever happens next it's given him some purpose again in his life.' Her soft voice on the telephone inexplicably raised goose bumps on his fore arms. 'Just how old is your grandad...?' He heard himself ask. When she replied he was taken aback. 'That's really amazing, he had the look of a man twenty years younger, even then his physical shape and his general outlook would happily grace any man in his sixties or seventies, what an incredible character he is...!'

'Yes, we are very proud of him, it was his knack and business know how that really made the family economically comfortable, he took Mick Lewis's early success and built upon it, invested wisely, bought a failing scrap metal business back in the fifties, it was just before the price of scrap metal took off, that's really the true source of the family's income and success today. He has trusted you Erich, I'm inclined to go with him on that, how are your arrangements for the diving expedition going?'

'At the moment I have much to do, need to get hold of my friend Gary today and find out what he needs from me. Later today I'm going to begin on the Breitfeld papers, then on Monday morning another trip to the newspaper archives, I've a feeling I may have missed something last time, just a hunch at this time, we'll see what tomorrow brings on that one. How about you, you're working this week you said?'

'I am Erich, I've an early start in the morning so I'm booked on the afternoon sailing, so should be back at my flat to catch up on my paper work ready for the morning by early evening, I'll leave you my telephone number for you to call me if you find anything dramatically interesting in the meantime…'

There followed some pleasant minutes of just chatting, the easy relaxed banter he found himself enjoying although much of the contents was trivia yet it stimulated his need to talk purely on a friendly social level with another person about life, the cabbages and kings without dwelling too seriously on themes or opinions. When he put the telephone down he heard a cautionary voice in his head warn him, he was warming to Sheila Lewis, an emotional experience he hadn't felt for a long time, now was not the best time to think about any involvement, there was too much to do and time was pressing. The domestic chores taken care of, another letter from the publisher an enticement inviting him to submit another story when he had prepared a synopsis for his next piece of work! Thought of an extended paper on Reinecke's story had already taken seed and form in his mind, first there was the present research and reading to do, establishment of facts and events those including though not only of the incident in 1944. There was a wealth of material, much more in Reinecke's adventures and travels when he had returned from captivity, these would need to put on hold, come later when the present task was completed.

In the evening, Barton sat at his old worn desk in the study bedroom, switching on the banker's lamp over the desk, he laid out the tools and material of his work. The Breitfeld notebook first, its leather covering was worn and stained with what appeared to be salt marks on the cover. It was not thick as the Reinecke diary had been, its pages numbered only one hundred and twenty sheets of hand-written notations. He laid this open at the first page and set it to one side. The envelope yielded only one sheet of typed paper, it was dated 28th December 1943, signed at the bottom by Gruppenfuhrer Konrad Liebnitz, Rennes with the stamp of the OKW. The order was brief and to the point, the bearer was to be given any assistance required in carrying out his mission in the interests of the Reich, with the full authorisation of the SS high command, any person or persons impeding or obstruction the execution of this order would be deemed an enemy of the state and be treated accordingly. The bearer's actions in whatever form were sanctioned by the R.S.H.A. Berlin (Reich Security Main Offices). Basically, it gave the bearer and open hand to do whatever was necessary to carry out his mission, Barton concluded that this would have included the brutal execution of a child. It seemed that in the event of any objection or protest on Reinecke's part would have seen this document produced indemnifying Breitfeld for any for overcoming anything which may have stood in his way. Barton placed it back in the envelope and turned his attention to the notebook.

This was a very different set of writings, clearly it was both the parameters of the mission with Breitfeld's own detailed chronicle of how he had become involved, as well in the later pages, for the shipment that he was charged as the responsible driving force and agent of delivery. Barton filled his pipe, the hand writing was legible, precise and clear which was going to make the work easier.

It began with Breitfeld's account of how the team of biologist he worked with had been contacted by the RSHA regarding a recent discovery in the Spring of 1938 of a mass gravesite near Koln, ostensibly this had dated from the fourteenth century when a wave of the Bubonic Plague had ravaged the land. The disposal of the bodies of the victims, at first had not been a problem, then as was gathered from contemporary sources as the sheer number of dead precluded any single burials, they indicated that mass graves had been dug in the nearby hills to contain the remains of some thousands of unnamed individuals. A group of these had been discovered and unearthed by archaeologists excavating a nearby earlier Roman site. Realising what they had found they abandoned the dig until the ministry for Reach Welfare had been informed, in turn they had recognised the potential for reinfection of plague disease spores if the remains were to be disturbed.

Instead of securing and sanitising the site with lime dust, at least official had taken it into his head that there may be something to be learned from examination of the bodies of the victims, therefore samples were to be taken for analysis by members of a team of biologists from the Dresden and Heidelberg universities. Among these, to lead the team, was the Oxford graduate and doctor of pathogenic research, Herr Jurgen Breitfeld.

Breitfeld described his exhilaration at being given this challenge, to examine a possibly living viral disease which dated back to over six hundred years of the decimation of populations. His team were given a brand-new laboratory complex to undertake their research programme with unlimited funds from the central Reich Office which had taken interest in the project. At first it was virtually impossible to safely isolate the disease from the samples taken from the corpses, then it was found that a few specimens yielded a viable living organism. The next phase of the research had determined that this pathogen could be traced to the specific pneumonic form of the plague, unlike the fragility of its relations, this was not only robust enough to survive, it could be cultivated into a pure form. The Breitfeld notes at this point gave testimony to his jubilation at having not only isolated and having contained the plague strain, he had found a method by which it could be cultivated and reproduced under laboratory conditions. He was ecstatic, the eccentricity now bordering on the insanity madness of what he had created. The next phase had seen the living disease suspended in a gelatin-based liquid solution, these capable of being stored as live depositories of the newly designed plague bacillus. Breitfeld had proudly presented his paper reporting with delight that the first thirty subjects had expired after having been exposed to vectors succumbing within twenty-four hours. He was pleased to submit his successful findings to the offices of the RHSA, where they were met with approval; the next question they had put to him was to answer if this discovery could form the basis of a viable biological weapon? Breitfeld had been overwhelmed by his recognition, with the accolades heaped upon him for his discovery and work. Of course, he had replied, it would be an honour to provide the Reich with a new form of malignant life form which could be used upon the enemies of his beloved leader, Adolf Hitler...!

Barton had to push himself away from the desk, the sheer horror of what he had just translated. Breitfeld had created a monster, a mutant version of a disease which would be unstoppable, created by carefully controlled bio-engineering to resist any attempts to counter its multiplication in the host's body, in fact it would thrive in conditions where other viral infections would fail. He found it hard to imagine, to take it what this would have meant in 1944, it would have been a plague of Biblical proportions knowing no antidote or defence it would have decimated the targeted population with infection in a matter of days, with an incubation period of hours and not days, spread in the atmosphere by aerosol droplets from the infected hosts. If it were capable of that kind of projected lethal course back then in the 1940s, what could it do with its mutated capability to the present living generations of people? The consequences were unthinkable, if this potent catastrophic creation were to be considered in still in existence and alive, then its presence and nature had to be known to the authorities as soon as was possible. If this was what Reinecke had unwittingly delivered to mainland Britain it may still be lying dormant waiting for the event to bring it back into its hideous life form. This cannot be allowed to happen; he would have to act upon this information. Two boxes containing eight phials had been loaded on the U-367 at St Nazaire.

The next part of the notebook dealt with the remainder of the consignment destined for Reinecke's U-367. Breitfeld described his liaison with Herr Max Schumann, an economist who had been recruited, according to Breitfeld, 'To spear head a two-pronged attack on the British monetary system.' Schumann's team had employed the best of engravers and forgers selected from the captive populations of the *special camps*; their purpose was to produce a near perfect as possible forgery of the English five-pound note. Not only would these be capable of passing all but the most minute inspection, they would be soiled and crumpled so as to resemble used notes to further avoid detection. Their target figure was to be a run of a hundred thousand notes with the face value of five hundred thousand pounds, these just the start of the operation. These suspect bank notes would be drip fed into the system of retail and wholesale commerce, at the first hint of discovery it was predicted there would be a nation-wide financial crisis as the numbers of notes in circulation increased flooding the markets causing chaos and uncertainty as confidence in the British pound dropped. Three crates containing quantities of these notes these would be part of the Reinecke consignment. The second part of Schumann's brief was in Barton's view, even more ingenious. A fine trawl had made throughout the German and occupied areas to identify and locate British gold coin, in particular gold sovereigns. Every coin that could be found or acquired legally or otherwise, was amassed into nearly the entire individual and state possession of such coins from every source identified by the Reich RHSA economic offices was brought to one stock pile numbering over fifteen thousand twenty-two carat coins, mostly from the late Victorian period up until 1914. There was a twofold purpose, one-third of a crate of bullion of five thousand coins would be used as readily exchangeable currency to fund activities on the British mainland once the forged bank notes had been introduced, these would represent a stable gold basis for both internal and external exchanges. The bulk of the residue was to be intended for deep storage, to go underground to await the time when money would be required to set up new modular branches of power in a post war Britain, whichever way the current threat to the Reich unfolded there would be the beginnings of the next order financially ready in place to draw upon by the new leaders once the fighting was over. Three of such crates had been prepared for the Reinecke expedition.

The remaining four boxes or crates contained an assignment of K98 rifles, plastic explosive and ammunition bound to supply the movement in Ireland, yet this was also a fall back plan. If Reinecke failed to land

Breitfeld and Schumann on the British mainland, then they and the cargo would be diverted in the fishing boat to Ireland. In the event of detection, all would be consigned with any objectors to the depths of the Irish sea, nothing could be allowed to fall into British hands, the men and vessels involved were expendable, success or failure with nothing in between.

Again Barton had to sit away from the note book and take stock of his feelings, the Breitfeld notes indicated the most wild and hair brained scheme he could possibly have imagined. The nature of the U-367s cargo was being revealed, in the simplest of terms a desperate damaging attempt by madmen, it would seem, to avert the consequences of an Allied success on mainland Europe, to create mayhem and sickness while Germany used the breathing space to develop further the V weapons and stave off a possible defeat in Western Europe...!

The following parts of the Breitfeld notes were dedicated to the numbering and the sequence of loading onto the submarine, then the same in reverse for their unloading at the rendezvous, the discharge into each section of the reception they expected on reaching the Wurm headland on the night of the 9th January 1944. Barton reasoned to himself, surely in this next part there is going to be revealed the destination of the boxes, the names of the people or organisations who were to receive them, in particular the five boxes successfully unloaded which were now unaccounted for. He poured himself a malt whiskey, a repacking of his favourite briar then set to face the final part of his task with some deeply felt trepidation. Breitfeld had made meticulous notes in St Nazaire, he ensured that each box was numbered in sequence according to how each was to be unloaded, the next sentences were gems, everything that Barton had desired and more. Breitfeld had ensured each box's content identified by the number he had assigned it. Simple yet effective, boxes 1, 3, and 5 contained paper money, the forged bank notes, boxes 7 and 8 the glass plague phials, 6, 11 and 12bullion, the remaining numbers 2, 4, 8 and 10 were bound for the fishing boat's hold. This was the order in which they had been loaded in preparation for their off-loading. Those containing the lightest consignments would come off first, the heavy loads left until last. In this way Barton could estimate the first six boxes would contain paper bank notes with the disease carrying light boxes, the bullion to come up last while the four assigned to the fishing boat would be the easiest to transfer vessel to vessel. It was a reasonable assumption therefore that the first six had been manhandled off the submarine and up the cliff as Reinecke had described with Gerald Lewis's confirmation that the other four had been successfully placed in the Lady Patricia's hold. One box had fallen from the cliff disgorging its contents onto the U-boat and Lady Pat,' the remaining two bullion heavy boxes were still on board the submarine when the alarm sounded. By simply arithmetic this meant that five, boxes 1, 3, 5, 7 and 9 were still to be accounted for, it was their whereabouts which now posed the problem of what to do next with the information he now held in his hands.

There was one last piece of the jig-saw tantalisingly waiting to be found. Barton cleared his desk for the night, nothing could be done now until the morning. He knew clearly what he had to do next, the thoughts he turned over and over in his mind as he had pored through the Breitfeld notes, then cross referenced once again with his own notes on the Reinecke writings in the diary. He needed to go back to the archives once more, to make sure there was nothing he could have missed in the first brief search. If he failed, if there were only the Breitfeld notes and the diary to go on, then despite whatever he may find with Garry this coming Thursday, there would be no choice but to hand everything over to David for his guidance on what must happen next.

33

Monday morning broke with some light rain. Barton did not sleep well this night, had suffered the numerous unwelcomed uninvited persistent thoughts running randomly through his mind, a hundred permutations of possible occurrences, sinister doom laden outcomes had insisted on being pictured in his mind denying him sleep Images in dreams half awake, crazy mixed up dreams of dead men and ghosts, of catastrophes, these had disturbed his thinking, impinged on his ability to gain any rest from his nagging thought processes. When the first light of dawn broke through the bedroom window the bird calls of the morning chorus, usually a pleasure, was hardly noticed. He studied his reflection in the bathroom mirror, a little haggard and worn, was that the first of grey appearing in his hair he asked himself? The exertions, both mental and physical of the past weeks were beginning to tell perhaps...? The weight of responsibility for the Reinecke revelations, the stumbling into a scenario acted out long before he was born, these resonating with the memories of a childhood where the father had only been but an image in an ageing photograph, it still sat on the shelf in the study where the smiling face of a uniformed man nearly half his age stared back at him. Would things have taken a different turn if his own father had lived? Again the *what if's* passed through his wandering idle thinking as he shaved, the reflection gazing back wasn't in too bad a shape he decided, approaching the forty mark, unattached, small amount of money in the bank and the prospect of life altering adventures to occupy his mind. Maybe it was a pretty good life after all! And, there was Sheila, the picture of her face crept into his mind's eye, well that could be an interesting development too, if, he played his cards carefully, but not to be hurt, get his emotional fingers burnt with misplaced trust or taken for granted as in the last time romantic affair when he had let his heart rule his head, absolutely not. No, tread with care this time...! He finished shaving, showered then prepared his leather writing bag with his notes and the pad ready for an early start. Over toast and coffee he read again the section of Reinecke's writings about the events on the Wurm, the shooting by Lewis of Breitfeld, the concealing of the body by Reinecke along with his Walther pistol in what appeared to be an empty unoccupied grave. The transcription describing the loss of the Juniper, the fate of her crew in the newspaper article in the week after the storm. This would be where he needed to pick up the trail.

By ten o'clock he was at the newspaper of office of the weekly publication which had reported the storms in the January '44 editions. After a brief explanation of his researching the period for an article he was writing, the issuing of a reader's ticket, he was shown to a small office where he could work undisturbed. Barton completed the form requesting access for the copy of the newspaper editions between January and March of that year. After a brief wait one of the young male trainee clerks brought him three large bindings containing the newspaper prints which he had asked for. Barton sat at the rickety little desk, unlacing the black ribbons securing the first large cardboard portfolio began with the pages of the first week of 1944. There was reports of local news until he came to the pages where he had found the entry on the storms and their effects, then the loss of the ship Juniper and numbers of her crew apart from the two men who were saved from the water. He carefully turned over the succeeding pages, each yellow with age containing little snippets of information, adverts for local retailers and service until in the 10th February edition he found a morsel of information that rang bells in his memory, he had passed over it on his last visit, it was only a very small piece probably added to fill up a page, the hairs on the nape of his neck stood up as he read:

'A thirteen-year-old local boy was rescued by an American serviceman in last week's weekend storms. Huw Henryd Thomas found wandering suffering with exposure, he had been lost on the Wurm in snow, was saved by Sgt L. Jones US Infantry. Sgt Jones who, with others had taken the boy by jeep to the new hospital in the Bay where a hospital spokesman said the boy was receiving treatment and his condition is improving.'

This could be the breakthrough he was looking for, the time and date were right, it had to be more than just coincidence, was this the 'boy' both Reinecke in his notes and Gerry Lewis had mentioned with is recollecting the events of that night? Barton took down careful notes of the date, the name of the child, Huw Henryd Thomas,13 years old. Reading over the following pages into the month of February, at the end of the month another brief article referred to the same boy, it merely stated the Huw Thomas, survivor of the January storms, had been discharged to the care of his mother having made a successful recovery, only two sentences yet it gave another date, the twenty second of February when the paper had been published. This was enough to go on,

Barton handed back the files to the clerk and made for home.

Laying his notes out on the desk, he arranged each of these in chronological order, the latest additions relating to the youth, Huw Thomas, a Welsh sounding name? Obviously this lad would have lived somewhere in the vicinity of the Wurm mountain and the headland, the paper had said that he was local, some quick mental arithmetic provided another teasing question, if this young person was only thirteen in 1944, he could easily be still alive, perhaps even living in the area? If the newspaper trail ended in '44, where to begin to look for some trace of this lad, his family, perhaps school records, the census returns for those years were possibilities, yet what about something much simpler? The local telephone directory…! No, he reasoned, that would be asking too much of the good fortune which had seemed to guide his actions so far, yet worth a try perhaps, there was nothing to lose! So Barton reached to the shelf above his desk for the recent telephone directories, laying these on the desk he began, with the aid of a magnifying glass, to trawl through the Thomas names, they were in hundreds, a popular surname in North Wales.

Nothing immediately came up in his first search, he tried with the initials, H with different versions of the name 'Huw' or 'Hugh'. Then in frustration he continued through the indexes where he came upon one name which contained the right initials, too good yet looked promising. This was in the section where businesses overlapped with the private numbers, here was listed *'H. H. Thomas & Sons, Greengrocer Whole-Sale.'* There was no private number listed, only the business address and number in the resort town's newly created commercial area. Barton sat back studying the entry, a family member, yet there had to be dozens of businesses with similar initials, but there was a number so worth a try, only the cost of a telephone call and quicker than another trip to the archives office or the town hall's register of births and marriages. Barton picked up the receiver and dialled the number, glancing at his watch, it was only three-thirty in the afternoon on a working day, there would have to be someone in the office he presumed, as it was a wholesale warehouse. The telephone rang six times then was answered by a female voice asking if he wanted sales or deliveries, Barton asked with a suddenly dry mouth if he could speak to Mr Thomas?

The voice at the other end of the telephone politely asked. 'Certainly, which Mr Thomas did you want to talk to? Our Mr Brian Thomas is out of the office at present, Mr Bryn Thomas is on holiday, there's only Mr

Huw Thomas in the office at the moment Sir…'

Barton nearly dropped the receiver, 'You have Mr Huw Thomas in the office, …now, …he's in the building?'

'Yes Sir, but if it's about orders or delivery you need to speak to his son, Mr Bryn Thomas, if you leave your number, I'll get him to call you when he returns later today…'

Barton felt his heart rate quicken, 'Mr Thomas senior, would that be Mr Huw Henryd Thomas…?'

'Yes, it is, but Mr Huw Thomas is very busy, I'm afraid he doesn't take the business calls himself, can I ask what this is about please…?'

Barton drew in a deep breath, composing his voice he said. 'Mr Huw Thomas doesn't know me, my name is Erich Barton, it's nothing to do with the business, I would ask to speak with him personally if possible, if you tell him please, it's in regard to an event back in January 1944, if you mention Sgt Jones that may help…?'

The woman at the other end f the telephone hesitated, 'If you hold the line Mr Barton, I'll ask Mr Thomas if he will talk to you, give me a moment please…'

Barton sat with the receiver pressed to his ear, if this was the right Thomas, what could he do or say if the man refused to speak with him, would that be the end of it? Holding the receiver, he looked through the window at the fields beyond as a minute passed, could this be another happy coincidence served up by good fortune rather than design? He was afraid to ask himself, to risk too much hope upon a quirk of the hand of fickle fate. He was almost unnerved, shocked when the telephone clicked back on…

'Mr Thomas will speak to you now Mr Barton, hold the line while I transfer you…' There was an audible click then a male voice answered…

'This is Huw Thomas, if you're a newspaper man Barton, I'm not interested, I'm a busy man, who has told you about the American Jonesey?' The voice was deep with a distinctive North Walian accent, not angry but a hint of annoyance in the tone of the question.

'Forgive me Mr Thomas, I don't want to intrude upon your time, I'll try to be as brief as is possible if you'll allow me, then perhaps you can consider what I'm about to ask of you?' Barton felt uncomfortably conscious of just how many times he had repeated this opening gambit with apologies so recently, to the different people he had come into contact with trying with each to justify and explain his motivation.

'Go on, but I warn you, anything to do with newspapers and I will put the phone down, is that clear...?'

'It is Mr Thomas. As said, to be brief, I have come into the possession of a diary written by a German officer of the name of Reinecke, with the contents I made contact with a family of a man called Mick Lewis who lived in the Irish Republic. Both made references to a night in the January of 1944 in which a young boy was involved as an innocent bystander. I later traced, through newspapers written at the time, I have to admit, these gave the name of a young boy who survived exposure on the Wurm in a snowstorm, the name given was 'Huw Henryd Thomas', I believe that that young man could be yourself Mr Thomas, if it is you, then I would ask that you may be able to help me fill in the gaps as to what happened that night...!'

There was a lengthy pause at the other end of the line, Barton could hear the laboured breathing as Thomas was considering his answer, despite the urge to add anything further he waited for the reply. It came with Thomas's voice mellowing from the terse earlier statement. 'If I answer you Mr Barton, I would first like to know what you intend to do with your information, you have told me a 'why' you are seeking answers to something long ago, but not for what purpose you have in mind. I've told you, anything to do with newspapers and this conversation is over, it ends here and now...!'

'Then let me be frank Mr Thomas, there is much more to this story than I'm able to tell you in a telephone call, that is neither fair to you nor does it help with what I am trying to do for people who are long dead. If it were possible to meet with you, then I could let you see what I have been able to gather so far, the document which started this search and the story of a long dead German flier called Dorn...?'

'Dorn, I know no one of that name. Barton I'm not prepared to continue this conversation over the telephone, I'll tell you that straight. Tomorrow however, I'm willing to meet with you and hear what you have to say, where are you staying?' There was a finality in the last words, Thomas controlling the dialogue under his terms.

'Thank you, Mr Thomas, I'm not staying anywhere, in fact I live locally. If you would suggest the time and place, I'll happily come to you...'

'Then not here, this is my place of work, this is my personal life and is not for sharing with my employees or anyone else. I will grant you an interview on my conditions, anything that I may say to you is held in the strictest of confidence, nothing that I may say will be used or recorded in any way at all, written or otherwise until I am completely satisfied as to the purpose of your research Mr Barton. You may come to my home, which will be convenient for me, however, I give you fair warning again, if there are any ideas of sensationalism, of papers, then I will ask you to leave. I'm going to allow you to come to my home as I don't like conducting business or anything else over the telephone without seeing the other person's face. Tomorrow, at two o'clock, it's my day away from the office, that is all I'm prepared to do at this stage of our conversation.'

'Then I'm grateful for your trust, I will do my level best to reassure you that my intentions are in sound taste, there is nothing devious about my request I promise you...'

The exchange concluded with Huw Thomas mutually exchanging telephone numbers with Barton giving directions of how to find the location of his home address on the outskirts of the Bay town. There was little to do now other than to plan for the meeting with this man whose recollections may now throw new light on to the shadowy missing parts of the Reinecke notes, of the recollections of the Lewis family passed down through the person of Gerald Lewis the older and his father Mick. More vital, any clues to the whereabouts of the boxes missing from the accounts of both sides.

There was much to think about in preparation for this encounter. Did Huw Thomas hold the information Barton so desperately needed to clear his mind for the next step in dealing with the prospect of a plague presence? As a thirteen-year-old at the time, how reliably accurate might his memory be of that night seen and remembered as laid down in the mind of a child? Barton finally decided that there would be little to be gained from conjecture, much would depend on Huw Thomas's attitude, his willingness to revisit those events, when he had made it clear he would curtail the interview at any point if he felt it was his prerogative to do so.

The remainder of the day was spent in transcribing his hand-written notes gathered so far in his research and travels into the beginnings of a typewritten format. At a brief guess this was going to run into hundreds of pages, the foundations for a book he was tempted to speculate upon whilst still wary of Huw Thomas's warnings about the withdrawal of any spoken contributions he may make. Barton telephoned Sheila Lewis in the mid evening, disinclined to chat on any trivia, only to keep facts, the promised update on progress with her to pass this on to her grandfather and her brother. Barton hoped he had not offended her with his clipped tones, there was just too much at stake on the meeting with Huw Thomas in the coming day.

34

Tuesday morning dawned as another clear day, Barton spent some little time typing up the notes from the previous day, then again prepared his writing bag for the afternoon's meeting. After a sandwich lunch he set out for the Bay town and the Thomas's home early. As he drove the difficulties which may mar the opening of the interview with Huw Thomas were at the forefront of his mind. Get it wrong in the first minute and he would be shown the door, he was quite clear on that as a negative possibility, the task would be to gently word the line of questions to capture Huw's interest whilst assuaging any reservations he might have in revealing the part he may have played in the drama which had left at least one man shot dead that night. Barton had taken the canvass top of off the Landrover, the Summery breeze coming in from the sea was refreshing as he drove down onto the coastal road following the contours of the coastline then up and over the hill to where the panoramic vista of the curve of the resort Bay town hove into view. It was reminiscent of a smaller version of the bay of Naples with trees lining the promenade into the centre of the main thoroughfare. Taking the directions given he took a left up from the sea front into a residential area, finding the road then the name on the driveway he was looking for, 'BRAMBLE END' it read leading into a short drive. As he pulled the Landrover up in front of a well-built cottage dwelling standing back against the walls of a small rock outcrop, he became aware of a spluttering exhaust sound, the man he immediately took to be Huw Thomas, seated upon a ride on lawnmower careering across about a half-acre of lawn under a stand of ancient pine trees. He caught sight of the Landrover guiding his way back along the parallel line he had just cut, pulling up on the drive beside Barton he cut the engine and climbed out of the seat.

'Mr Barton is it…? Was expecting you but have taken advantage of the good weather to get a trim done today, you found your way here then…?' Huw Henryd was not at all as Barton had imagined, the voice on the telephone yesterday had suggested a big man, suited, shirt and tie. The Huw Thomas before him stood no taller than five foot four, was a slender built energetic looking man somewhere in his later years with a mop of grey hair, dressed in old well-worn blue jeans and an open necked check shirt, he could easily be taken for the gardener Barton mused to himself as the other reached toward him and gripped his hand powerfully in his.

'You're welcome here Mr Barton, before we begin do I have to repeat what I said to you yesterday?' Huw stood with his hands on his hips dispelling any notion of a gardener with his clipped and crisp businesslike tone of voice.

'No Mr Thomas, I'm quite clear about what you said, I'm grateful for you're seeing me on your day off and I promise if you will bear with me and hear what I have to say then it may put your mind at rest as to why I have asked to see and talk with you.' The other man fixed Barton with a thoughtful gaze for a moment, then continued.

'Fair enough, come, we might as well be comfortable, I've built a terrace at the back of the house, we can sit there undisturbed. Do you want a tea or coffee?' There it was again, that slight North Walian accent, direct bordering on the brusque.

Barton followed Huw around the corner of the cottage to where a stone flagged patio area led up to the open kitchen door, there were a number of wooden armchairs with cushions laid out around a matching large circular table. Huw disappeared into the kitchen calling back, 'Was it tea or coffee Mr Barton?'

Barton took one of the low armchairs, 'Coffee if you please, as it comes milk and sugar...!'

'Fine, be with you in a moment...' Huw could be heard bustling about in the kitchen, then appeared carrying a tray with two chunky steaming mugs and a plate of biscuits, 'Here, made yourself comfortable have you? Now, tell me Mr Barton what's this all about...?' He sat himself opposite Barton, took a sip of his coffee and nodded for Barton to begin.

'Well Mr Thomas, I seemed to have told this story so many times over these recent weeks I'm beginning to sound like an old gramophone... I'll be as frank and as honest with you as I possibly can, please stop me at any time if you want me to explain any details, you have to understand that I've been living this story in my mind since May of this year, I'm liable to forget that for anyone hearing this for the first time it may sound incredible, even in the realms of fantasy Mr Thomas but here goes...'

Barton went right back to the beginning, to the involvement with the finding of Dorn, the association of ideas with his own father's fate, through to his meeting with Reinecke then his journey to Ireland and his time spent speaking with Gerald Lewis and his grandchildren; he left nothing out relating the details as described by Reinecke with the additions filled in by the Lewis family, it took an hour before he finally rested looking for Huw Thomas's reactions. The man had neither interrupted nor expressed an emotion while Barton had given his account, he had sat very still, his gaze never leaving Barton, not even a nod or any acknowledgement that he had comprehended the saga he had just been told. Then after nearly five minutes of contemplation he broke the spell of silence which had descended heavily over the both of them.

'I thank you for your long and detailed account Mr Barton, you have cleared up for me personally, so many questions to which I've had no answers or explanations for nearly all of my life. I think it best if I begin by telling you a little about me to set your records in order. When I was a boy of no more than six going on seven, my father was killed, so I was told, in an accident. My mother, alone and penniless, married again to an evil man, a living devil who abused and beat her, kept her pregnant and took a delight in torturing me physically and emotionally at every opportunity. There was no one to turn to or to help in those days, we lived in a cold damp cottage not too far from here, where this man, Ifan Evans, put us through living hell every day of our lives. There was no way out, no escape from the brutality, the abuse, the poverty. If you've ever known what is like to be hungry and desperate every day of your life Mr Barton, then you might understand but somehow I don't think ordinary people can imagine what that is like, we called it 'the reign of terror'. He drank any money coming in, stole what little my mother had even when the babies were hungry, he did that to us.

When the war came things became even harder, he'd lost his job, took it out on us and continued to borrow steal or beg to keep himself in drink money. The Americans came, for many of us this was a Godsend, there was money that could be earned doing small jobs, we called it being a 'gopher', you went for this or that for pennies. If I earned anything doing jobs, he would steal it, not just take the pittance but threaten me with the children's home if I didn't surrender everything to him. I did manage to keep bits for my Mam and the other children but at the cost of being slapped about with my Mam getting a dose of it too. The man you have found out about in the newspaper clipping was Sgt Lem Jones, to everybody he was just 'Jonesey', one of my Yanks. He was a good man, he was walking out with one of our neighbours, the Owen's girl, their daughter Peggy, she, in her way looked after me, saved my life, if it hadn't been for Peggy's quick thinking I wouldn't have survived that night. I knew nothing about Germans or Irish fishing boats, all of that is news to me, what I did know that night was that Ifan Evans told me that he had killed my Dad! He had murdered him by pushing him to his death then telling everybody that it had been an accident, but he told me how he had done it and how he took pleasure in that. I couldn't take anymore, he hit me about that night, and my Mam, then told us that he was leaving, going off somewhere new… I couldn't let that go, a man who had admitted murdering my Dad, beating my mother, living like a parasite on other people's lives, I just broke so I followed him, I got my mates, Henry and Ronnie and we followed him up the Wurm to where he was meeting the Martin brothers, Bill and Reg, these two were of the same type as Evans, steal rob and cheat whenever they got the chance. We followed Evans up through the snow to the Martin's house, watched them load their lorry then when they left driving up onto the Wurm, we followed them. It was snowing really badly, my two mates had to turn back, Ronnie as he was scared Henry got a good hiding for being out late. We had called ourselves the 'Gassy Arabs', we were the army which was going to deal with Evans! On the day, I was on my own but was so boiling with hate and red rage, it drove me on. I wanted to settle with Ifan Evans for all the hurt and misery he had caused us, and, now for the murder of my Dad. So I followed their tyre tracks in the snow, eventually I came upon them outside the old church at St Mary's, there he was, they were with other men I didn't know, men loading the boxes which you have talked about onto their truck. I was cold, so really very cold, I couldn't feel my fingers or my feet, my head was pounding, I felt as if I would pass out and miss my chance, I needed to get Ifan on his own.' Huw paused, his eyes moistened, he was clearly going through some torment with the retelling of his experience.

'Look Huw, if you don't mind me calling you by your first name, do you want to leave it there, I really don't think you should distress yourself…?' Barton asked gently feeling the waves of emotion pouring from the other man.

'No, what's your first name Mr Barton…?' He wiped his eyes, shaking his head to clear his thoughts.

'It's Erich, Huw. Please feel free, but I think you should have a break now…'

'I'll tell you when I need a break as you put it Erich, no, I didn't realise how much I needed to get this off my chest, I've been carrying it so long. I never told my wife when she was alive and my sons know nothing of this secret I've been concealing since 1944, so if you are game I'm going to go on…'

'Then take your time Huw, please stop at any time if it gets too much…'

Huw nodded then wiping his eyes again went on, 'I needed to get out of the cold so I climbed over the church wall near my Dad's grave, nearly ended it when I fell into an open grave, then managed to get to the church door, thank God it was open, they never locked church doors in those days. I closed the door behind me and tried to find somewhere just to warm up a little when the door banged open and two men came in, one was Bill Martin, then a third followed. There was some kind of argument, I can't tell you what about, I was shaking so much and one of them had lit a candle, then I must have moved one of the wooden seats, they heard me. One of the men shouted at me to show myself, I stood up, a tall man I couldn't understand what he said, pointed a gun at my face, it looked enormous like looking down the barrel of a drain pipe, one of the other two men got in the way, stood in front of me, the candle went out, at the same time there was an explosion then another and I just waited for the pain…! It didn't come though I couldn't hear, I was deafened by the bang, the man who had fired the shot was laying on the floor, blood coming out of his head, I couldn't move with fright. Then, one of these men, the one who had stepped in front of me, dressed in some kind of uniform took me to one side, he asked if I was alright, I couldn't hear what he said, my ears were whistling, they seemed to be talking about what to do with the dead man's body, the one that was going to shoot me, for some reason I remembered the grave I had just nearly fallen into, so I told them. I can't tell you how, but they picked up the body, they just did and they carried him outside to where the grave was open near my Dad's. Then I remembered Ifan, and I started to make my way back.

By then the Martin brothers had loaded up their lorry and were for some reason frenetically scrambling to get away, they had started up their lorry and it sped past me in the snow. I went over to the gap in the wall above the cliff, there had been no sign of Ifan coming up to join the Martins. Then, he appeared coming up the last few steps with another man carrying another of those boxes. At that moment there was a blinding brilliant flash of light out to sea, suddenly I could see everything clearly, then followed a loud bang. The man nearly at the top dropped the crate, it must have been really heavily as it pushed Ifan back and almost over the cliff edge, I saw my chance, I jumped over the man on his back the ground, I stood for a fraction of a second above that swine then every fibre and morsel of hate and anger in my being went into that kick into his face! I heard his teeth crunch; I saw the look of naked fear on his devil's face as he teetered for a moment then fell backwards into space. I heard him scream all the way till he hit the bottom…!

Then, I was spent, I caved in on myself and started to shake, the two men dealing with the body in the church reappeared, they said something I couldn't hear, then they too were gone, back down the path to the sea. I was barely putting one foot in front of the other, following the tyre tracks again but this time feeling dead inside, I had just killed a man…! No matter the cause or reason I had murdered him in the same way that he had murdered my Dad. I felt nothing at all. In front of me there was a ball of flame off to the left, the tyre tracks led across there and I followed. The heat was intense, nothing could have survived that fall, it was like looking down through the gates of Hell, a furnace was raging down there the heat of it melting the snow all around the sides of the quarry. All I could do was manage a few steps back to the roadway, there I just stood shaking, I was at an end and could not go a step further. That was when Jonesey, Peggy and gunner Bob turned up, I must have passed out and don't remember anything more of that night other than feeling somehow being bumped about as they must have put me in Jonesey's jeep. I just lost all consciousness; it was days before I came around in hospital. Then Jonesey, Peggy and my Mam were at my bedside, that's all I can remember I'm afraid, no Germans, no Irishmen and no submarine…' Huw sat back in his seat and was breathing deeply.

'Did you see Jonesey or Peggy to talk about this afterwards Huw, how about the other man you mentioned, 'Gunner Bob' I think you said? Barton did not want to press Huw; he had the most vital piece of information now.

'I saw Jonesey once more, he came to the hospital, he gave me this…,' Huw reached around his neck showing a coin on a silver chain between his finger and thumb, it was an American quarter dollar, 'I had it pieced, have worn it ever since. Jonesey sadly was wounded in the D Day landings with the 4th Infantry Division, he was very badly injured on Omaha beach, he lost a leg and was badly scarred, as a badly wounded

GI Jonesey was sent back to the States, we never saw him here again. Gunner Bob was tragically killed when his field gun carrier was hit, he had been with 30th corps on the approach to Arnhem in the same Autumn. Norah, his then girlfriend and fiancé, Peggy's older sister went on to marry one of the other yanks, the one called 'Dutch', he came back in the Summer of 1945, they were married a year later, last I heard they were living in Chicago and had a tribe of children. And last Peggy, dear Peggy… She never got over Jonesey, she lived in that same old cottage after her mother, Mrs Owen passed away. Peggy was there until she was moved out when they demolished the cottages to make way for more luxury flats. Peggy was given one of the new flats the council was building in town for local people, she was working at the library in the town hall well into the late fifties everybody knew her. Then one day she let people know that she was going to the States. From what I heard she had had a letter from her sister, Norah, and within a week had booked her ticket on a steamer out of Liverpool, by the end of the month she had left, was gone! That was way back, and I never heard from Peggy again, maybe she did find and meet up with Jonesey in the end?' Huw took another deep breath and stared up at the heavens.

'What about you Huw, what happened to you next…?' Barton was aware of how much this had cost Huw, to reach back some sad and tragic memories from his distant past where so much had lain undisturbed for many long years.

'Me, well, hospital took a long time to get me together again. While I was in there, the baby Megan, Ifan's last with my Mam, caught measles, there was nothing that could be done in those days, the cottage was damp and mouldy which would have done nothing to help. Little Megan is buried in the new cemetery on the other side of town. My Mam didn't last long after that, she passed away with pneumonia in the Winter of 1944, we buried her with my Dad, the church helped arrange it. Ellen and Dafydd were taken in by the Children's Board when Mam died, they both were adopted and as far as I know are still around somewhere. I couldn't do anything to stop that happening, Ifan Evans got his way in the end, I was placed in the Crafnant Children's Home. I was there until I was nearly seventeen, then after a bit of bother with the Law, they offered me a choice, Borstal or the army, I chose the army and did my three years' service to his Majesty. When I came back, times were still hard, but I'd saved a little money, I rented an allotment, bought potatoes cheap, then sowed them, the first crop I sold and bought more. Then another allotment, this time vegetables, I bought a second-hand cart, got a street trader license, then when I had enough money behind me rented a shop. I found by then you could go to the Liverpool markets, buy cheaply and sell for a fair profit back here. I made my living that way into the sixties, every time I raised enough capital, I invested it in increasing the turn-over, more shops, vehicles to deliver. In the 1970s I went into the wholesale business, had the warehouse you visited yesterday built, bought this house, took my sons into the business, financially we didn't look back. My wife, my best friend, my Maureen, passed away two years ago this coming Christmas. So, Erich, that is it that is my story, yet I have an idea, pictures are clearer sometimes than words, how much time have you got today?' Huw was standing, fishing in his pocket for a moment. 'Come with me…!' It wasn't a request; it was a demand. Huw took Barton over to his carport where his own vehicle was standing, a well-tended white 1970s MGB roadster. 'I don't apologise for my indulgence in this little luxury, in this weather this old lady is just what's needed. Jump in Erich…!'

Barton had little choice, he had worried about the level of Huw's despondency as he had come towards the end of his story, suddenly he was animated once more and they were motoring down into and through the Bay town with the distinctive exhaust rumbling behind them.

Huw drove up through the end of town onto the road he had climbed so many years before in pursuit of Ifan Evans and the Martin brothers. He drove expertly over the twisting bends as the car climbed to the upper reaches then out onto the well-made road, through the cattle grid onto the pasture fields on the top of the Wurm mountain. Just before he took the right turn down to St Mary's on the Mount, he pointed towards the summit, 'That's where Jonesey had driven in the snow looking for me… And this…' he pulled the car over to the right bumping onto the grass for a few yards then stopped, 'Come with me Erich.' He was out of the car looking back expectantly as Barton joined him. They walked on another hundred yards and halted on the lip of a steeply sided quarry working, there was wire fencing on stout poles across the edge to the drop with a notice fastened saying 'Dangerous Cliff'. 'This is the Druid's Pit Erich, this is where the Martins met their end, all that they had on that lorry went up with them, look down there,' he pointed towards the sides of the pit over a hundred feet below, 'you can still see the scorch marks even today, everything here was burnt, blackened by the heat of the blaze for years afterwards, that is what happened to your consignment of boxes, they were incinerated along with the Martins…!'

Barton had to see this in close up, he followed the barbed wire fence to the down to the lower section, climbed over and carefully made his way down the steep side to the bottom of the quarry workings slithering on the loose scree as he went. At the bottom he walked back to where he was standing with Huw over a hundred feet above him. There was little to see other than a few twisted pieces of metal, an axle, rusted over with the remains of the wheel at either end, blackened and probably left because of the weight to lug it back up the cliff. Apart from that only some scorched rock evidenced the fire which had raged here. He looked up at Huw, imagined the force with which the lorry and its contents must have hit the ground, then the fire contained in this tight circular pit. This is where the Martins had met their untimely end, it was also where the five boxes from the U-367 had been reduced to ashes. Barton's relief was so overpowering, it took him minutes to compose himself for the return climb to join Huw.

Huw led him back to the car before he could ask or say anything, 'I know what you must be thinking, one more visit then you can ask me anything that you like. Back in the MG, Huw reversed back onto the road, then drove forward, down the sloping hill to the church which lay at the bottom against the cliff edge. They drew up on a tarmacked apron in front of the church. Barton saw at once the wall along the cliff edge, the opening, now blocked with a yard-high padlocked wrought-iron gateway. 'No one uses that pathway any longer, the erosion over the years has taken the path away, it's really dangerous down there unless you're a goat...' He said opening the oaken wooden gate into the churchyard. He took Barton over to the left of the entrance, up to the boundary stone wall then pointed to a headstone. 'This is the grave of my father and mother,' Barton could see the faded inscription in the marble, 'To William Henryd Thomas died 1937, his wife, Eira Thomas, passed away December 1944, together in eternity...

Barton was lost for words, yet Huw appeared quite content that finally his parents had been brought together in this place. 'My respects to both of your parents Huw, is this why you brought me here to see this?'

'No Erich, it's this...' he walked on another half a dozen paces and pointed to another headstone, this one in weather worn black granite, 'here is the final part of your puzzle I'm thinking, the end of your trail, it lies here...'

Barton focused his eyes on the headstone, it read part in English and part in Welsh, *'ER COF EZRA LLOYD-WILLIAMS, 1858 – 1943 YN 85 MLWYDD OED. YN FARW RHAGFYR 18th 1943 RIP.'* It did not seem to make sense, the eighty five year old elderly man buried in this grave had no relationships to any of the other characters, or did it…? He turned to meet the smiling face of Huw Thomas.

'That's right Erich, your missing man, apparently a German, lies here, underneath his host, the late Mr Ezra Lloyd-Williams…!' Huw waited for Barton to respond and was not disappointed.

Barton felt that he was reaching the end of a long and arduous journey, the whirl of events of today overtook, even exceeded the expectations he could barely have hoped for. He was within a few feet of the remains of the man, whose actions had set in motion a train of events which could have cost the lives of thousands, but for the unexpected appearance of scruffy little schoolboy bent on a crusade of his own. What conclusions might have emerged from the exchange between the Martins and Breitfeld that night had not Huw Henryd Thomas intervened with his diminutive presence? Would Breitfeld have accepted some compromise, paid off the Martins to ensure the delivery of the deadly plague phials to their unsuspecting victims, if they had been as successful in their impact upon the people and troop concentrations, would it have caused a delay in the second front that Summer of '44? It was all conjecture, an academic series of 'what ifs', which could have quite feasibly altered the course of history, if it were not for the intrusion of a poor, malnourished and abused child who had had the courage to pursue then to confront his tormentor. Fate or destiny, call it what you may, had stepped in changing the well laid plans of the bigger players in the game.

'I don't know what to say Huw, it's not often that I am lost for words, here, things have come together in such a short space of time, I'm not sure I'll ever be quite the same again. There are one or two things I do need to share with you after seeing these sites, where the thing I had only read about and imagined happened with real people, you were there, innocent as you were, I feel you have a right to know a little more about what you had stumbled upon when you took your revenge on Ifan Evans. Was his body ever found, what did people think had happened to him?' Barton looked across to where Huw was still leaning on the headstone of Ezra Lloyd-Williams, his face suddenly showing his years as the lines around his eyes and mouth deepened.

'No, he's at the bottom of the sea, his body never came up, was never found… You need to be clear about Ifan, Erich. It was not revenge, it was justice for the things that he did. Now, with your filling in the gaps as to why he was here to meet with the Martins, to do even more harm, for money nothing else, just his selfish greed. Then I have no regrets, if he was here now… I like to think I would have it in me to do it again. The Martins too, look what they were doing? Selling out to the Germans to make a fast profit regardless of the suffering they would cause. To answer your question again, I repeat myself. No, nothing was ever found of Ifan Evans… He had told his drinking cronies that he was leaving so people assumed that's what he had done being the man that he was, up and left abandoning his wife and children in the middle of Winter. 'Good riddance' was the comment most of the locals made and there was never any investigation made to find him, he had just disappeared. Now, c'mon, we'll get back to my place, you can tell me there whatever it is that's playing on your mind…'

They walked back past the door of the church, on impulse Barton tried the iron handle, it was locked…! Barton raised an eyebrow to Huw who answered before he could voice the question.

'Vandals…! No one comes up here much these days, so it's kept locked unless they have a service or a funeral.' He raised an arm and swept over the graveyard, 'Very seldom these days, there are very few of the older people, of their descendent families still living in the area these days.'

'What about in the church, there must have been bloodstains after Breitfeld was shot, surely someone would have noticed?'

'Not necessarily, things happened so quickly that night, if the door were left open, animals would have got in, even sheep looking for somewhere to lamb out of the weather. There would have been little left a month later when poor old Ezra was laid to rest.'

'And the bullet marks, two shots were fired, if one missed then there would be a hole somewhere in there where it struck…?' Barton tried to imagine the sound of the shot, the bullet ploughing into woodwork or plaster somewhere in the building.

'Again the answer is probably not, remember, there was no one left here who knew anything about what had taken place, why would anybody come searching for a bullet mark without reason? Yes, it's probably still there, I certainly am not going to ask for the key to start looking Erich…'

They passed through the gate to where the car was parked, Huw pointing out as they went that the churchyard had closed for burials many years before once all of the available space had been taken up. Only those families who held the deeper grave plots were permitted to inter their dead here, even then only providing there was room left in the family graves. Huw had himself recently made sure that his own place had been secured, he would eventually be placed here with his mother and father when his time came. The gulls were soaring on the thermals above their heads, lifting effortlessly into the breeze calling their piercing cries as they drifted seawards across the cliff face. Barton paused at the wrought-iron gateway to the path down to the sea, he stood on the loose stones beside the gate, resting his elbows on the top of the stone wall. He felt time slip away, he was in the exact same spot where Huw had stood all those years ago, he was looking at the turn in the path where Ifan and Schumann must have emerged out of the darkness when the star shell went off behind them. This was where Huw's booted foot had sent Ifan to his death, where the chest of coins had followed him down onto the U-367 and the deck of the Lady Patricia. The surface of the sea was sparkling in the light from the late afternoon sun, small white horse waves chased each other on the otherwise tranquil waters. Somewhere here directly ahead of where he stood, within range of the naked eye, the hull of the U-367 lay on the seabed. It could be but only yards from his present point of vision, Reinecke had made notes to the effect that she had gone astern from the cove below under this very cliff, she had turned then was struck by the warship's bows. That location, as a guess, had to be within a radius of no more than a half a mile in either direction of the finger of rock where Reinecke had stood watching the death of his boat.

The ride back to Huw's Bramble End home was pleasantly relaxed, Huw taking time to point out places of interest as they passed by, where the old dance hall had been, now a block of flats, the area where the Americans had created their base, where the motor pool had been, the PX and the barracks, now more luxury flats here too covered the grounds where those structures had once stood. Huw took a short diversion to show Barton where his family cottage had once stood, the seawall where Jonesey had walked with Peggy, where Huw's own story had begun before the loss of his father, lastly they passed the site where the gas works had once stood, a modern busy industrial park now occupied area, any evidence of its earlier purpose long buried beneath the new foundations.

They arrived back at Bramble End where Huw parked his MG back under the car port, then invited Barton to join him in the lounge part of the cottage. It was spacious and comfortable with matching green leather buttoned armchairs and settee, a well-used open log burner fireplace hinted of winter nights with a crackling fire. There were oil paintings on the walls of local scenes, yet, Barton noticed, none of the usually expected photographs was in evidence. Huw busied himself in the kitchen and brought in a tray with more coffee and a plate of sandwiches.

'If you think for a moment that I made these, you're wrong. I have an order brought up from town from one of those new shops that do sandwiches to order, these are tuna and sweetcorn. I do little here Erich but tinker I have to confess, yes, in the working day you'll find me in my office where I still wear a suit and tie, oversee some of the deals, then, when I'm here alone I just laze about, I potter around on my own. I don't even do the housework anymore, I have a wonderful lady who comes in twice a week and looks after the household, not quite a housekeeper but very efficient. The rest of the time, the gardens, my reading, I've never been one much for socialising even when Maureen was alive, we tended to keep pretty much to ourselves most of the time. I have shunned company Erich, for that I probably have a name for being a miserable old fool, I couldn't care less what anyone thinks, I owe no one for what I have made and the life which I have created around me. My two boys have their families, their part in the business so I'm left with time on my hands, time to think and remember.'

They sat and ate in silence with the early evening sun beginning to throw shadows from the trees over Huw's earlier work on his lawn. He finally put his mug down on the coffee table and said to Barton.

'Whatever you want to tell me, then you can do it now, I have managed to get off my chest the burden I have carried all of these years Erich. When you called the office yesterday, I had an intuition that it would be something to do with Ifan's death, that somehow that spectre had come back to haunt me at last in these the final lonely years of my long working life. In one sense I was right was I not, you're sitting here now, but you're not a journalist are you Erich, are you a scientist of some kind, what is exactly is it that you do?'

Barton instinctively felt the mellowing of Huw's attitude towards him, it had begun prickly, defensive almost, now, after only hours the man's manner was warm, affable even friendly. What was it about his meetings and newly formed relationships with white haired old men which somehow generated their acts of confession he asked himself?

'I am a writer Huw, as I have told you. Not perhaps the most successful but I make a living. Mostly it's stories which I unearth then elaborate on into print for the human-interest stories. Mostly my work goes into magazines, occasionally I admit, I have sold copy to the weekend newspapers these however are not sensationalistic there on human lives and experiences. I am certainly not a scientist unless you count an 'O' level in biology?' Both men saw the funny side of this, 'You had asked I think Huw what I intend with this story, I had told you all of the important land marks and travels to gather information up until my coming here today. Now, I have brought you into this, have involved you, there is one piece I need to add, this I feel as a responsibility to you for being so forthcoming despite the cost to yourself.' Barton waited for a response from Huw…

'Erich, you have arrived here today, unexpected not in my plans at all for this week, we have spent some valuable time together, I have told you things no living person knows yet I have trusted you as an instinct. I tell you now, I felt sure that your arrival would see the dredging up of things from the past, that even now once the word is out, then I will be held responsible for a murder. Yet, all I feel is a tremendous sense of relief, I have had this hanging over me all of my life, now I feel it has lifted with the details you had uncovered with your research. What more can you possibly tell me that is going to alter my way of thinking at this time of life? In reality I am a little like King Lear, I have nothing left to do, just fool myself that by going into the office and pushing a pen that I am being useful when I am not, I'm a nuisance past his prime. One of the worst things about the passage of the years Erich, is that one day you wake up and say to yourself 'Do I serve any purpose at all for anything of value to anyone any longer?' Now you tell this old man, me, something which will make it all seem worthwhile again when all that was left was memories and a garden, I'm all ears…'

Barton saw the earnestness in Huw's face, the lines, the whitened hair the glint of enthusiasm fire again in his eyes. 'The boxes we have talked about Huw, the five which were loaded onto the Martin's lorry, three of those boxes contained forged white five pound notes, a face value of perhaps a hundred and fifty thousand pounds, another never made it to the lorry, that one that was dropped by Ifan, that one contained gold bullion it was lost. The other two on the lorry held a biological weapon, glass phials of plague virus which were intended to be purposely spread to infect the population with a deadly silent killer. Indirectly Huw, when you turned up and threw a spanner in the works, you probably saved the lives of countless thousands of people. Stopped the country's economy being thrown out of gear by the insertion of forgeries which would have taken months perhaps even years to detect and remove from circulation. So you see Huw, it was worthwhile, you served your country in more ways than one as much as you could have as a serviceman in the fighting forces, you're a hero Huw…!'

Huw Henryd burst out laughing, he held his sides with mirth, 'Forgive me,' he said whilst trying to catch his breath, 'But that is the wildest stories I've heard in a very long time, Erich Barton, if you have done nothing else you've made an old man very happy, you've given me the belief that I did something right…!'

'Barton hadn't expected quite this response, 'It's true Huw, whether you like it or not, what you did helped the war effort, it really did save lives…'

'Then I believe you, wish someone had told me at the time…! Well Erich, this good fortune comes at a price to you, if everything that you have told me is true, and I have no reason to believe otherwise, then now I want in, I want to be a part of this. You have talked about Gerald Lewis, he's still alive, his children who are part of this too as they now have this knowledge, I want to meet them! You know Erich, we should be a team, not just expecting you to go about finding the pieces, we are the pieces and it would be better if we were to get together as we each have a stake in this fabulous Reinecke story…?' Huw's face beamed, the light in his eyes now afire with enthusiasm, he had found a cause, a focus for his being.

'I think you are right Huw, for my part, when I am writing this up I see no point in mentioning Ifan's fate, it has no bearing on the course of events and except for yourself there are no living witnesses. That much I can promise you. The Lewis's do have an interest, Sheila Lewis works over at Bangor, she and I had intended to meet, she can put it to her grandfather that if he is able to make the trip, then he can be invited over for a meeting of the three of us. I'll make the call tonight and float it as an idea, could they come here or would you prefer a neutral meeting place, say in town Huw?' Barton's own feelings were very much that his own responsibilities for deciding where they go next with the information would benefit from a sharing of minds.

'I have plenty of room here as you can see, my few work commitments can be passed on to my boys to deal with, mightily grateful they will be too…! Where and when do we start…?'

'With the telephone call tonight, then, much depends on what may be found when Gary and I have a look at the seabed off the headland on Thursday. If we are successful, then the first part of the promise to old Reinecke will be have been achieved without compromise, his boat, his crew to be found, to give them a place with perhaps a service over where their remains are known to rest.' Barton knew time was now at a premium, things had really gone so quickly he could hardly believe how much had been accomplished in such a short period of only a few days. If, it was a big if, Thursday's weather was true to the forecast, if the sea condition were as calm as they had been today, if, there were so many ifs Barton worried that his well of luck would run dry.

'Huw, I going to get home and make some telephone calls, I've only a day before the dive on Thursday and there are practical things to do. I'll give you my card with my address and telephone number, we'll speak again over the next twenty-four hours when I've been in contact with the Lewis family. Here, my card.' Barton passed over the small business card and Huw turned it over in his hand.

'Your first name, Erich, is this how you spell it? Huw asked raising his eyebrow.

'It is Huw, before you ask, yes, it's not the English spelling, my mother named me and she was Austrian…' Barton had given this explanation more times in his life than he could recall, school, then repeatedly later in adult life.

'Don't worry Huw, you'll get used to it, I almost have though it's taken most of my life to do so. Right, I need to get off home to begin to make some calls, I'll ring you in the morning with news from my talks with the Lewis family. Huw followed Barton to the Landrover casting an appraising eye over the vehicle as they walked.

'You have a preference for older girls too it seems, this one has seen some wear in her years?' Huw patted the bonnet as one would pat a dog.

'True, she's still reliable as the day I bought her, wouldn't trade for one of the newer models, this is an old and trusted friend…! Until tomorrow Huw, we'll talk in the morning.'

Barton climbed into the driver's seat, with a wave of the hand turned the Landrover towards home, to the list of tasks to be tackled in the evening.

Huw Henryd watched him go with mixed feelings, he had confronted his demons, the years of waking up in the middle of the night in a sweat. The nightmares where Ifan had appeared again having somehow survived the fall and had come back to haunt him with his presence. The memories of his mother, with bruises on her face while carrying a baby on her arms. All of these spectral images drifted back through the corridors of his mind, as vivid as there were when they were laid down in the brain of his childhood. He had meant what he had said to Barton, if time could be reversed, then he would do it again with little regrets.

After an early dinner that evening Barton got to work on the telephone calls, the first being to Sheila giving an update to the day's meeting with Huw Thomas, the unexpected fate of the Martins, with the resultant lifting of the tensions over the plague containing crates. The relief between them as he spoke was palpable, so much had hung in the balance while they had contemplated the survival of the threats to humanity these terrible man made creations had posed, the implications of such a meaningful report to the authorities with all that it would entail. Now however, an immense cathartic release in the clearing of such responsibilities from their collective consciences. Gerald Lewis would not be considered as a participant in an intended genocide, the tangible hard material evidence was vapourised. Sheila said that she was free the next day, perhaps they could meet for lunch? Despite the urgency of the time element he was taken again by the soft almost melodic feminine burr of her voice, he needed little urging to concede defeat, they would meet at the Red Lion pub in the village near to where he lived. Barton gave her the directions, and, she seemed genuinely excited at the prospect of another face to face meeting, ostensibly to discuss the progress made in gathering information yet he thought he detected another arcane agenda in her voice tone. Next was the call to the older Gerry himself, he had answered the telephone in person after only three rings, had he been waiting impatiently for such a call Barton asked himself? Again Barton outlined the findings of his visit to Huw Thomas, related the events of the day to Gerry as he had done with Sheila. He sensed how the older man must feel at this positive outcome, the relief at the news, the immediacy of the plague threat was over, no longer an imperative demanding disclosure to powers in authorities above and beyond their control. When Barton went on to share Huw's suggestion that they meet, his request that each of them to be regarded as a 'team member', he was surprised when Lewis not only readily agreed but quickly was asking when it would be convenient for him to come over and join them in Wales…? Barton gently suggested that they wait until after Thursday's expedition to the sea off the headland. This was accepted, Lewis saying Sheila would be coming home for the coming weekend, he could travel back with her on the Sunday evening then come over to the Bay town on the Monday morning. Would make arrangements for his grandson Gerry junior, to look after the house and the land until he returned. He seemed enthused, despite his years, he like Huw, was taken with the idea of such a team approach, that he too would have a part to play, an obvious personal interest in the outcomes as they were unravelled. Lastly, he needed to call Gary Johnson. All had gone according to planning they had made the week before, Gary had the boat ready for Thursday morning, she would be fueled up the evening before by Gary's twenty-year-old son Richard, he would be coming along to pilot the boat whilst Gerry and Barton concentrated on the diving preparations. This was a sound inclusion to the original plan, young Richard was a reliable competent sailor, Barton had known him since early infancy likeable lad with a sense of humour, Richard knew the vessel as well as his father, another member had been added to the team! The remainder of the ensuing conversation was around the gear needed for the dive, Gary's equipment was all in good order, regularly checked. He had a spare single air tank for Barton to use, a wet suit if needed, his only concern was with Barton's limited experience at depths over fifty feet. They had dived together before, always under Gary's firm guidance and supervision, whilst Barton was an above average swimmer, he only had half a dozen sea water dives under his belt. As a competent amateur, was aware of his own inexperience. The proposal which he outlined was for Barton to remain on the Megara whilst Gary did the preliminary dives, they would then join forces to examine anything of interest Gary would find, preserving Barton's dive time. Barton assured him that his own wet suit, his mask and set of fins were all in good useable order, he would happily accept the offer of the air tank along with Gary's well thought proposal for the dive strategy. There was nothing more to do regarding Thursday except pray for the present good conditions to continue on the day. Barton spent the rest of the evening returning to his earlier note translations, the cryptic little comments he had made in the first stages were now enlarged to draw the witness testimonies to add and enlarge their recollections of happenings to the expanding written journal of events. It was after midnight when Barton eventually turned in, pleased and content with the leaps of progress he had made today with Huw's generous verbal contributions, this time he had no problem in dropping into a deep sleep soon after his head touched the pillow.

35

Barton's alarm clock sounded the hour at eight o'clock, Wednesday was going to be as relaxed as he could make it, no insistent imperatives to get anything under way, with the prospect of a leisurely lunch to look forward to at mid-day. For the first time in days, he felt positive, optimistic in approaching the next and these final stages of his research and explorations. His morning shower he took a long unhurried time with, enjoyed the minutes spent under the refreshing force of the massaging water. Towelling his tousled hair dry he turned to the mirror to begin shaving, the face smiling back at him had recovered some of the boyish enthusiasm of earlier days, not enough though to stop him nicking the skin causing blood to flow, a curse escaped his lips, the effort had been in vain, the look of the bumbling yokel had returned uninvited... He shook his head, further attempts at smartening his appearance would serve no purpose, donning a pair of fawn moleskin jeans with a crisp blue shirt he was ready for the day. The rest of the morning sailed by with domestic chores to be carried out, by mid-day the cottage was as spruced as it could be, with a last glance around Barton picked up the keys for the Landrover sitting on the patch of land beside the cottage, with the canvass tilt down again he set off for the Red Lion meeting at one. The drive through the lanes over hung with leafy green trees took no more than five minutes with Barton pulling into the pub car park just before one o'clock. There were a few other customers already seated at the rustic log tables dotted outside the entrance, each with a broad umbrella sunshade giving shelter from the warm September sun. Barton went into the bar, saying his, 'Hello,' to the landlord Simon, and asked for a table for two. Back outside he picked a table distanced from the other diners and settled down to wait. It was only minutes before an elderly open topped Volkswagon Beetle arrived on the gravel parking apron with Sheila Lewis at the wheel. She did notice Barton at first, busied herself in the driving mirror before climbing out with that grace some women possess for extricating themselves from difficult positions with poise, reminiscent of a Siamese cat Barton mused. He stood up and waved, she returned the gesture and joined him at the table. Barton was conscious she was wearing a white linen two piece suit, which may be a little vulnerable in the rough log seating he had chosen, Sheila declined the invitation to dine inside, brushed out her hair and smiled at him over the top of her aviator style sunglasses.

'This will do fine Erich, no worries, these clothes are tougher than they look, like me… I love this place, is this your local watering hole then…?' She opened the conversation in the same low feminine tones he had taken a liking to when they first met.

'It is, though I don't get over here as often as I would like, especially when the weather is as balmy as today, any problems finding the place…?' He was conscious of the nick on his cheek which suddenly felt like a large and livid gash.

'Not at all, the directions which you gave me were pretty good, only got lost once, it's only taken me twenty-five minutes to get here from leaving the flat in Bangor, do you like the car…?'

It occurred once more to Barton that there were coincidences everywhere in his recent life, another old car, tidy and neat it was true, definitely a female type vehicle, pale blue with darker blue leather seats, 'It's very 'you' isn't it, how long have you had her…?'

'She is a he, I call him 'Conrad', strong and reliable, my grandad bought him for me when I was a student, that was six years ago, my first car, and I still love him to bits. Little like you and your ancient Landy I think, we have something in common, a deep regard for old things…!' Sheila said this with laughter playing on her lips, now let's order, I'm famished, what do you recommend?'

They pored over the lunch time menu before both deciding on a smoked mackerel salad with garlic bread and a glass of Chablis. As they were waiting for the meal to arrive, she turned to back to him again locking his eyes with hers.

'Now tell me everything, you met with this man, 'Thomas,' he has given you his version about what happened with my grandad?'

Barton was at pains to explain in detail the brief report he had given over the telephone. He omitted nothing, emphasising once more the important evidence that the fears over the survival of the Martin lorryload were ended with the incineration of the vehicle, its load and the two men. It would be in bad taste to toast such an event, yet Barton was tempted to raise his glass at that point.

Barton went through Huw's recollection word for word as much as he remembered it happening. The particular focus of interest for Sheila was the part where Huw, awaiting execution by the man Breitfeld, had his life saved by the intervention of her great-grandfather Mick Lewis! Huw, his family, his business, in fact everything to do with him could never have taken place if Mick had not shot Breitfeld in that moment before in the church, he would have certainly callously murdered a young boy for no other reason than that he was presented an impediment to be disposed of…! Sheila had tears in her eyes as Barton confirmed this as a truth, even more so now that Huw wanted to meet with the family of his saviour Mick, with his son Gerry, the only other living survivor.

Lunch arrived was served onto their table by a female waitress with a flourish and an 'Enjoy' before disappearing. While they ate the conversation moved to lighter themes, Sheila gazing across at Barton, was delicately forking a mouthful of mackerel to he lips, she viewed his obvious pleasure in her company with some satisfaction, he was putting on no show for her benefit she decided.

'Tell me about yourself Erich, in these few days all we have talked about is the diary and history, what about you, what makes you tick, what kind of person are you under all the research and deep plans for long dead people?'

Barton paused mid-way between breaking off a chunk of hot garlic bread, I'm not sure how to answer that one, there I times when I'm not sure I know myself. I'll try, but you're going to be disappointed if you are waiting for an exciting answer. I was an only child; my father was killed when I was only a boy of six, so I never knew him. My mother brought me up single handed living on an RAF widow's pension. As my mother was Austrian, she encouraged me to learn languages which paid off in years to come though I was never a good linguistic student. Went to university and came home with a decent degree in Roman and medieval history, began to get into freelance writing in my early twenties when working in a factory to pay the bills, then when my work began to sell, albeit small time, I found that I could afford to give up the drudgery of manual work, keep my hands clean. Having said that it was a valuable learning experience being with men and women in the eight to five dull routine day in day out.' Barton hesitated before going on, the next part might not be well received, especially if Sheila was anything like a devout catholic. 'I met a girl when we both at university, I was reading history, she psychology. We got together when I found the factory job, we set up together, had a tiny flat for a year then decided to get married, it just seemed like the right thing to do. My mother was elated, her' people were not so thrilled, her father was a police officer who had risen through the ranks, I was a humble factory worker with no prospects. We see-sawed through the next five years growing apart as our interests differed and evolved, Judith, my wife then, developed an interest in line dancing would you believe, she was good at it too getting into a local demonstration team she began to travel all over the country, then Europe with her friends. Ultimately, she found someone else, a fellow line dancer, I know it sounds trite but it's true, she said she wanted some excitement in her life and that was the end of it. A costly divorce followed which wiped me out financially, however I was free to do my own thing so started seriously on my writing career. My mother had gone by then, she never really got over the loss of my father. There were no children in my marriage to Judith so was saved that kind of heart ache. I rented the cottage where I still live, so gradually became financially viable again, this time taking more care with what I spent it on. My interests, well sorry to have to tell you they are boring I'm afraid, never got into any sort of sports when I was younger, I dabbled with Karate for about five years, nothing exciting there. Have a deep abiding interest in social history, the kind I write about. Material things, you've seen my Landrover, only other things I have kept over the years are a number of Roman artefacts which I had early on in life spent my spare money on, a collection of base metal coins from the time of Augustus to the late period of occupation of Britannia in the fifth century, nothing fancy, all of my small selection of ancient things show signs of wear, of human usage, I hold these in my hand and wonder about the people who have held them before me, tried to imagine who they were, what kind of people, what they thought, what they dreamed about hundreds sometimes thousands of years ago.' My bad points, well Sheila, there are too many to list, I don't have a television, do love classical music, have a leaning towards good folk songs, the artists who perform them, I do refuse to be brain washed with the modern stuff that's mostly groans and wails. I forget where I put things regularly and I enjoy an old and well used briar pipe for contemplating when I'm writing…

'Erich Barton, you're a romantic and a dreamer, when you talk about your collection of things a look comes over you, it's like listening to someone totally engrossed with his chosen interests, much like boy's will have collections of Dinky toys or Meccano, in your case it's ancient pottery I assume, and the coins dating from bye gone ages. What about your ex, Judith, do you ever see her now, was there anyone else for you afterwards…? Do you have someone now to share your dreams with?'

Sheila let the question in the tail hang in the air while Barton formed a reply.

'I guess you're right about the small boy, I don't think I ever really grew out of the dreams or romantic ideals, I have no intention of changing Sheila, I'm happy with my thoughts. In answer to do I see Judy anymore? No, not if I can help it, every time I did it generated a bill. Afterwards, there have been a small number of dalliances which were fun while they lasted, nothing serious though, just didn't have the magic or the chemistry I suppose. And you, a girl with your looks and intellect, there must be men beating a path to your door...?' Barton knew this was opening up a new direction to their course of thinking, Sheila had tested the water relating to his female interests, his counter question was doing the same thing in repost.

Sheila sat back in her seat and put down the fork, sipped her wine before replying. 'Like you I had a succession of student affairs, they came to nothing as I never met anyone who really interested me, the boys I dated seemed shallow with little on their mind other than frenzied personal gratification. There were two more serious relationships after I graduated, first when I landed my first lecturing role. I had a two-year fling with a fellow lecturer, a married man. A year later another with an older man, it went well for a while but his life was buried in the academic quests for knowledge, we had no future together parting amicably, he still teaches in my department and we are still on good terms. Recently, nothing, I meant what I said to you about Polly, she's the only love affair in my life at the moment...' Now it was Sheila's turn to wait for a reply, she was studying Barton's face for his reaction to her frank account.

Barton was feeling relieved, there had been no indication either way at his tale of the failed marriage and seemingly trivial interests in life in general. He began to feel some genuine humour rise from deep inside his being, somehow it seemed good to have that admission out of the way. Sheila appeared just a little uncomfortable herself, did she too have some reservations about disclosing intimate secrets? 'Swap you Polly for my Landrover...?' He regretted the juvenile words as soon as they were uttered...

'Not a hope Barton,' she said tossing her hair, I'll let you keep your old trusty charger, I'll keep my mare...! Erich, a more serious question, tomorrow, the trip to find the submarine, I want to come with you...?' It was more a statement of intent than a request, she again waited, another sip of the wine, then an expectant look of enquiry played about her face.

'Why Sheila? Everything is arranged with the boat and my friend, why would you want to come on what is going to be a near hour journey in choppy water just to get there, we are leaving at ten o'clock in the morning, catching the falling tide is crucial to the visibility in the water at what maybe fifty to a hundred feet. There can be no delays or we miss the window of opportunity, can't you see... I can't change things now...?'

'I know, I'm well aware of just how fine the time frame is, I have no intention of jeopardising that need. My great-grandfather sailed into those waters all of those years ago at night in the Lady Patricia with my grandad Gerry, he came out again with Reinecke on board, he saved two sailors from drowning putting his own safety on the line. That, Erich, is why I want to be there, this one chance to see this place where this all began. I believe I have every right to make the request, you said yourself, we're a team now...!' Gone was the smile this time her eyes bored into Barton's with purposeful intent, this was not a sudden whim, it was a carefully prepared strategy in advance of their meeting.

Barton too sat back in his seat, this he had not expected, there was the tiny male part of him which without prejudice had discounted the notion of a female member on board the boat. It wasn't his craft anyway, it was Gary's Megara, how would he respond to the prospect of a girl getting in the way as an observer with no functional role to play? 'I hear what you're saying Sheila, there are problems here I have to consider, the vessel is not mine, it's m friend Gary's boat. Then there is the time, crucial as I have said, we need to be cast off and heading for the river estuary before ten in the morning, there is no room for error, you would be reliant on the traffic coming out of Bangor being in your favour, we cannot wait for you on the quayside at Conaway, it just can't be done... I am sorry but short of parachuting from Bangor, I have to say no...' It had to be said, there was no way to soften the blow, the next thing might be a girlie flood of tears, he hoped not but he was ready for it...

'Then I'll stay over Erich...' She held his eyes with hers.

'Stay...? Stay over, oh great, this means that you'll have to go back over to Bangor, get what you need then come all the way back to look for a hotel...'

'No, I've thought ahead, I've brought a toothbrush with me...!' The smile on her sensual lips was back, impish and pixie like it revealed a dimple in her cheek. The breeze caught her hair ruffling the long dark tresses back across her shoulder, Barton became aware that he was thinking despite himself, she really was quite beautiful, in a manner elfish and mischievous beyond his experience.

'You've brought a toothbrush...! We're going to sea in a small boat, and you brought a toothbrush...? Look at your clothes, you can't wear those Sheila, you'd still need to change into something more suitable, the answer has to be still a no...' Barton was slightly incredulous, the image of Sheila on the deck of Gary's boat clad for an evening out with the girls, unbelievable...

'I've brought some things with me, they're in the boot of my car...' She fired back without ruffling her composure.

'You planned this Sheila, without telling me...!'

'I prepared which is quite a different thing, now will you say yes...?'

'Then we will have to find somewhere for you to stay, the nearest would be here, I think they have rooms for guests...' Barton was giving ground and he knew it.

'I could stay with you,' Sheila said purposely and very slowly, 'you said your cottage is comfortable, do you have a spare bed...?' This time she just laughed aloud, 'I've packed my pyjamas too...'

Events more had moved apace taking Barton off balance again by the speed with which things happened, yet, there was something else, the thought of spending the evening with Sheila was a thrill to his senses, the cottage was warm and friendly if tiny, there was wine chilling in the fridge, this could be an unexpected yet welcome development.

'Sheila Lewis, you're a brazen woman, what am I to do with you, you can have your way but God help me if old Gerry gets to hear of this, I've seen his shotgun...!' They both enjoyed the good humour, after finishing their lunch left for the cottage wit Barton leading the way. Sheila parked up beside the Landrover on the patch of ground next to the cottage and fished her bag from the boot of the VW following Barton inside.

'You can't get lost, it's only got two rooms downstairs, two bedrooms and the bath room upstairs...' Barton said as they entered and stood at the foot of the narrow staircase, 'This is the lounge, back there is the kitchen, have a wander round if you want...' With natural curiosity Sheila did just that. When Sheila had completed her mini tour of the cottage, she came back downstairs to find Barton sat on one of the settees searching for appropriate music to put on the music centre. 'Hope you're ok with Borodin, I find him really relaxing, can I get you a drink, tea coffee or whatever...?'

'No Erich, thanks but I'm much too full after lunch. I see what you mean about your views from your desk, these are inspirational. I don't think I would get any work done if I had that to stare at every day. The lanes, the fields and woodland, the countryside here reminds me very much of home, it's really lovely.'

As the evening approached Barton cleared the large wooden table and placed upon it the nautical chart he had shared with Johnson. Smoothing the paper flat he pointed out the Wurm headland, in particular the finger like promontories pointing northwards from the cove beneath the cliffs. Tapping his finger on the depth soundings in a half-mile radius around the base of the cliffs.

'This is where we are going tomorrow, before I forget I need to ring Gary and give him the news you are joining us, keep your fingers crossed Sheila, as I said to you earlier, it's his boat and he is in charge of everything that happens on the water in the morning...'

'Show me where the church is on the chart Erich, I'm keen to see where great-grandad saved the young Huw, doesn't seem to show up on here?'

'No, this is a nautical chart, here however is a large-scale OS map of the area, St Mary's is clearly marked.' Barton placed the OS map over the chart and point out the church on the cliff above the hidden Merlin Coves at their base. Tomorrow we'll get a better view from sea level, the church, if you really want, I could take you there when we get back tomorrow evening, or even Friday if you're free?'

'I'd like to, very much. I am free Friday, there's little work for me this week so I cleared it with my line manager to have the rest of the week off, I'm due back at Greystones on the Friday night sailing as usual though, I need to spend some time with Polly... You do understand Erich...?' She said this as if expecting Barton to make some comment about her need for quality time with her mare.

'Of course, I'd have been surprised if you did otherwise. Now, check the clothes you have brought for suitability, I'm going to ring Gary before it gets too late...'

Sheila laid out the clothes she had brought, a pair of working jeans, a polo necked blue jumper, denim jacket, the ubiquitous small makeup bag necessary for all of her gender with a pair of trainers to complete the set. Practical rather than fashionable much to Barton's relieved approval. As the evening drew on, the long shadows beginning to fall they prepared a simple meal of cheese and tomatoes toasted on freshly cut bread, Barton opened a bottle of Chardonnay from the chiller as they relaxed over the talk on the plans, the hopes for what tomorrow might bring. Sheila asked to see Barton's collection of artefacts and Roman coins, to his pleasant surprise she extrapolated her knowledge of the Roman period of occupation in Wales based on her own area of Celtic studies. The period of early struggles in Wales for freedom firs from the invaders through to the early warlords and princes of Wales influenced by Romanitas. In this they had common ground with Barton taking great pleasure in showing her his clay oil lamps dating from those time along with the coinage produced and used in the area by the common people, he referred to the local Celtic tribesmen, the budding Welsh, who had worked for their Roman overlords for the copper coin in payment contrary to the common belief that they had been purely slave labour. This shared area of interest and knowledge stimulated the conversation, the time passed quickly by. With a glance at his wrist-watch Barton was suddenly aware it was nearly eleven o'clock, mindful of their early start he told Sheila he would make them a night cap before they turned in. Sheila had popped upstairs, had changed into tartan print pyjamas by the time he arrived back in the lounge with a malt whiskey each to end the day. There followed more lazy rambling talk between them before Barton remembered neither of them had put up the tops to their cars. Sheila gave him the VW keys, he went outside and began to arrange first the tilt on the Landrover, then tackled the VWs pram cover. This proved a little more tricky than he had imagined, it took some minutes before the clips were in place and he was satisfied it was weather-proof. Locking both of the vehicles he returned to the pleasant warmth of the lounge. Sheila was stretched out on the settee with her head resting on a cushion, the empty whiskey glass still held in her hand. Barton sat down on the matching opposite settee gazing at this young woman in repose. He rethought his earlier first impressions of Sheila Lewis, she was undeniably a very attractive woman, even with her eyes closed, her lips open in slumber, she had a soft feminine beauty which had captivated him. Her wide-ranging knowledgeable intellect coupled with a broad sense of humour added to the comfort, the relaxed feeling he felt in her company. Barton rose quietly, went to the cupboard under the stairs coming back with two tweed throws, he gently covered her sleeping frame, pausing as she stirred in her sleep, he gently prised the chunky whiskey glass from her fingers before tucking the throws over her body. He stood for a moment looking down at her features so relaxed in sleep, her dark hair framing the lines of her face. Before switching off the light Barton studied her face once more, asleep she looked vulnerable, almost a childlike innocence on her features, he was severely tempted for a brief passing moment to place a kiss upon her forehead, shrugging off the impulse he resisted the juvenile urge. This was not the 'sleeping beauty' of fairy stories, this was a very real and sensuous mature young woman, his responses to her, his own feelings, would be governed by discretion and respect her personality demanded. Satisfied with his resolution of the conflicting emotions he had presented himself to solve, Barton tip toed his way upstairs to his room and bed. It had indeed been a memorable day, quite unplanned yet the outcomes had left him with warm mellow feelings. He was at ease with this young woman, had derived much pleasure from just being with her sharing the very ordinary simple things which made the day go round, her intelligent manner, her laughter, he could become too easily smitten, this here he knew, yet didn't care, it was a marvellous feeling, a feel good factor which he didn't want to come to an end with the finding of Reinecke's U-367. Yet, he was consciously aware how it played upon his mind, he had not sought the start of a relationship, it had just evolved out of their meeting at the Lewis home in Greystones, this was not the time to begin a romantic entanglement with a woman he had met only days ago, there was a need to temper foolish temptations with the demands of reality. Tomorrow was another day, for now, he needed to sleep, resist the deviations in his thinking and to remain focused on the purposes of the day ahead.

36

Thursday morning broke clear and bright, sunlight filtered through the bedroom window, the rays of light dappling the walls with the shadows of the gently waving leaves from the apple tree in the garden. The dawning of the big day, Barton stretching, yawned and turned over luxuriating under the duvet. The say bolt upright, Sheila…? There was the distinct clink of crockery coming from downstairs, his lounge radio was on, the muted sounds of the early morning programme drifted upwards. He pulled on a pair of jeans and went down to investigate. Sheila was in the kitchen humming along to a song on the radio.

'Morning sleepy head, I've got breakfast on the go, coffee, boiled eggs with soldiers, Marmite and marmalade, how's that suit you…?'

Barton caught sight of Sheila still clad in her pyjamas busy in the kitchen, the aroma of coffee and freshly toasted bread hung appetisingly in the air. Sheila had tied her hair back looking as fresh as if she had just stepped out of the gym, with a flourish she produced a laden tray with the makings of breakfast.

'How did you sleep? Sorry to have left you like that but you seemed so peaceful I didn't want to disturb you…' It seemed a good place to start.

'Fine, it's me that should apologise, I must have drifted away while you were outside, did you cover me up before you went to bed…?' That beguiling smile was back on her lips as she tilted her head on one side questioningly.

'Of course, wouldn't have wanted you to freeze, it gets cold up here in the nights. Breakfast looks good, you obviously found everything you needed?' He answered.

'I did, as you said yesterday, it's impossible to get lost here, everything is at hand in your kitchen, I thought I'd let you sleep before waking you with my using the shower and getting ready for the day. It's nearly eight o'clock, you tell me what we are going to do next Erich, I'm just the passenger…?' Sheila sat herself at one end of the large farmhouse table, Barton at the other, they talked over breakfast of the time they would leave to meet with Gary, the things they needed to take with them. After breakfast was finished, the dishes washed and put away, Sheila took the first turn in the bathroom taking with her bag and change of clothes. Barton was surprised that she emerged only twenty minutes later, other females he had known took up to an hour and then some before being satisfied with their appearance. He noted the wear she had chosen, jeans and denim looked appropriate, though not strictly an outdoor expedition garb, it would suffice for the trip. He took his own turn, showering at the same time smelling the distinctive scent of her shower lotion, the female smells left lingering in the bathroom. For his own part he showered and shaved quickly, chose his own worn jeans and a faded sweater with rope soled sandals for the trip. Back downstairs they poured another coffee while Barton laid out his gear. Wet suit, mask and short flippers with a weighted belt to counter buoyancy. A small knife on the same belt and a wide lensed rubber lamp with a line attachment. A towel and his canvass safari jacket completed the set. By nine o'clock they were ready to go, Sheila had fixed her hair into a ponytail secured with a band, she shook it standing with one hand on one hip whilst dropping the other.

'Will I do Mr Barton…?' She said coquettishly with pursed lips.

'You will, you look a treat Sheila. Now about my friend Gary, he's a little earthy at times, I wouldn't want you to get the wrong impression of him. His son Richard is a good lad whom I've known since he was newly born, very like his father in many ways, highly dependable and reliable. Gary's wife left him some year ago, though they're still married technically, Gary has nothing to do with her, Richard however keeps up regular contact with Angela, his mother. Don't be drawn into any talk about her… We are to meet them on the quayside in Conaway at ten, the boat trip will take maybe an hour to get to the headland off the Merlin Coves, then we will make a series of exploratory dives, all being well. I think we'll take the Landrover Sheila, if necessary, we can park it on the foreshore where we are to meet the Johnsons. Are you ready…?' He said, hefting his bag containing his gear and the charts and maps he had packed. 'Then we're off…!' Barton reversed the Landrover out, with Sheila aboard they set off for Conaway.

37

The weather was, as forecast, bright and sunny, little cloud with a clear blue sky. Barton drove down the valley towards the beach before turning up onto the road Westwards to Conaway some six miles away. Glancing across to their right the sea condition appeared perfect, the surface placid with only small rollers coming in on the receding tide. Sheila leaned across to him as they drove, taking in the broad vista of the coastal area they were passing.

'Do you know Erich I really enjoyed last night, it was fun to just relax and chat, you won't believe this, but I haven't done that for a long time. I'm really looking forward to today, it's an adventure isn't it? Exploring the unknown, being part of a quest to solve a mystery, I'm so thrilled at being part of this, excited by what today may bring. Am I making sense...?' This was said in honest manner, her face bore an expression asking she wanted him to believe the words spoken.

Barton was actually enjoying himself too, the pretty girl beside him made him feel good, a little resentful even of the envious looks other male drivers gave as they passed the open topped Landrover ambling along at a sedate thirty miles per hour. It was a pleasurable feeling, *'Carpe Diem'* came to mind as he drove with one arm resting on the open window his sunglasses perched on the bridge of his nose. Twenty minutes later having crossed the bridge into Conaway town, Barton took the Landrover down the narrow streets onto the quayside, there was some parking space next to the town's medieval wall near where there were a variety of small boats pulled up on the shingle. Seagulls flew overhead in numbers, searching for any scraps of food crying their calls as they swooped over the new arrivals. They were hailed by Gary Johnson and his son who were jogging over the shingle to meet them. Johnson came up extending his hand to Sheila.

'This must be Sheila,' he said with a wry grin on his weather-beaten face, 'the woman who has led the pious Erich back on the road to being human. Very pleased to meet you Sheila and welcome to Conaway. Here's my boy Richard, don't take any notice of his appearance, he always looks like a ruffian. Here, Richard, say hello to Miss Lewis, friend of your Uncle Erich…!'

Richard Johnson came forward a little timidly, conscious of his wild shaggy hair and matching beard in comparison with Barton's clean-shaven appearance.

'Hi Uncle Erich, good to see you and you Miss Lewis, I hope we can look after you on board…'

Sheila took the initiative, 'Heaven's sake, 'She said with that captivating Irish burr, 'It's Sheila, Miss Lewis makes me sound like an old spinster schoolteacher…!' She shook hands firmly with both men, not a weak effete grip but in a businesslike manner. 'Where do we go from here Gary?' She added directing her gaze to the older Johnson.

'Follow me, I think you're going to find this interesting, the Megara's fueled up, all of our gear is on board and we're ready to go…!' Johnson led them a few yards to where a large three-metre Avon inflatable tender was beached on the shingle, she had a powerful Mariner outboard engine hinged to the wooden transom at her stern which Richard patted as he made ready.

'Don't worry Uncle Erich, we've got plenty of power here for rough seas. If my Dad chose the Megara, he let me choose this beauty…!' Richard smiled with obvious pride at his ownership of the Avon as he prepared to cast off from the beach.

Richard invited Sheila to climb in then pushed the craft out with Barton and Gary joining her as soon as she began to float clear. Richard waded out beside them and climbed aboard at the stern. Gary pulling in the line which had secured the tender to its beached mooring, coiled and stowed it then turned to start the outboard engine as they began to turn lazily adrift in the current. It fired on the second pull of the cord, holding the tiller bar pointed the tender out into mid-stream. 'There she is Erich, the Megara…' said Johnson proudly, 'what do you think…?'

Johnson's cumbersome looking craft was a converted Fletcher fishing boat, at twenty-nine feet in length with a beam of eight and a half feet powered by a 200hp diesel engine, she wasn't a pretty vessel, she was a working boat adapted and fit for purpose. Her working area had been adapted to give deck space for handling diving paraphernalia, her square wheelhouse sat squat amidships. Johnson seeing the frown of consternation on Barton's face as he gazed at the ugly looking blue painted 'Megara' riding at her anchor, saying.

'Don't be fooled by her appearance and good looks, she's sea going Erich, powerful and can even handle rough surf, I promise you she's really safe. And… she carries life belts, how's that for tailor made for the job…!'

'I guess you're right…' Barton voiced with some apprehension in his reply, 'Wasn't Megara one of the three Gorgons, those horrific sisters who turned men to stone with one look…?' Barton quipped as he clung to one of the rope grab-handles on the side of the inflatable. Johnson merely laughed, unruffled by Barton's comments he guided the tender between other moored craft as they puttered out into the stream to where his rather chunky looking boat swung at her anchor.

Johnson neatly piloted the dingy alongside the tubby Megara continuing unabashed. 'Yup, true she was fabled to be the more ugly of the sisters, seemed fitting somehow but I'm rather fond of the old girl…!' Johnson patted her gunwale as he tethered the tender's painter to the stern of the Megara. Passing Barton's gear over to Richard who had already clambered aboard, putting a hand-out to Sheila who frowned politely ignoring the offered hand as she climbed unaided onto the broad stern decking. They stood on the gently moving deck to take stock of their surroundings, the quayside with the many craft of different sizes riding at anchor or at their moorings around them.

'Sorry about that…' Barton had noticed Sheila's refusal of any assistance, 'He probably thought you'd be a little off balance, he was only trying to help…'

'You seemed to have forgotten Erich, I come from a long line of fishermen, salt waters in the blood…! I wasn't being rude; I just want to be treated as a team member and not a helpless female…'

Barton, nodded, held Sheila's arm pointing over the stern, 'Look there Sheila, that quay is where your great-grandad Mick came in that morning with the survivors he saved from the sunken ship. Here, on this beach, is where Reinecke must have come ashore with the Irish priest, Father Liam Heggarty. Up there on the quay itself is where your great-grandad helped unload the sailors he saved. Do you know, it's giving me cold goose bumps just thinking that we're in exactly the same place where these things happened…!'

Sheila Lewis took in her surroundings remembering not only her great-grandfather, her grandfather too had been aboard the Lady Patricia when she sailed into this harbour, in the cold, the storm and the fear of getting caught, trapped here so far from home… She couldn't help the tears that welled her eyes, running down her cheeks. 'I do Erich, it's a really strange feeling. I wanted to be with you today so much, I didn't anticipate how much just being here would move me. If the ghost of old Mick is looking down on me, I hope that he's not disappointed. I'm glad I am here Erich, I have no belief in the supernatural or things going bump in the night, but you're right, it makes your skin tingle doesn't it, I'm not afraid of whatever is going to happen next…' Sheila meant every word, deep within her were being stirred feelings for her kin who had braved the elements to be in this exact place. It wouldn't have changed much despite the passage of the years, there was no sign of new building or development to spoil the character of the harbour, if one could turn back the clock she was sure that she would see the figure of her great-grandad, the man Reinecke, they had talked about so much, here near this very spot. A shiver coursed its way down her spine at the thought.

Barton was tempted to reach out and put a comforting arm around her shoulder, when he was saved even as he raised his hand, by the call from Gary to his son telling him to 'cast off'. Richard untied the Megara from her floating buoy, immediately she began to drift down river into the current, going with the flow of the falling tide. Sheila turned to Barton looking deep into his eyes, 'Thank you for that Erich, I felt you reach out and touch me…' Before he could say anything in reply, she raised herself on her toes, and kissed him on the cheek.

Johnson was now in the wheelhouse whilst his son secured the tender's painter to the Megara's stern. He beckoned Barton and Sheila to join him. The engine had fired, the wash of the propeller began to turn the water white as they got steadily underway into the main river channel of the harbour basin.

'Come on in both of you, I've got some things to show you once we are out in mid-stream, here, put your paper work on the chart table Erich, there's my own charts on there with the route pencilled in. I called at the harbour master's office this morning, he's got a copy of where we're bound, I told him for some sea bed exploration which he seemed happy with, I've given a return time at the latest for 20.00hrs this evening, we can be in touch by radio if we get into any difficulties. Does that allay your fears, I saw you were a bit put out by Megara's unpretty looking outline, you're right, she's no sailing yacht that's true, I do promise you though, you'll enjoy the day… we're going to have some fun, it's going to be interesting, c'mon Erich, cheer up…!'

Barton couldn't help smiling at his friend's boyish enthusiasm, ever the optimist, a born adventure seeker. 'Ok, we're in your hands from now on in, where are we heading first?'

'We need to clear the top most point of the Wurm where it reaches out into the Liverpool Bay, there our bearing will be an East by South East heading until we stand off the cliffs above the Merlin Coves, should be easy going, the weather conditions so far are as predicted, if the sea is as calm as this all the way then we should make good time...' Johnson indicated on the chart on the table for Barton to follow the course he had laid in pencil from the harbour to a square search area North of the coves.

As the Megara cruised into the narrows towards the river estuary, Johnson pointed out the features of interest sliding past them, to their left as they approached the narrowest point between the two shores he pointed his finger to their port side where a new marina was under construction, 'There Erich, during the latter part of the war, the time when your friend, Mick Lewis sailed into here, was a hush, hush development for the building of some parts of the Mulberry Harbour for D Day, it's a wonder he wasn't challenged given the security in those days. Up there to our right is the remains of the castle which once guarded the river back before the days of the Norman conquest. And, here, along the water edge were fish weirs, the source of income for the people and later taxes for the king in their working days, we're sailing through history Erich, the Romans came here and later the Vikings too...!' So Johnson merrily continued on with his version of local history as they cleared the estuary following the channel out into the open sea. They reached the point of the Wurm headland an hour later on a mill pond calm and placid sea with only a gentle swell rising under the boat. As they turned onto an Eastward heading, the looming cliffs of the Wurm began to rise up towering two hundred feet above them. At the most Northerly point these were sheer drops into the sea below, seabirds thronged the ledges of the cliffs, their shrill noisy cawing crying out a warning as the Megara sedately ploughed through the still surface of the water below the tender twenty feet behind bobbing in their wake.

Johnson let Richard take over the helm as he stood over the chart, Barton had been on deck laying out his gear beside that of Johnson's, satisfied that all was in order he joined the others in the broad wheelhouse. Sheila was bent over the chart, following the pencil marks with her finger asking questions about points Johnson had marked with a cross, he in turn explaining that these were the key areas where he intended to focus the dive, four marked points at varying distances from the eastward most mouth opening of the coves. As Barton came in through the open-door he reached over onto the instrument panel in front of the wheel, he tapped on the top of a grey monitor the size of a small television set into the surface of the control panel.

'This little device we are going to find useful, it came built in when I bought the Megara, her life before as a fishing boat relied to a great extent in finding fish shoals, this box of tricks is a bit like a small sonar, it lets us see what the bottom is like as we pass over, any unusual features come up as a grey outlines, here, you can see we're passing over something now, probably the remains of a wreck of some sort, there are fish here too… We may get some limited indications as to any irregular shapes on the seabed, we won't know for sure until we go down to take a look.' He looked up expectantly to see the interest in Barton's face.

'Does this mean we can pin point a wreck site from above then Gary, is that all we need to do is to conduct our search backwards and forwards within the grid you have marked out until we get some kind of reading or am I being just too naïve…?' It was a fair question, the instrument was limited in its accuracy, giving hints at mass which bounced imaged back from the depths and not the photographic imagery of the more advanced form of technical equipment.

Johnson nodded his head in agreement, 'Although this may save us a great deal of time, it's not a substitute for the human eye. Here right now, we've got about sixty feet under the keel, it will increase, deepen as the tide comes in, if you look closely at the reading this shows an undulating bottom, we could end up with our search being in anywhere between forty to a hundred feet of water, I'm hoping for a workable depth of around fifty feet if we're very lucky.' Johnson held up his wrist showing the divers watch, 'I think it's about time for us to get ready Erich, hope you've brought clean underwear as there's nowhere to change other than the deck… hope Sheila is not too shy…!'

Barton and Johnson went out onto the after deck and began to strip their clothing to don their wet suits, Sheila spent time viewing the scenery, fascinated by the cliff tops as they passed under the majestic rising mass of limestone. She saw above them high on a rocky shelf, the lighthouse building, its windows catching the reflected light of the late morning sun. Then, in the near distance, atop the rise of the cliffs directly ahead of them, perched on the edge of an almost sheer drop to the sea, the wall of the church, with its small tiny spire and cross a recognisable silhouette against blue sky. At the foot of the cliff, the three rocky fingers of the promontory reaching out into the sea came into view as they closed the distance nearing the first marker on Johnson's chart. Johnson and Barton re-entered the wheelhouse clad in their dive kit, with a quick check with the chart, the visual sighting of the landward salient reference features they had known to look for said to the others.

'I think we're here, we are sitting about half a mile off the Merlin Coves, the depth below us is eighty feet rising towards land to probably sixty feet, the lowest point of the tide is due in forty five minutes, we need to be in place for my first dive if we can by then. Now Erich, what kind of dimensions does this U-367 have that you're looking for?' Johnson was now in his professional element, his demeanour becoming serious as they approached their first objective.

Barton quoted the details from memory of the information he had gleaned on Reinecke's U-367 type. 'All U-boats of this class are around the same standard size, she would be sixty-seven metres in length, a beam of six point two metres with a draft of some four point eight. There will be no forward deck gun, they were removed for this class of the U-V11Cs. The conning tower amidships rises up with the two periscope shafts one behind the other, there's usually a radio mast to the right-hand side of the bridge area where the watch would stand when at sea under operational conditions. Aft of the conning tower was something they called the '*bandstand*', in reality this was a gun platform for their anti-aircraft Oerlikon armaments. In other words, she's a considerable size, anything that big must surely stick out on your sonar?' Barton had done his homework; in his mind's eye he could see the vessel as she would have appeared underway at sea.

'Not necessarily so my friend.' Johnson shook his head slowly with a knowledgeable smile playing about his lips, 'It's never as easy as that, we are looking for something which has been on the bottom for decades, it may be covered with silt or sand as the tides have changed the layers of the sea bed. She certainly will be covered in marine life, anything which may have grown on top of her or collected over her those years. Don't expect a pristine version of your sub to be sitting on the bottom waiting to be discovered, it will have changed over the years Erich, don't be too disappointed at what we may find, it'll be a wreck and in poor condition. Right we go on...! Richard, will now take us slowly on the grid pattern I have worked out, overlaid over the chart based on your description of event taken from the Reinecke diary, we are going to start at the top right hand corner, the most Easterly point on the chart, then work back on ourselves half a mile before running back and forth in parallel lines as we close into the immediate area off the coves. All set? Sheila, you may get a better view from the bows or your welcome to keep an eye on the sonar, your choice, take my binoculars…'

So it was for the next half an hour they patrolled westward then turned reversing the course back to the furthest point of Johnson's grid. All were aware of how close they were to the beginning of the turn of the tide in just over an hour and a half, ninety minutes of clearer water, then the sediment would be disturbed once again reducing visibility. They had just turned onto the second run when Barton noticed a grey irregular blotch edge on its way onto the fringe of the screen, something was beginning to take shape, to appear on the sonar monitor, still shapeless, yet clearly some form of a large mass on the sea bed, he quickly called Johnson's attention to the screen. They were right over it…!

Johnson acted immediately calling, 'Stop engine Richard, hold her in this spot, I'm going down with a line attached. Erich, you pay out the line as I go, we're at just under sixty feet so could get lucky on our first run…!' Johnson had donned the air tank, dipped his mask in the water and was already to go sitting on the port gunwale with his back to the sea. Mask in place he gave the thumbs up to Barton and tumbled into the sea backwards. A moment to get his bearings, waved a glove covered hand then was gone. The trail of bubbles marked his descent into the pale green water, the sea's surface mill pond still as Barton paid out the line. Then they waited as the line went slack…

The minutes seemed to drag by, then the line in Barton's hands tightened and jerked several times, Johnson was coming up, the line needed to be retrieved at the same time so no snags were allowed to foul either him or his equipment. Johnson's head broke the surface eight feet out from the boat, he allowed himself to be drawn in by Barton steadying recovery of the line.

Johnson pulled himself up onto the deck, Barton taking the weight of the air tank. He pulled away his mask and mouthpiece. 'There's something down there Erich, but I don't think it's your sub. There's a vessel lying under us well over on her side half buried in sand, she's got the remains of a wheelhouse and a deck gun forward of her bridge, all badly mangled up. Covered in all manner of marine growth, whatever it was, looks like it's been down there some time…!'

Barton did some quick calculations, looked up towards the cliffs to get a bearing. 'Which way was she pointing Gary...?'

'She lays in the opposite direction to us, towards the East parallel to the mainland...' Johnson said closing his regulator to save air. Do you want me to go back for a second look?'

'God's Holy teeth Gary, I think you may have found the Juniper...! If it is, we need to move on this same line another four maybe five hundred feet and search a pattern in that area, if you have found the Juniper, she would lie where she came to rest after she struck the U-367. Can we shift the Megara over in that direction?' Barton was really excited by the find, was this yet another run of the incredibly good fortune which had seemed to guide all of the efforts in this unbelievably complex multi-faceted story?

'You heard the man Richard, take us ahead slow, Erich, keep your eyes on the monitor, the clock's ticking, take Sheila with you, her eyes are younger than yours, she might spot something you may miss...!' Johnson readied himself as his son took the Megara ahead at minimum revolutions.

Both Barton and Sheila were glued eyes fixed inches away from the monitor. The seabed dropped away to eighty feet then rose again, seventy, then sixty then fifty. A long flickering grey mass slid slowly into view, blurred at the edges, indistinguishable in shape but long laying across their line of travel.

'Stop engine Richard, hold here, go a little astern if you can...!' Barton could hardly get the words out, Sheila stood utterly stone like staring at the shape on the monitor as Barton scrambled back to Johnson. 'There's something under us now in fifty feet of water, it's laying at right angles to our course and heading, what do you think Gary...?'

'I think I'll go and take a look that's what I think, don't leave without me...!' He was gone again over the side. This time the minutes were agonising, the line paid out then stopped, time stood still, then more line was taken, then more. A pause, a long pause, then the line jerked, Johnson was coming up...!

His head broke water again close in towards Megara's side, he pulled his mouthpiece out and lifted his mask. 'You'd better come and get your feet wet Erich; we seem to have got something interesting this time...!'

Barton fumbled with his fastening fins, then hitching the air tank onto his back, dipped his mask into the water and bit onto the mouthpiece, it was clear. He sat himself on the gunwale as Johnson had done minutes before, Sheila came out of the wheelhouse hurrying over to him.

'Take care Erich, come back safe whatever you find…' She put two fingers to her lips then touched them to his. 'I'll take care of the line, trust me…'

Barton fastened the face mask went over the side into the green water, it was much colder than he expected taking some time to acclimatise himself and for the wet suit to do its work insulating his body. It took a moment to orientate himself to the negative buoyancy, then with his breathing steadied he calmed his movements into the rhythmic breathing through the mouth piece, he watched as the bubbles began floating upwards, to flow in silver chains in time with his breathing. His nostrils were closed off by a pincher on the bridge of his nose, he was now breathing and expelling air through the mask. He let his body weight begin to stabilise then catching sight of Johnson beside him, nodding he was ready to go, they slowly began their descent together only metres apart. Sheila watched as the two men ducked beneath the surface, following their progress under the green water as they disappeared into the depths. She paid out the line noting the white marks every six feet musing to herself her grandfather's explanation of the fathom marks on the line, four fathoms, then eight, they slowed at the ninth mark, fifty-four feet then a gentle pull as they moved on the bottom.

Beneath the water below her, Barton and Johnson were heading headfirst vertically towards the sea bed, it was eerily calm with only the sound of the escaping air and the hiss of their regulators. As they had approached fifty feet the light began to fade yet the water around them was remarkably clear, the temporary visibility allowing them to see quite well about twenty to thirty feet in all directions. Johnson had been right about the slack water respite they were given when the lowest point of the tide stilled before beginning to turn moving the water again. The sediment particles were drifting slowly down unmoving in the temporarily stilled water. Johnson tugged at his arm, pulling him after him as he swam with strong lazy strokes from his fins, this time horizontally across the undulating sand of the seabed. Then, it reared up in front of them, the silhouette of a grey monster loomed up in the green watery light. Much bigger than Barton could possibly have imagined in his dreams. A wall of metal covered in barnacles, with densely packed marine growth covering the steel of her decks and upper works. Small shoals of fish meandered their way over the sunken hull cruising lazily through the iron work of the rails surrounding the gun platform behind her bridge. The two divers, as they were rising, could see what appeared to be the conning tower of the submarine, cloaked in fronds of seaweeds clinging to the with the two periscope shafts rising above her bridge, the remains of old strands of fishing net, were hanging in the water like the trailing vines from a tree. The wreck was at angle, she was lying on her starboard side, the upper works clear but much of her deck and hull under sand. Johnson was pointing out something on the side of the pressure hull in front of them, it appeared that much of the metal must have been covered until fairly recently as there was much less marine weed and growth on the lower parts of the exposed hull plates, it was possible that the U-367 had been mostly covered with sand until something, tide or currents had disturbed the depths, shifted the sands exposing the bulk of her hull. Out of pure impulse, Barton pulled the knife from his belt, reversed the blade and hammered the haft on the steel plate before him, an ominous echoing boom resonated coming from within, he became suddenly aware of just how terrified his reaction might be if there was an answering banging from the other side of the plates, the area where the control room had once been the scene of so much activity. There was none. He had frightened himself with the thoughts of the men trapped inside, if it were possible for the hairs on his neck to stand on end under water, they had just done so. He shivered, despite the wet suit, quickly pushing away the images forming in his mind, shrugging off the macabre dark nature of the thoughts he had provoked so deep in within himself, the stuff of nightmares... They swam forward again with measured strokes conserving energy, very slowly keeping to within touching distance of the steel plates, circling around the sunken submarine from the tip of her prow, along the surface and sides of the boat's steel decks to the tail where her starboard stern dive fin, buckled yet still recognisable as it rose up out from the sand. Barton was surprised at this, he had expected only shingle or a rock-strewn bottom, this, on the contrary, was a seabed composed mostly of yellow fine sand... They both paused, hanging upright in the water as they gently held position scissoring their fins, coming to rest just aft of the remains of the fishnet entangled weed strewn bandstand. The Oerlikon cannon's barrel still pointed upwards towards the surface, draped with snagged fishing lines and netting, festooned with weed. Behind the bandstand, three metres towards the stern, they made a stark discovery. Here, clearly visible, was the evidence of the massive amount of mortal damage the keel of the Juniper had inflicted upon the starboard pressure hull. The steel plates were bent, ruptured, buckled and stove inwards, the result of the terrible weight of the five hundred and thirty tons of the Juniper's final deadly ramming speed charge impacting into her port side. Somewhere on the other side of these plates lay the grisly entombed remains of the forty men, of Reinecke's doomed shipmates. Barton watched as the silver bubbles from his air tank drifted upwards in chains towards the surface, in this moment of calmness, his thoughts unto himself were of a profoundly sombre nature, they had found the physical proof of the manner of how the boat had died, the killer and the victim within a few yards of each other in what must have been the death agonies of both men and machines. The U-367, Reinecke's boat and her crew were no longer lost, they had been found. The wrecks of both boats were no longer missing, their resting places were now known and could be marked. Barton and Johnson circled the wreck once again, awed by the same numbing silence in which the dead U-boat had lain undiscovered for so many decades, from a time in which neither of the men finding her had been born. Both Barton and Johnson at the same time, felt united in the mutual feelings of deep sadness, the profoundly distressing knowledge of which both were now aware, that this U-boat had lain here on the bottom, with probably many of her crew still trapped alive inside her behind the closed water tight doors when she had finally settled on the sea bed. These disturbing imaginations recoiled at the mental imagery of the men, of such a slow impending death; humanly appalled by the thoughts of these same young men trapped, with no hope of deliverance, alive yet helpless awaiting their inevitable slow tortured ends when the air fouled then gave out, the water rising flooding the compartments. What terrifying inescapable thinking must have gone through their conscious minds as each would have had to face the utter despair at the prospect of such an impending lingering and horrendous death. This and the certainty that they would remain where they were, unknown to their families, in an unmarked watery grave at the bottom of a merciless sea?

Barton found his way hand grip over hand grip up the side of the conning tower. The old fishing nets trailed across him as he moved causing him to proceed with care lest his tank became entangled in strands, or the long fronds of sea weed gently moving in the water in front of his mask. A larges Black Wrasse wriggled its way through the growths around the cramped bridge floor. Barton gingerly found his way up and over on to the right hand side of the bridge where the captain would once have stood when the U-boat was at sea; for some long seconds he held the front rail with one hand, the other clutching the remains of the diamond shaped radio mast to his right, Reinecke must have stood in this very place innumerable times in 1944, when this boat was at war. He had probably stood here when he had guided the U-367 into the Merlin Coves on that night of the 9th January, it would have been from this viewpoint he would have witnessed the crates being unloaded off the foredeck from the torpedo hatch now concealed beneath the weed and sand which now covered her deck like a shroud. The small steering wheel was still in its place, the binnacle housing for the compass with a thickly encrusted mantle of barnacles, the cover of the speaking tube to the control room below... It was enough, Barton could feel emotions rising within him he did not wish to confront in this terrible forlorn place. He turned to find Johnson floating on the outside of the conning tower, only feet away in the water watching him, his eyes behind the glass of the mask showed an understanding. Johnson nodded his head then gestured upwards with his gloved hand in a questioning manner waiting for Barton's response. Barton took one last look around below, there was little more to see of the U-367, it was time to let her return to rest in her grave. He made the thumbs up signal to Johnson, returning the nod to his friend who in turn jerked the line to Sheila three times signalling they were coming up. Both men pushed themselves clear of the entanglements of the conning tower and began the ascent together in a cloud of shimmering silver bubbles.

They broke the surface of the water side by side three metres from the Megara's gunwale, Sheila was taking in the line hand over hand with one foot braced on the gunwale as she coiled the rope as it came in metre by metre.

She shouted across the water, 'Are you both ok?... Did you find anything...? Her relief at their safe return was palpably obvious as she reached over to take the weight of the air tanks as they made for the three-step dive ladder platform at the stern.

Johnson pulled his mask off spitting seawater, 'This is Erich's show Sheila, I'm going to let him tell you, c'mon Erich, have you got the strength left to climb aboard unassisted or do you want a hand up...?' He laughed out aloud that piratical laugh, then slapped the water with the flat of his hand splashing Sheila with droplets.

Ten minutes later they were sat on the after deck of the Megara sipping a hot coffee from a Thermos flask Richard brought from the wheelhouse. Barton had related, step by step, their dive to the wreck, their inspection of the sunken hull, her condition in the water fifty feet beneath their feet. Johnson had added his appraisal, when Sheila had posed the question of the possibility of the U-boat being raised, recovered from the water, he had been emphatic in his response.

'She's a grave Sheila, for all of those men still on board her, she is their resting place and shouldn't be disturbed, they lie here together, as they were so very close in life in the cramped conditions in which they served and then died, they should be allowed to remain together as they are now in death. It would be a sacrilege to attempt to disturb that boat now after all of these years, leave those lads together where they belong...' Johnson's words were meaningful. It was a heartfelt statement, none of the others had any inclination to argue with his sentiments. He continued, 'You know Erich as do I, if your notes are accurate, if Reinecke's account is to be believed, that there are still two crates aboard the U-367 with a king's ransom in gold bullion still on board, then if word of this gets out there are certain unscrupulous individuals and institutions who would give their eye teeth for this information, they would have no hesitation in desecrating the vessel for what's held inside her...! What are you going to do about that as a possibility, as a result of what we have found here today...?'

Barton had already had these sour sullying notions insert themselves uncomfortably into his conscious thinking, Reinecke's hopes for the finding of the U-367 would be blighted, marred by the greed ridden attempts to salvage the gold from her hull, to rip the hull open to rob and desecrate violating the purity of the wishes of the dead captain for his crew. 'Then we must take all measures necessary to withhold that part of the discovery, I think we can all agree the boat, with her dead should be left intact. We can put this before all of us when we meet together in the coming week for discussion in finding our way forward. For my part, I am inclined to believe we have to put our discovery before the authorities in order to attempt a war grave registration for the submarine, once done the wreck site will have some protection. Until then we each must take great care that none of what we know leaks out to anyone other than the six people involved, do we all agree?' There was no argument or comment from the other three, each gave their common assent to maintain the secret of the location and contents of the wreck.

Sheila had moved away to the stern, she was using Johnson's

binoculars to study the entrance to the coves, saw the opening to the inlet where she knew from Barton's account, was where her great-grandad Mick had sailed the Lady Patricia into the natural harbour those many years before, she called over her shoulder not taking her eyes from the binoculars. 'Could we take the Megara in there, my great-grandad took the Lady Patricia in, Reinecke his submarine, could we do the same, I'd dearly like to see where they were when things went so wrong?'

Johnson came to stand at her side, he took the glasses from her and took a close look for himself at the waves slopping around the inlet entrance, 'I've fished off of those rocks over there Sheila, it's dangerous believe me, even in this calm water I'm not sure I'd be as brave as your grandad Mick to try it even in these calm seas, I don't think I can justify risking the Megara, we've accomplished so much in such a short time… What do you say Erich…?'

Barton joined them, gazed across the water focusing his eyes on the waterline where the cliffs met the sea. He gave the idea some thought, it was certainly true, they had succeeded beyond his wildest dreams, even cause him to think that in some way, everything that had fallen into place so quickly must be due to more than just pure luck, was there a guiding force in this somewhere, were matters being manipulated beyond their level of comprehension? No, he was a realist, yet there was a temptation here to go with the flow of good fortune.

'Could we take the tender in for a brief exploration Gary? According to Reinecke and Gerry, Sheila's grandad, there's a shingle beach at the back of the cove, if we beached there, we could have a quick look around to satisfy Sheila, my own curiosity too? The tide's still low, the waves are negligible, we turn back if it starts to roughen up…?' Barton meant it, his curiosity was very much aroused, he was on a distinctive high after the finding of the U-367, this would be the icing on the cake…

Johnson called Richard over, they discussed the details of Sheila's request, Richard's opinion was very much that they were in safe water, that he would take them in a little closer, he would hold the Megara at station, they could then use the tender for the approach to the inlet. His only caveat was to limit the time to no more than an hour maximum, by which time the tide would have well-turned conditions could worsen at a moment's notice.

'Alright Sheila and Erich, you have a point, Sheila must put a life belt on, Erich keep your suit on, bring your snorkel and lamp, if there's any hint of danger I will pull us out immediately agreed…?' He waited for the affirmative response before continuing, 'Ok, take us in Richard, you two get yourselves ready, this time Sheila you might get your feet wet…!'

Johnson pulled the inflatable tender in close to Megara's port side, untied her line whilst holding onto the stern cleat to steady her, then folded out the outboard into the water from its securing point on the transom. Sheila and Barton took their seats in the rear, Richard was keeping the engine ticking over as the Megara drifted without way until they were safely aboard the tender heading for the inlet a hundred yards off the Megara's stubby stem. It was a short journey, the outboard engine puttering under Johnson's nursing hand as they wend their way between the rocks guarding the entrance, above them the gulls circled screeching their cries at the invading intruders to their domain. As they cleared the first sharp rocks, it became clear just how much space there was inside the inlet, much wider than it had appeared out at sea. The rock walls on either side rose above them, sheer without any visible ledges or handholds below the tops some twenty feet above the tender. The sound of the outboard now was echoing off the stone of the walls as they made their way deeper into the natural harbour, Johnson took them alongside the wall to their left, just before they fell into the shadow of the overhanging cliff, he pointed out a corroded frail iron ring in the wall, beside it were the rust marks of where the rungs of the steel ladder set into the wall had once offered the way up onto the ledge, there was nothing now, only a few pieces of corrosion were left. Barton saying as they moved past.

'This must be exactly where Mick tied up the Lady Patricia, alongside her here would be where the U-boat unloaded her cargo…!' He said looking up the path the iron hand holds had once been in the rock leading to the ledge above.

Further in the tender beached onto sand. Barton had expected shingle, they pulled the tender up out of the water conscious of the rising tide now. There was little to see in the cavern beyond, Barton switched on the powerful lamp he had brought, Sheila's breath caught as a pair of green eyes peered at them from the darkness at the back of the cave, it coughed…!

'What the Hell is that…!' She blurted out, startled by the sudden movement under the green eyes.

Johnson laughed aloud at Sheila's obvious consternation, 'That my dear Sheila, is a local resident, it's a grey seal, she's probably got a pup back there with her. Don't worry, quite harmless unless we threaten her baby…!'

Sheila's reply contained a number of expletives, although she saw the funny side of her reaction, yet in her mind thought to keep the seal's presence in mind, especially if it made any attempt to move in their direction. She gazed intently at the remains of the iron ring, the marks of the long gone hand holds, her great-grandfather had been here, here grandfather Gerry too, this place could not have changed, it was exactly where they had been, when this story and the mission they had embarked upon had moved to its critical conclusion. They could have died here…

Barton waded into the water a few feet, he looked back at Sheila and Johnson who stood on the sand with a questioning raised eyebrow.

'Are you thinking what I am thinking…?' He called to Johnson, his words echoing off the walls and roof of the cove.

'I am, Sheila can you take care of the tender for a few minutes, Erich and I have one last dive to do…?' He looked carefully at Sheila, then dismissed the notion of the vulnerable female, she'd be insulted.

'I can, I've been around boats since I was a child, you two, what can you expect to find? There's nothing left there after this long time; the wrecks are out there yes, and that was something else, but if you want to paddle, the pair of you, then I'll look after your boat, just for a few minutes then, I'll get bored standing here…?' Whilst she was entirely confident of her own ability to look after the tender, the presence of the seal however, left her with some small misgivings…

Barton and Johnson waded out then began to swim as the bottom sloped away from them into the deeper water where the iron ring was above them. Barton had brought his lamp with him, he trained the beam below them, the water was clear, the bottom appeared to be about twelve to fifteen feet down. Johnson was fixing his mask back in place adjusting the snorkel attachment, Barton did the same. All that they were leaving behind from the previous dive were the weights on their belts, their flippers, their swim fins. Barton filled his lungs and dived down, with a few powerful kicks he reached the bottom, around them the bottom was remarkably clear, sand instead of the expected shingle again met the beam of the heavy rubber clad lamp. They swam side by side across the inlet, it was much the same, am expanse of flat sand. Nearing the wall on the way back Barton rose for a breath then dove down again, this time with his nose almost touching the bottom, there were shells from a variety of crustaceans, some good-sized crabs scuttled out of the way. Just below the place where the ring sat on the wall above, he experimented by brushing the floor of the inlet with his hand, there was only inches of sand, below was the firm flat surface of the bed of the inlet, there was nothing to be seen… Until, on the fifth wave of his hand something bright glinted as he disturbed the layer of shells and sand. He needed another breath of air, surfaced at the same time as Johnson.

'Gary, come down here with me, I think I may have found something…!' They both went back down-side by side, Barton's lamp focusing on the spot he had left moments ago.

They both made the same movement, waving the sand to uncover the layer below, there it was again… Barton's finger closed around the object, he turned it in the water allowing the sediment to fall away, it was a coin, a very bright and shiny coin they both exploded to the surface, Barton handing the coin over for Johnson's inspection…

'It's one of those from the crate that dropped onto the U-boat and the Lady Patricia…!' Barton gasped for breath, 'Gary, there may be more, how could they still be here, this should have been washed away surely…?'

'Erich, I think that your dead right, they would have cascaded into the water right here. They are heavy enough to have stayed on the bottom, then been covered by sand and silt. There was a really heavy Summer storm while you were in Austria, it might be it removed the sand again, tomorrow, next week, it'll all wash back in again. Are you game for another look…?' Johnson was now definitely riding the waves of success as was Barton. He called over to Sheila waiting near the tender, 'Hey, don't go away. We've found something again…!'

They dived back down and for the next twenty minutes between coming up for air, they search the floor of the inlet around the area where the Lady Patricia had been moored. Both men were now nearing exhaustion but were exhilarated with their findings, as they waded out of the water towards Sheila Barton shouted to her…

Sheila, we found the gold your great-grandad missed, it's fabulous, it was still there, and we found it…!' He realised that he was shouting, jumping up and down at the water's edge where it had risen and was floating the tender. 'Were done here, don't you think Gary…?' The other man's smile broke his face into a broad grin.

'Tell you the truth Erich, I'm completely done in, I'm spent, it's going to take all my strength to get us back to the Megara, our times up too, Richard will be starting to worry… You take the tiller, I'm taking the back seat.' Johnson sat himself in the bow end and let Barton take over the engine and tiller for the return journey.

It was an animated conversation that Sheila and Barton having pulled the tender back into the water and got the craft under way. They laughed and hugged one another, as if a goal had just been scored in a football match…! The mood was jubilant as they chugged back out to where the Megara lay waiting for them. It took some minutes to get themselves and the tender secured back in good order, the outboard stowed with themselves safely once more aboard the Megara. The three of them joined Richard in the wheelhouse as he held position juggling the Megara's engine revolutions until they were ready. Setting course for Conaway, Barton and Johnson congratulated themselves, they had between them, retrieved a total of eighteen gold sovereign coins from the bottom of the inlet, each bearing the distinctive royal head of Queen Victoria…! Barton laid these in rows on the polished wood of the chart table for inspection. Richard, his patience to see what they had found already frayed, took some time to gaze at their haul in something like awe…

'Dad, you've been doing this for years, you've never once come back with anything like this, it's fabulous man…!' His youthful exuberance showed in the beaming smile on his face. 'Are we worth a fortune now, do we get to keep these or do we have to declare them to somebody, you know, treasure trove and all that…?'

Johnson paternally patted his son on the shoulder then softly punched his arm, 'The first thing is we need my curious son, is to have our meeting with everyone involved to decide on what to do next, that's Erich's province. The object of today's venture was to try to locate a long lost wreck, that we have accomplished in an unbelievably short space of time. These coins, as they are, belong to no one; they were not lost as in a legitimate manner, with a stricken ship foundering, these are the spoils of war. By some twist of fate, the odds of which I can't begin to calculate, they were laying on the bottom waiting for us to pick them up, that is nothing short of a minor miracle…' He picked up one of the coins, turned it over in his fingers, the sunlight coming through the wheelhouse glass catching the glint of the gold in his palm. The surface was smoothened by the action of years under water, the shine of the gold however untarnished. Others amongst their collection were virtually unmarked, their embossed head of the queen clear without wear. 'I know nothing about the price of gold,' he said to everyone, 'My last reading on sovereigns like this was that they were fetching around three hundred pounds apiece on the collectors' markets, the gold value alone is high, these are twenty tow carats each I seem to recall. Multiply that times eighteen, then I think we have a tidy sum here gang…!' Johnson broke into his Long John Silver piratical laugh again, 'A fair day's earnings seems to me…?'

Barton was a little more sober in his reply, 'It wasn't for the money, none of us expected this, it is however a marvellous bonus on top of our unusually good fortune. These coins we found must have dropped between the Lady Patricia and the U-boat, others may be still there as many will have clattered off the deck of the submarine into the water on the far side…'

Richard was quick, asked on hearing this, 'Does that mean there may be more to be found Dad, could we go back and look again…?'

'No, there may be odd coins still there, but I don't think we should tempt fate when it has been good to us, the sea gave up these to us, in conditions that will probably never occur quite the same again, we should be grateful for our good fortune and leave whatever may be left where it is…'

Barton admired his friend's moral goodness, his lack of greed at the prospect of searching for more of that which they had gained. 'We've done what we came to do, we should be satisfied with our success, we're not treasure seekers, we have a purpose, that part of the mission is yet to be accomplished when we inform the admiralty where Reinecke's U-boat lays today, in my opinion that will bring this matter to an end…'

The others agree with him, Barton was about to go out onto the fore deck to watch the estuary come into view when Johnson held onto his arm, 'There's one more thing Erich, I was keeping this until last, when I went out under where the sub would have been, I was searching on the bottom with my fingertips, I found three coins almost immediately all together, then, believe this if you will, in the soft sand my hand closed on this, I didn't find it, it found me, I swear it was the strangest thing Erich. I kept it as I'm sure it will mean something to you, put your hand out…!' Johnson put his hand into his shirt pocket and then held his closed fist over Barton's outstretched hand, he dropped something into the waiting open palm...

Barton let out an audible gasp at the sight of the small metal object in his hand, not as well preserved as the coins, some white corrosion on the metal, the black paint at the centre almost all gone, the swastika was still visible with the date 1939 embossed in the lower branch of the medal, the reverse still held the clasp and pin where it had been secured to the uniform... It was an Iron Cross... *Reinecke's Iron Cross...*! If Barton had needed one more convincing piece of hard evidence which tied up with the accounts in his diary, this was it, the medal Reinecke had tossed overboard when Mick Lewis had told him to get rid of any incriminating features which would have given away his identity if they had been challenged... The last piece of the puzzle had finally been slipped into place...

38

The Megara had docked at her moorings in Conaway, their homeward bound voyage had been a pleasant uneventful cruise passing the channel markers back to the harbour, as the miles had flowed into their wake the mood had lost some of the initial elation after the success of the finds. Johnson and his son had piloted the return journey from the wheelhouse, Sheila and Barton sitting on the fore deck as they turned in the river basin before tying up to the Megara's buoy marker. The evening sun cast shadows across the surface of the water, on the quayside there was activity as some local events were taking place, people were standing on the quay with glasses in their hands. As Richard secured the Megara, Johnson pulled the tender alongside putting the outboard down ready for their short trip to the shore.

'Do you want to join in the fun Erich, it's the Autumn fayre, music and entertainment with the pub open on the quay...?' Johnson looked as tired as Barton felt, it had been a very long and demanding day in more ways than one.

'If you don't mind Gary, I've got some calls to make to our friends, my gear to stow away, I think we'll give it a miss this time...' He meant it, he felt drained both mentally and physically, there was much he wished to commit to paper whilst the vivid short-term image memories were still fresh. They had neglected to bring a camera, that which they had were the mental pictures in the vaults of their imagination, he was acutely aware of how these would decay or corrupt even with a short passage of time. He desperately wanted to get these on paper as soon as was possible.

They puttered their way to the shore, unloaded their respective gear onto the wet shingle, Richard pulling the tender out of the water before tying her up to her shore anchor. It was enough, they stood in their small group, people joined in the knowledge of the deep and solemn affair to which they had now each become a part of. Sheila hugged both Johnson and Richard as left the tender on the shingle, they were turning to take their leave, when Johnson walked quickly back, grabbed Barton bear hugging him.

'You were right you old sod, there were times I thought you were on a fool's errand, now, I'm convinced, you were on old Reinecke's sacred mission, and look where we have ended up! Take these coins with you Erich, till we decide what to do with them.' He handed over the small canvass bag into which he had put the eighteen sovereigns, 'I'll be in touch with you during the next few days. Drive careful, and… take care of this girl, I think you've found something very special yourself…!'

Sheila was tempted to say something funny, instead she kissed his cheek, 'Pirate…! The next time we sail in your boat it'll have the skull and cross bones flying from the mast. Thank Gary, it's been a really memorable day, I'm grateful for you letting me on board, it really has meant so very much to me, we'll be seeing you very soon Gary.' She waved to Richard still fussing over the tender, blowing him as kiss…

Barton fired up the Landrover with their gear in the back they made their way up through the town over the bridge and on the road home to the Barton's cottage in the hills. As they passed through the main road through the town on route to the cottage, Sheila noticed a Chinese restaurant, she pulled at Barton's arm saying.

'Can we? I don't feel like a sit-down meal and I don't fancy cooking anything tonight, but a take away would be fine, how about you…?' That soft burr was back in her voice having been missing all day, how could he resist? Twenty minutes later they were back on the road with a large bag containing a selection of varied delights picked at whim from the menu. Barton stopped briefly at an off license just before the end of town, complemented their coming dinner with two bottles of good Italian Chianti.' Minutes later they pulled the Landover in beside Sheila's VW, hands grasping the makings of the meal firmly between them heading indoors. The cottage was chilled by the evening air, Barton set alight the log fire already made in the iron dog basket in the ingle nook. It caught quickly, within minutes began to crackle as the dry logs ignited. They laid the meal out on the table, Barton produced two wine glasses and popped the cork on the Chianti. They both chinked their glasses, the contents disappearing in easy swallows. Barton filled them once again, sitting at the table he lit the candle stick in the centre, the warm glow casting pleasant shows on the white walls as they hungrily devoured the spicy Chinese dishes. After, with the remainder of the meal disposed of, the dishes washed and put away, Barton flopped into his soft leather sofa, brought out his pipe and began to fill the bowl with tobacco from his leather pouch.

Sheila came in from the kitchen drying her hands as Barton blew a cloud of smoke from his first pull on his pipe.

'Erich, enjoy your pipe, I'm going to have a long shower, it's been an incredible day hasn't it...!' She smiled at him in his obvious state of pleasurable enjoyment the effect of the Chianti warming and relaxing the both of them. 'Pour me another, I won't be long...' Sheila giggled to herself as she ascended the stairs, with below in the light of the fire, Barton sat with his arms draped behind his head as he laid back across the sofa's cushions.

'Take your time, I'm not going anywhere. I'll open the other bottle and put some music on...' He called up after her.

Barton browsed through his music discs, selecting one, placed Rimsky Korsakov's Scheherazade suite on the music centre, sitting back with glass in hand, to let the gentle strains of the violins introduction waft over his mind enjoying the mellow tranquil ambience as the wine and music took effect... Any thoughts of working on his notes had fled for the moment. Sheila would need to call her grandfather this evening, he felt that he must do the same with Huw in to give them both updates on their recent discoveries of the day. It was time to relax with the mental foot from the accelerator for a while, he felt they had earned some small respite from the activities of the past days...

Sheila came back down the stairs twenty minutes later dressed in her tartan pyjamas vigorously towelling her hair, pausing as he reached the bottom saying petulantly.

'One thing your cottage doesn't have Mr Barton, is a drier for your lady friend's hair...! Where's my wine Erich...?' She asked in that slow low burr with which he had become so enamoured. She dropped onto the sofa beside him, one leg folded under her as she continued to rub her hair dry. Barton passed her a recharged glass, Sheila taking a long sip said, 'God how I needed that Erich, I was going to suggest...' A jangling of the cottage doorbell interrupted her sentence before it could be finished. Who the hell is that at this time of night...?'

Both stared at each other quizzically, Barton rose putting his glass down on the coffee table, turned off the music, then switching on the porch outside light he said with annoyance,

'I haven't a clue, but we'll soon find out...' He peered through the lounge window, another vehicle was pulled up onto the parking patch beside their two cars, hard to make out in the darkness but it was a big car…

'Erich, if it's your ex, then I'd better leave…' Sheila put her glass down was half risen from the sofa when Barton opened the door… There was the murmur of voices then a figure, taller than Barton, ducked through the doorway into the lounge.

'Sheila Lewis, is it yourself I'm looking at? Now would you look at this, I didn't expect this at all, at all…! Where's yeh clothes girl, you look far too much at home here I'm thinking. Erich me lad, you're a dark horse and that's a fact, you with me granddaughter and her in half her clothes an all…!

'Grandad…?' Sheila stood up both eyebrows raised.

'It is, I couldn't wait, got young Gerry to bring me over and here we are…' Gerald Lewis the older stood with a broad grin on his face, a twinkle in his blue eyes as he beamed at the two of them in their obvious embarrassment.

Barton was taken off balance, a second later the younger Gerry appeared beside his grandad, 'Come in, come in, if we'd know you were on your way I'd have got something in for you, when did you arrive…?

'We got off the ferry at Holyhead only an hour ago, you'd left me your card Erich, with your address, young Gerry got a map out and here we are. I thought I'd surprise the two of you… You did say I'd be welcome any time did you not…?' The old man was enjoying every minute of the drama he had created. 'Now, if that's a good wine that you're slurping, would I be imposing on you if I asked if you had anything a bit stronger for an old man…?' He burst out laughing with that deep rumble from somewhere down in his frame.

Barton and Sheila had no choice, the old man was here, Gerry the younger looking every bit as if he too was amused at their discomfort…

'Gerry, about Sheila being here… We've only just got back from the expedition today, there has been no time to arrange anything and…' He was cut off by the older man.

'What this I hear, do you not find the girl pretty, is she not good company with her love of all things interesting and more, are you ashamed of being with my granddaughter Erich Barton? And there's me, silly old fool that I am, thinking you were a friend to be trusted…'

'I do, I mean I am pleased, I'm… Oh God I don't know what I am.

Take your coat off the brothers Grimm, find yourselves a seat. No, I don't have a good single malt, I do have however a bottle of Hennessy Cognac which I was saving for next week but what the hell, will that do…?' Barton was relieved, old Gerry wasn't going to fly into a rage at finding his granddaughter half undressed in the home of a philanderer, he was immensely taken with the jape he had played in catching them both unawares. If anything, the old rascal looked elated…!

An hour later, with both of the two Gerry Lewis's installed on one of the sofas with brandy glasses in their hands, Barton and Sheila began their account of the past two days culminating with the finding of the U-367 and the recovering of coins with Reinecke's Iron Cross from the cove. Barton placed these along with the Dorn Luftwaffe identity tag and pay book on the coffee table. They made a sad collection of objects, Gerry sat and stared at hem then reached for one of the sovereigns.

'So these have come up from the same box that broke over the Lady Pat on that night, I was there, I remember the shower of gold from the heavens, my Dah and Finn collected all that they could, they couldn't have known how many went into the water. And. Reinecke's cross, it is just incredible you should find that, the poor man, he could have kept it on him, no one would ever have known…' The older Gerry's voice had just a hint of melancholia as he spoke the words.

Barton and Sheila's evening had been turned upside down by the arrival of the Lewis's, anything which may have evolved over the course of their time together now placed at the back of their respective minds. Taking the initiative, he called Huw Thomas who was delighted with the results of their endeavours. He asked Huw, that as Gerry was with him here at the cottage, he might like to speak with him in person. The two men spoke animatedly on the telephone for nearly half an hour. When Gerry finally put the receiver down, he looked up at the faces around him, again his face wreathed in smiles.

'Small change of plan, Huw seems to think we can easily bring the meeting forward to tomorrow as we're all here, Friday, in the late morning. He's going to lay on lunch for us at his place, he's offered that young Gerry and I can stay over with him tonight, says he's got plenty of room. This, I'm sure will be a relief for the two of you…' He peered around the lounge of the cottage, 'I've the feeling we might be a little cramped if we imposed ourselves on you for the night, young Gerry and I have brought some things in the car so we have all that we need. Now, I think it's time to say good night to you both, unless, Sheila, you want to come with us to Huw's...?' He let the question hang in the air with one eyebrow raised in question.

'No grandad Gerry, I'm going to stay here, Erich will take care of me...' Sheila nodded at Barton for support for her decision.

'Right, then we'll be off and see the two of you in the morning...' Her grandad seemed quite satisfied and rose to leave.

As they made their way out into the night and over to where the younger Gerry's Mercedes stood beside Barton's Landrover, Gerry the younger took Barton's arm, speaking quietly as his sister chatted with her grandfather her arm in his as they walked.

'Erich I apologise, truly the old man suddenly burst in on me, told me to get our passports that he had made a booking on the ferry, crafty old bugger did it all on his own. I had minutes to arrange for one of the hands to look after the farm then we were on our way, him clutching the card in his hand saying, "we're going to surprise them..." Please believe me, I had no part in putting this together, you must be beginning to get an idea what he's like.' Gerry the younger was sincere and Barton believed him without reservation. They shook hands as both men got into the car. As the Mercedes pulled away with the older Gerry's arm waving out of the window, Sheila came and stood beside him, shivering still in her pyjamas, Barton put his arm protectively around her as they walked back towards the cottage, she didn't resist putting her head on his shoulder.

'I think he likes you Erich, I've never seen him take to someone before as he has done with you, he trusts you...' She said the words quietly and with feeling.

39

The good weather had broken when Barton awoke in the morning. Rain trickled down the bedroom window with the wind tugging at the branches of the old oak tree in the garden. He turned yawning to find Sheila's arm draped across his chest, she, still in a deep sleep her eyes closed her breath coming steadily through her slightly open lips. He gently raised her arm so as not to awaken her placing it under the covers before very slowly getting himself up to stand and stare out of the window at the rain-soaked garden with green fields in the downpour beyond. Barton had one of those rare moments in his life of overwhelming wellbeing, where everything seemed just right, the deep desire to hold onto the warm mellow feelings which seemed to course through his whole being filling him with a contentment hitherto unexperienced in his adult life. He told himself in rational terms, it's purely chemical, endorphins, enkephalins, this was the feel-good factor yet even with the logical explanation he knew deep down he had no wish for it to end. Staring back at her sleeping form he was acutely aware that despite the warnings he had repeatedly made to himself, something had changed, and he could never be quite the same again.

Barton shook himself wide awake, today was going to be the day when, with the meeting of all of the 'team members' everything was approaching a conclusion to the events of the past months. Could he go back to the way things had been before, the odd piece of writing, the occasional cheque in the post or did he sense within him the need for something more permanent in his future existence? He ran his fingers through hi tousled hair, much to think on… First, get started Erich he told himself, my turn to make breakfast…!

When Sheila came downstairs a little while later, she smelled the aroma of coffee finding Barton had been busy making omelettes and toast. Fresh orange juice stood chilling on the table, he stood back with a flourish, 'Voila…!' As they ate breakfast Barton noticed a white envelope on the coffee table amongst the debris from the night before, wiping his lips he rose and picked it up.

'*SHEILAGH LEWIS*' was written on the front in heavy black

handwriting, Barton handed it to Sheila, 'Where'd this come from, I didn't notice it last night?' He looked at Sheila expectantly…

'That's my grandad's writing, it's Gerry's, he must have put it there before they left…! I didn't see it either Erich.' Sheila put her fork down and rubbing her hands reached for the envelope. She opened it taking out a single sheet of paper folded around a cheque which fluttered onto the table among the breakfast things. My God…!' She said reading the words, 'Erich listen to what my grandad Gerry has written…' She read out the brief letter as Barton poured their coffee.

'My Dear girl,

I've been doing some deep thinking over these past days as I have waited for news from you. I've thought about my life, how the years have passed by so quickly leading up to this time when the events of the past have caught up with me at last. I'm of the mind to give you a start in life now rather than for you and your brother to have to wait until I'm gone, I'd miss all the pleasure of watching you enjoy your life. So dear Sheilagh, here's some money to spend on what you will, no strings attached just go out and have some fun with it. Make an old man very happy my dear.

Your loving Grandfather.

Gerald.'

Sheila picked up the cheque and turned it over in her hand, it was written for the sum of twenty-five thousand pounds…! She looked up into Barton's eyes as a tear trickled softly down her cheek.

'I told you he was a mad old fool, now look at what he has done…!' Sheila wiped away the tear and forked vigorously at her omelette.

'Then I wish that I was fortunate enough to have a mad old grandad, I think he's one of a kind Sheila, there's some genuine love and care behind his gift to you, accept it for what it is, a token of his affection for you… How come he spells your name that way…?' Barton pointed to the lettering on the envelope.

'It's the Irish way, after my maternal grandmother, she was Sheilagh too I was named for her… Funny, I never thought you'd think it was any other way Erich… Anyway, you can't talk, 'Erich' instead of Eric or Erik…'

'That's not fair Sheila, my mother named me, she pronounced my name as *'Ayrish…'*, a little difficult for some Anglo Saxons so I've been happy to have it sound like Eric… Less confusing for all…'

They talked and chatted over the remainder of breakfast, they recounted the sudden invasion of her grandfather and brother Gerry into their intimate attempts at privacy, with some laughter at Gerry senior's mischievous plotting to rudely surprise and embarrass them both. After they showered and changed for the day. Sheila keeping her jeans and denim jacket with a fresh white blouse underneath, Barton also jeans with a heavy check shirt, then his leather bag containing all of the relevant papers notes and paraphernalia related to the Reinecke diary. By eleven o'clock they were ready to drive over to meet the team at Huw Henryd Thomas's home.

40

They had decided to take Sheila's car, the rain had eased off a little, yet it was still wet as they backed the more practical VW onto the road and set off for the Bay town. Barton was unsurprised with Sheila's obvious driving skills. A little aggressive when they reached traffic lights, she gunned the VW past the driver waiting at their left through the lights with a racing change through the gears. They found their way to Huw's 'Bramble End' home finding young Gerry's black Mercedes parked on the gravel outside. Huw met them at the door coming out with an umbrella to shelter Sheila, leaving Barton to make his own way in the light drizzle of rain. Huw greeted both jovially.

'Your grandfather and I should have met years ago, we've had a fine time this morning reminiscing, we get on well with much in common he and I. Now, come on in out of the wet, we're all in the big lounge, my good lady is in the kitchen preparing lunch for us, I had a notion you might prefer fish, it being a Friday an all, is that ok with you both...?' Huw had obviously considered the likelihood of guests from the Republic observing the recommended obligations of the faithful in his choice of fare. The two older and younger members of the Lewis family were seated on the deep sofas, with the senior Gerry looking extremely comfortable and relaxed, Sheila caught his eye and shook her fist at him with a smile on her lips, in return he put out his tongue at her much amused by her stern look. Beside the Lewis's another long sofa stood empty. 'That is for your friends Gary and Richard, they should be with us any minute, they called half an hour ago to say that they were just leaving home. Sure enough, a couple of minutes later another set of tyres could be heard crunching on the gravel of the drive with Gary and his son climbing out of Richard's green Mini Cooper. They too trooped in taking their place on the vacant sofa. Barton looked around the room, here were gathered everyone who had become involved in the Reinecke saga. The journey that had begun with a young airman's body being found in a wood, the trip to Austria, the meeting with members of the Dorn family, with Bruno Reinecke and his beloved Inga, Ireland and the Lewis family, then Huw Henryd. It had all come together ending with the meeting of all of these interested minds in this room. Barton couldn't help remembering his early trip alone to the Austrian village, the beginning of the quest which had gathered people as it progressed through different counties and across times. Now, they were all seated here together, expectantly, it looked as if Huw, being the host, was now expecting Barton to open the discussions which were about to follow, with the six members of the team present eagerly waiting for him to begin. Barton looked around at each of the faces, feeling once again the responsibility for having begun the story which they now would bring to an end. He opened his bag and put everything which he had brought with him onto Huw's large wooden coffee table, laying out his notes, the papers, then the objects he had accumulated along the way. The eighteen bright coins sparkled in the light, the medal and identity disc sombre reminders of the dead men who had worn them, those men whose spectral shades Barton seemed to feel standing here beside him in the room causing the fine hairs on his fore arms to stand on end. It was time to make a start…

Barton took them back to the beginning once more, recounting each step of the journey allowing questions or expansions on details of the tale as it unfolded before them. The search under water being the culmination with the older Gerry asking many questions about the seabed, the two wrecks which they had found. Eventually, after an hour of talk, Barton brought his verbal account to a close with the open question before them now being what to do with their many findings, who to approach to pass the necessary location details of the wrecks to the authorities. Barton mentioned his friend, the police officer, David Strachan as if it were not for him telephoning on impulse Barton that day in the early Spring, then none of this would have happened. The consensus was that everyone was in agreement, Strachan would be the person to begin to test out the official reaction, who might point the way as to where they went next with the information which they had accumulated, the facts which they now had in their possession. The objective now after all of their combined and collective efforts, would be to seek official war grave status for the wreck of the U-367 and her crewmen, to mark their place in accordance with their captain's last wishes. Everyone enthusiastically agreed that this now should be brought under way as soon as Barton had sought David Strachan's views on how to progress the matter. The next important aspect would be how much of the story would it be necessary to release, the destruction of the plague phials, the death of the Martins, the man Breitfeld and his end?' This was a prickly area to probe, there were obvious discrete confidences known only to Huw and Barton which were to be kept strictly between them. There was the Lady Patricia's illicit voyage across the Irish sea in that Winter of 1944, again it was agreed that some discretion must be exercised in revealing the part Mick and his son Gerry, had played in the receiving of the dubious contraband and arms from the Germans in a time of war, the welfare of the dead and the living would be best served by an economically tailored version of the factual events thus preserving the elderly Gerald Lewis from the prospect of any examination by the authorities on either side of the Irish sea. At this point in their discussions, Johnson cleared his throat noisily, raising his hand to catch the attention of the other members of the team.

He began in a serious tone, 'There is one more vitally important factor we have to include in our thinking here. There is the loss of the Royal Naval ship, the Juniper, along with the thirty-five officers and men of her crew. If the Juniper had not rammed and sank the U-367, she might have got clear, escaped with her cargo and story into the open sea to prey upon shipping again. The end of this story would be quite a different matter if she had survived along with the banker Schumann, and officers and men to tell a very different tale from that of Reinecke's. We need to think about those British sailors who also lost their lives on that night, they were defending their country from an armed aggressor, this we must not forget...' Johnson had thought long and hard about this factual reality it had worried him; though so much of their attention had been focused on the German captain, the fate of his U-boat, there were British lives which had been lost directly as a result of the German's carrying out a raid with the specific intent ultimately planning to purposefully kill and maim great numbers of innocent people.

Barton broke in, 'There were two survivors apparently Gary, perhaps we should go further and try to find out what became of them...?'

'I can add a little information there,' said Huw leaning forward on his sofa seat, 'I was in the hospital when those men were brought in from Conaway, I didn't remember much at the time, I was out of it, the nurses talked about the to sailors who were in the male ward next door to me. One poor man lasted days, then sadly the oil that he had swallowed killed him. The other I seem to remember was transferred somewhere else the week I was being discharged from hospital...'

'That's right,' Johnson came back quickly,' I did a little digging myself, after the first sailor had died, the one remaining man, a rating named Jenkins, began to lose his mind, they tried everything to calm him down but he was a nuisance at night shouting over and over that they had hit a mine, that there were men in the water still to be saved. Apparently, the doctors had no choice but to have him transferred over to the then mental establishment at Denbigh, there was little understanding in those days about the trauma mental disorders affecting servicemen. He was there until he died five years later the U-367 claimed her last victim…! The Admiralty never had the chance to interview either of the two men, both were in a pretty poor state when they were rescued by Mick's boat, Jenkins's balance of mind was affected, he was all that was left of his ship's company, his rantings about the hitting a mine were in part accepted, the Juniper's loss put down to probable "enemy action", probably that she had struck a sea mine either dropped by parachute or deposited by a sub. The Admiralty could close the file on the Juniper with that cause as sufficient explanation for her loss.' Johnson eased himself back in his seat, the knowledge which he had just imparted had an obvious effect upon the others, particularly Huw and Gerry senior. No one spoke, this was a disturbing yet very real facet of the events of January 1944, one man had spent the remainder of his days in a psychiatric unit, driven mad by what he had witnessed.

Gerry sat quite still before speaking, 'I saw those two men, I saw the state they were in when my Dah and Reinecke pulled them aboard. I never knew what became of them, no way of knowing I suppose, I am so really saddened to hear their fates, my Dah did what he thought was right, but the mark was already upon them…' Gerry made the sign of the cross as he spoke the last words, the sadness on his face very clear to his companions.

'I'm sorry Gerry, I did not intend to cause anyone distress. I did feel a responsibility to contribute those additional pieces of the human story in bringing everything together, here, today…' Johnson felt genuinely remorseful for what he had felt he must do, it would have been wrong to allow the others to live with only part of the story, the tragic pieces need to be included no matter how painful. There was a common empathy for his motives, each however remained with their thoughts a little longer before Barton spoke again.

'I thank you Gary, that couldn't have been easy but it needed to be said, does anyone have any questions or comments on these things Gary's just told us…? No, then we press on…'

The objects on the table now received the attention of all, each relieved to change the theme away from the thoughts uncomfortably risen by Gary's words. Huw Thomas began, made it clear he sought nothing material from the efforts of the research the travels Barton had made collecting and collating the information for their meeting. In similar vein Gerry too, said that he had no need for anything material, the gold sovereigns to be left to those who found them in his opinion. The medal and personal items relating to Dorn and Reinecke, to remain with Barton. Again there was a common agreement, the younger Gerry too feeling as he had played no part in the recovery, he didn't feel any entitlement to any monetary gain the proceeds might fetch on the gold market.

Barton took Johnson aside for a moment, then after a few brief words announced their joint suggestion to the group. Each member of the team of six received one of the gold sovereigns apiece to mark everything which had been achieved between them, no matter how small or great had been their contribution. This was happily received, with the consent of the other four adding their caveat in saying the remaining twelve coins, or their gold market value, should be split between the members who had crewed carried out the sea searches with the dives on the wrecks. Here Barton and Johnson being the principal participants, with shares to Richard and to Sheila. Any additional proceeds to be used to foot the bill for the hire of the Megara, the total costs of the dives on the wrecks. This as a motion being carried with no one in dissent nor having any other suggestions. Barton gave to each member a gold sovereign leaving the remaining twelve upon the table. There remained little now other than to bring matters to a close. It was left with the next step being for Barton to make contact with D.I. David Strachan, to set up a meeting for the first talks to progress Reinecke's wishes into reality under way. The effects of the information Johnson had disclosed still weighed heavy on their minds, the thoughts of the man, the rating Jenkins, being confined for the rest of his days in a Victorian asylum for no crime other than being the unfortunate survivor of a disaster. Barton was aware of this, knew they needed to lighten the mood so on a cue from his host, announced dinner was being served in Huw's dining room. The six trooped into an elegantly furnished dining room set with a large table with a chequered red tablecloth. Huw's housekeeper cum cook, Mrs Collins, had laid out a cold lunch of carved meats, salads, garnishes with fresh French sticks still hot from the oven. There was something to everyone's taste, an hour passed in pleasant talk with some pleasing reminiscing and the sharing of memories between the older members.

By four o'clock it was time to leave. Johnson and his son the first to go, then followed by Gerry and his grandson. It was an emotional parting, Huw and Lewis held their hands in a long handshake, Lewis offering Huw to come over the water and spend some time with him on his land in Greystones. Huw, exchanging numbers and addresses readily agreed, they would be meeting up in two weeks' time. Young Gerry brought the car round and they were off to catch the early evening ferry from Holyhead. As he came round to open the door for his grandfather, he paused, reached into his pocket and said.

'I owe you an apology Erich, I suspected you of having the wrong motives when we first met, you've proved differently. This... 'He offered his hand placing his gold coin into Barton's palm, 'Was no thanks to me, I think you should keep it with the others, my small contribution to your hard earned outcome, you keep it my friend...' He had that same boyish wide smile on his face as he had that first day in Greystones, 'Take care of my sister Erich, she's precious to us...!' Another handshake then the Mercedes crunched on the gravel as they started for home. Barton and Sheila said their goodbyes to Huw a few minutes later, it was clear he had every intention of making them welcome at his home in the near future, Huw's life had taken a turn for which he had waited a very long time to come about. His past demons had ceased to plague him with their nightly visits, for this he felt indebted to Barton's including him in bringing matters out into the forefront of his thinking, the laying of the ghosts which had haunted him these past years since the passing of his beloved wife, Maureen. Huw followed then over to Sheila's car, the rain had stopped, a watery sun shone through the trees. Huw became very still, then animated again he reached up to his neck and took the quarter dollar coin on its chain from around his throat. 'I've a mind you should keep this with the other pieces of your collection Erich, it's in good company there, another part of the story which came together through your work. When Jonesey gave me this all those years ago, I kept it, a talisman, now I think its place is with these other mementoes of the past. If anything happens to me it would just be lost, I'd rather this stays with you...' He placed the coin in Barton's hand without the chain.

'If you are sure Huw, then I'm honoured, if you ever change your mind, then I'm just holding on to it for you.' Words here somehow didn't seem adequate; Barton took his hand in both of his and shook it warmly.

They waved Huw Henryd goodbye promising to keep him informed of the news of the overtures to Strachan which was to come in the following weeks. Sheila guided the VW down the drive to the main road, there was some small measure of time to kill before returning to the cottage. Sheila had some little time before her sailing on the late ferry to follow her grandad and brother, back on the main coastal road they decided to retrace the drive up to the Wurm where Huw had taken Barton just days before. As they drove the climb up the steep road then onto the flat area above, Barton pointed out where the Martins had met their end. Then, parking the VW where Huw's MG had sat earlier, got out to look at the view over the stone wall and gate at the sea below.

'This is where it all began isn't Erich, I can feel it. The idea that here, where I'm standing, my great-grandad Mick trod this same path... It's uncanny but I feel him here somehow...'

They walked hand in hand through the gravestones to where Huw's parents were laid. Then Barton showed her the stone with the name Ezra Lloyd-Williams, Sheila took some moments, aware that the other man lying in this grave had met his end at the hand of her grandfather. Yet, she felt comforted by the knowledge that the man they had just left, Huw Thomas, would have been killed in cold blood, had not Mick Lewis not acted when he did and saved a young boy's life. They had stayed walking on the Wurm for nearly an hour exploring the edges of the cliff tops along the sheep tracks before retracing their steps to drive back to Barton's cottage. Sheila packed her few things into her bag, was ready to leave by nine o'clock with plenty of time for the ferry sailing.

'I don't know how to say this Erich, these past days, so much has happened, it is as if we've been caught up in something which took on a life of its own. I'm not sure I'll ever be the same again. And you, is this how your life is going to be, a series of adventures, doggedly following the stories you intend to write...? Digging up tales from the past then bringing them back to life with your pen...?' Although the smile was on her lips, her face was solemnly serious.

'Six months ago, Sheila, if you had asked me that question, I might have said yes... Now, there is still so much left to do, when we have overcome the next, and hopefully final barrier with David's assistance, then I think I will be able to answer you honestly... Until then, just bear with me a little longer, I need to get my head back together.' Barton meant every word, there was but one more agonising hurdle to surmount, then with a clear conscience, the commitment he had made to Reinecke's memory would be accomplished.

When Sheila was ready to drive off to catch her sailing on the late ferry, Barton walked with her to her car. She was dressed in a fawn coloured trench coat with the belt knotted at the waist, he couldn't help but think she looked adorably like a mysterious female agent from a spy thriller. Then, spent some time in a long embrace before she pulled herself free.

'I have to go Erich; I'll miss the evening ferry… If you had asked me to stay, then I would have done, but then you know that don't you… I know just how much this *promise* you've made means to you, maybe when it is over, we can begin to think about the future instead of the past…' Her voice was husky, again that low feline brogue which raised the goose bumps on his arms…

Barton watched the VW's headlights pick out the trees in the lane before finally disappearing over the hill towards the distant village where they had lunched but days before. He stared up at the starlit sky, the pin pricks of light in the velvet of the blue heavens… Was there some guiding force in all this? He teased himself, or was the course of life just a series of unpredictable happy accidents, like the random firing of a pin-ball machine…? He walked back, alone with the many randomised thoughts flowing through his mind. Time to collect his ideas and thoughts into some semblance of order. There were indeed things to do, first on the list would be to bring up to date his chronological journal of the events from Dorn's fatal mission in 1940, through all the twists and turns up to the present day. Included integrally now would be the Lewis and Huw Thomas recollections along with Johnson's melancholic findings relating to the last crew members of the Juniper. This was beginning to read very much like a book in progress and he hadn't yet touched upon the other parts of the Reinecke diary, the years which followed, these were waiting to be explored…

The first light of dawn crept through the bedroom window as Barton, at last, put his pen down, closing the well-thumbed diary once again. The written pages of notes piled up on his desk as he had numbered them as they flowed from his pen. These in turn would need to find their way into hard typed copy before he would be ready for any meeting with David Strachan. In front of him the Iron Cross and Dorn's identity disc lay on a square of green baize, beside these was the Eagle quarter dollar Jonesey had given to Huw in 1944, remaining gold coins from the dive made up the rest of the group of objects, he touched each of thoughtfully with his fingertips, if only they could speak? Time for reflection, reaching for his old briar pipe and tobacco pouch out of the desk draw, he packed the bowl with tobacco then lit the mixture blowing a fragrant cloud of smoke into the air where it drifted towards and through the open window. A dog barked in the distance, from the small holding across the fields, blue smoke curled lazily above the dwelling in the growing morning light. Barton put on his safari jacket and made his way into the lane outside, not bothering to lock the door, he meandering along the narrow roadway taking in the new day with the bird song floating across the fields in the early morning countryside, the awakening of another day. A few hundred yards along from the cottage, a fox appeared dragging its kill across the road, Barton was downwind, he stood very still and watched as it struggled with the carcass of a rabbit half its size. Then it became aware of him, was gone, leaving it's prey on the grass verge at the side of the lane. Barton pushed the little corpse with his toecap into the hedge where the fox had disappeared. Perhaps all life was like this he thought, fighting to achieve, only to have fate intervene and snatch the fruits of one's labours? He took his time wandering back to the cottage, picking a switch from the hedge he whipped the grass, dragged the tip along the gravel as he walked. As the sun rose over the horizon, he neared home, it was time to sleep, get some rest then begin the list of things to be done this day.

41

It was mid-day when Barton was aroused from his slumbers by the telephone ringing at his bedside, it was Sheila. She quickly told him that on the return ferry crossing, Gerry senior had begun to feel unwell, his condition had worsened with his grandson calling for their doctor as soon as they had arrived home at Greystones. Old Gerry had taken on a little too much, the excitement of the past few days had brought on some form of a minor suspected seizure, he was now in hospital confined to bed where his condition was to be assessed by a neurologist. Barton felt for Sheila's obvious distress, though her voice was level and calm he detected the concern for her grandfather, especially so given his grand age…

'Do you want me to come over Sheila…?' He offered genuinely worried that his own enthusiasm had contributed to the old man's over taxing himself.

'No, not at the moment, he's comfortable with orders not to get himself worked up for any reason at all, you know what he's like Erich, he's not a good patient, has no respect for doctors, they'll have to tie him down to stop him getting out of bed. I'll keep you posted on how it goes over the weekend…'

Barton put the receiver down, he liked Gerry Lewis, with his sense of humour, the twinkle in his eye when he was taken by a whim of mischief… However, nothing would be achieved by undue concern until he had been given the once over by the medics. After lunch he settled back at his desk and pushed on with the writing, he now had a fairly comprehensive word map of the Reinecke story laid out on paper, he could navigate his way with page headings through the years of the man's life bring the saga up to date with the recent events. Next, he picked up the telephone and dialed David Strachan's home number. It was answered after half a dozen rings. Barton gave another rendition of the course of the travels and people he had met over the weeks since they had last spoken. Strachan listened patiently, when Barton had finished his story asking a number of pointed questions, in particular about the U-367's cargo.

'You're saying this consignment of plague carrying boxes were destroyed at the time Erich, how can you be so sure, were there witnesses…?' Strachan was impressed by all of the other aspects of the Reinecke story, yet openly stressed his concerns over the details regarding the fate of the Martin brothers and their truck. He asked Barton for the names of everyone involved, he seemed particularly interested in the name of the American Sgt L. Jones, known as Jonesey. Strachan questioned Jonesey's involvement, where might he have ended his days? Barton filled in as much as he could from his notes, however leaving out the parts where Mick Lewis had shot the man Breitfeld, the drama at the top of the cliff with Huw Henryd Thomas, and those suspicious boxes taken aboard the Lady Patricia. Strachan finished with the suggestion that Barton keep this story firmly under wraps until he could arrange a meeting with the appropriate authorities.

'I'm serious Erich, what you have uncovered could have far reaching ramifications at many different levels, hold onto it until you hear from me will you?' He was extracting a promise from Barton and he knew it…

Barton agreed, 'The salient thing here David, for all of the people involved today, is to get the sunken wrecks marked and registered as war graves, we hadn't really thought further than that, I hear what you're saying, I'll keep it to myself until I hear from you…' He put the telephone down, a little unnerved by his friend's response. Yet it made sense, if the story got out the media would focus on the horrific prospect of a plague outbreak, the rest of the news would be treated as just so, so… Not as sensational as a threat to life on a Biblically massive scale.

The remainder of the day was spent dealing with the necessary trivia of domestic chores, some shopping needed to replenish his depleted stocks of food. The cottage a tidy up after the visits of the Lewis family. In the evening he returned to his writings, as he wrote he pondered on Strachan's obvious concerns, was this last stage going to be so difficult to overcome where everything else had fallen into place so smoothly…?

42

The Sunday came with little to remark apart from a call from Sheila to say that her grandfather had improved a little, it appeared he had suffered a small stroke, fortunately neither his speech nor faculties were effected though he was unsteady on his feet. Sheila would be returning on the late ferry, while she had lectures to conduct through the working week intended to call over on Thursday evening, they made a date for dinner together on that night. Barton told her of his call to Strachan, of his concerns at David's response. The positive news was a beginning had been made, now it was wait to hear again from David as to what was likely to happen next.

Barton didn't have to wait as long as he had expected, he had the call from David Strachan early on Tuesday morning, David had set up a meeting at his own office for Wednesday in the afternoon at one o'clock, this was to be with two officials figures who he said, were anxious to meet with Barton as soon as was possible to arrange a meeting to discuss his findings. However, Barton was to come *alone,* with none of his associates to be informed at this stage, he, Barton, was requested to attend bringing all of his evidences, anything which was relevant, especially the lengthy notes he had made, this was to be treated as a matter of some serious urgency…!

Barton put the telephone down and considered this development, he had expected a meeting where at least Gary would be present to confirm the visual description of their discoveries. He asked himself why this sudden need for secrecy, where the intention was to bring the story into the open apart from the obvious involvement of Mick and his son Gerry? Barton felt a distinct sense of unease beginning to form in his mind, logically however the best way to tackle this would be to attend the meeting at David's office with an open mind before allowing himself to speculate on possibilities. He shrugged his shoulders reaching again for his notebooks and the bulky Reinecke file, he needed to complete the final paragraphs of the journal ready for Wednesday's interrogation by the people in the authorities David had contacted…

43

Barton arrived early at the main police headquarters where Strachan had his office. He did not feel comfortable, explaining to Sheila and the others that he had to attend this meeting alone had not been easy. All that he could do was to try to outline the clear instruction he had been given in David's telephone call. It had left a sour taste as each of them had played significant roles in collecting the threads which had led to the complex yet comprehensive account he had put together from his notes and talks over these past months. The detailed description of the underwater search would have benefitted from the inclusion of photographic evidence, this had been a remission on his part not for see how important this might prove to be. However, with everything he carried with him he believed he could give a detailed fair account from start to finish. Barton presented himself at the front desk just before one stating that Detective Inspector Strachan was expecting him. He waited for only minutes before Strachan came down into the reception area to collect him.

'Thank you Erich, I hope you weren't kept waiting, I've been talking with our two visitors for the last hour, they arrived this morning, I warn you they are both officious individuals… C'mon, let me take you up to my office…' Strachan was his usual friendly self yet Barton detected a certain unease in his manner as he led the way up climbing the stairs two at a time. Shown into Strachan's office, Barton was met by two formal looking grey suited men standing in conversation at the window as he entered. The older of the two, a tall man in his fifties with the all too distinctive bearing of an officer greeted him.

'Ah Mr Barton, thanking you for coming, let me do the introductions. I am Major Duncan Craven, my naval colleague here is Lieutenant Commander Charles Hewitt, we both, respectively, represent our branches of the military intelligence services, you don't need to know any more that that at this stage. David Strachan, I believe you know so no need for an introduction there. We won't take up too much of your time Mr Barton, so we'll get started straight away. If you will take a seat at D I Strachan's desk perhaps you will be good enough to give us a verbal account of where all this began, take your time…'

Barton sat on one side of Strachan's desk, the men Craven and Hewitt on the other side with Strachan sitting back, almost as an observer. He took a deep breath mentally and physically, how many times had he told this story, he was beginning to lose count. Making himself as comfortable as was possible, he began from the beginning, again...

It took over an hour and a half to recount the story beginning to end, neither man interrupted nor made any comment, they both had open note pads on the desk which seemed to be filled with information which they appeared from time to time to cross reference with what Barton was saying. At the end of his rendition, Barton felt hoarse from this latest retelling of the saga, he politely asked Strachan for a drink which caused his friend to apologise for not having done this at the beginning, picking up the telephone ordered refreshments for them all before they continued. Coffee and tea arrived and was served. Craven had taken the lead at the beginning when they were introduced, now his naval colleague Hewitt took over, stirring his teacup slowly he began.

'You are aware I'm sure Mr Barton, of a document called the Official Secrets Act...? His manner was curt and precise, not a hint of friendliness, his close clipped hair meticulously groomed manner gave off the aura on one who was used to absolute obedience. He waited for Barton's reply.

'I am, though I don't see how that has any bearing on what I have brought before you today, and I might add, the intention here is quite clear, to lay to rest the men of two ships who hitherto have no official recognition in either of the two opposing services as far I have been able to discern, despite some extensive research...'

Hewitt shook his head, 'Oh it does indeed Mr Barton, we have long been aware of the mission of the U-367, her recorded history in the Kriegsmarine archives ended in the January of 1944, so it was to be left until you began your amateur endeavours to dig up the past. What was missing from the records was the exact nature of the research the man Breitfeld and his associates had carried out, much of the paperwork was destroyed before Allied Intelligence could get their hands on it in 1945; the SS made a thorough job of concealing their plans to wreak havoc on the economy and the unsuspecting civilian life in this country before the end of the war. It reality it would have served no purpose other than to prolong the human suffering as revenge upon the allies for bringing an end to their regime. The prospect of resurrecting this hideous menace in the modern public eye cannot be allowed to come to be a reality, you have inadvertently uncovered a social time bomb Mr Barton, it would have been better if you had not interfered and left it lay as it was...!'

Barton felt the anger rise within him, all that had been achieved, the good that had come of the wishes of old Reinecke, the submarine found, her place marked along with that of the Juniper and the men who had served in her, this now questioned by these stuffed shirts afraid of the spectre of truth being revealed. 'The cargo the U-367 was carrying has been accounted for, the threat of the plague went up in smoke, it was all incinerated in a blaze which took the life of the men who were carrying it, I thought we had gathered enough evidence to make that clear, the boxes and what they contained did not constitute a threat once they were destroyed... There were witnesses to their being consumed by fire before they were taken off the Wurm...'

'Very true Mr Barton, we were able to trace the American sergeant Jones who saw the event, it was he who rescued the boy Huw Thomas. It might be of interest for you to know he lived on after he arrived back in the United States, survived his injuries. He was followed there by the woman Peggy Owen, she married him and believe or not he still lives, another survivor and although now a frail very old man, yet was able to cooperate with our investigation with our friends in the American CIA, he confirmed the truck carrying infection bearing boxes were eliminated in a "fireball" as he put it. We haven't been sitting still since we were alerted to your interest here...' Hewitt looked to Craven beside him who gave his nodded agreement.

'Jonesey was alive?' This was incredible, Barton immediately thought what Huw's reaction might be to this news? 'So, what are you telling me, is that I should drop the story, and those of all of the people involved, what of their interests in this...?'

Hewitt interrupted, 'It's a little too late for that Mr Barton, news got out very early on when you started to pry into the past, they once used to say, "Walls have ears...", they still do. There are too many people involved now who have knowledge about the U-367, yes you have found her and the remains of HMS Juniper, we can do nothing about that now as it has become fact. What we cannot have are speculations about an active fifth column in this country in 1944, this with the further fact that an enemy could have and did successfully bring into this country a device which would have catastrophic effects; that we must suppress along with any myth which may take root in the public's imagination... That Mr

Barton is how it must be allowed to remain with some adjustments brought about by your discoveries…'

'Then what about the wrecks, their status as war graves, you can't take that away from those men or their memories for God's sake…?' Barton was now finding it difficult to conceal his frustrations, was all of this then for nothing?

'Not at all Mr Barton, the U-367 will be marked on Admiralty charts as a war grave, she will be protected from interference with a perimeter which must not be crossed by civilian divers unless they wish to risk the severest of penalties. Royal Naval divers are, as we speak on route to seal the vessel permanently, no one will be able to enter or disturb that wreck site from now on. The Juniper in the same manner, she too still has ordinance on board which needs to be made safe, it would seem when she went down all of her depth charges had been armed, they may still be viable despite having been down there for so long; we are still finding and destroying sea mines left over from that period, believe me. Her captain, Lieutenant Commander Stewart Penrick, will be posthumously honoured who by his actions in sinking the U-boat with the saving of many lives of her prospective victims, history Mr Barton, will record his heroism and that of his ship. The rest of the story Mr Barton, it never happened either officially or unofficially, do I make myself perfectly clear…?' There was a veiled threat in Hewitt's tone with Barton finding little room for him to manoeuvre.

'My work, my account, the Reinecke diary…?' He had the gut-wrenching feeling Hewitt or Craven would demand the old man's diary.

Hewitt leaned across the desk, 'Let me see the evidences we have asked you to bring with you today Mr Barton, I believe these include the original diary and the notes you have made?'

Barton reached into his brief case and put on the desk his hard-backed file of written notes, then the Reinecke diary beside them. Hewitt raised his hand saying.

'That will be enough, the other odds and ends are not relevant, may I…?' He said reaching for Barton's notes. He flicked through the pages then handed the file to Craven. Hewitt picked up the diary, placed it on the desk in front of him then taking a pair of reading glasses from his pocket began turning over the pages slowly. He paused occasionally, made some 'Hmm' grunts then brusquely put the diary back on the desk.

'This, this diary or journal is all that you have, all of your notes are in reality suppositions based more or less entirely on what is written in these pages… Yes?' Hewitt breathed the words out with the question left hanging in the air.

'Well yes of course it is, there are other accounts from the other people who were there, Lewis, the boy as he was then Huw Thomas…'

'Hear say Mr Barton, wishful thinking not hard cooperating evidence of any substance, you must see that surely…?' Hewitt's eyebrows were raised as he had stated what appeared to be an obvious truth…

'No, I can't believe that to be the case, the people I have spoken with I believe have given honest account, and the diary, you must see how specific Reinecke's words were in describing everything which he had witnessed…?' Barton's frustration was getting the better of him as the very basis of his work was being taken apart, systematically dismantled discredited.

Hewitt tapped the cover of the leather diary with his fore fingers at the same time saying, 'These Mr Barton, officially are no more than the eccentric ramblings of an old man, they weren't even written at the time of the event, he may have been the victim of false memory syndrome. Therefore, the Reinecke diary has no testable statements, it's a fairy story Mr Barton…!'

Barton struggled to find the words to express his personal indignation and the slight which had been pointed at Reinecke. 'Then what would you have me do Commander Hewitt, just ignore it, pretend nothing of this ever happened…?'

'Then comply with his wishes, he told you to destroy it did he not? Then write your story Mr Barton, keep to the human aspects without reference to plots and intrigue. We will of course take great interest in anything you may publish, reserve the authority to take action if necessary seize or prevent anything which suggests you insist on breaching the confidences which I have just explained to you in detail as are not permissible. That's all I have to say, Major Craven and I are in agreement having discussed the whole matter of the Reinecke affair long before you arrived here today… Then I think that we are done here… It's been a pleasure meeting you Mr Barton your enthusiasm has been remarkably impressive, please don't take any personal offence when sincerely I say I hope we don't have to meet again…' Hewitt pushed the diary across the desk towards Barton, 'Please Mr Barton, do take this souvenir with you. DI. Strachan will see you out…' The Reinecke affair had been officially closed…

Strachan was apologetic as he took Barton back down to the reception area, making it clear that all he had done was to relay everything Barton had told him, that he had no idea of what Hewitt and Craven had had in mind prior to the meeting. Barton walked away from the police headquarters to where the Landrover was parked, his old leather brief case containing his notes and the diary clutched firmly under his arm. His mind was reeling at the events of the past two hours, they, who so ever they were, had intonated they had him under some kind of surveillance for these past months? There were now more questions than the conclusions and the missing pieces for which he thought, he had so successfully, perhaps even a little too egotistically, found valid answers. One thing he had now resolved, had decided in full frank contemplation of the stark awareness of the comments made in and during the course of this harrowing derogatory meeting with Hewitt and Craven, they had inspired him, he would begin to write the draft for the book, he even had its prospective name in mind, it would be entitled, *"The Reinecke Journals"*…

The drive homeward found him deep in thought, he took the roads driving on autopilot, only when he arrived back at the cottage did he surface from his thinking on all things to do with Reinecke, as he had espied Sheila's VW parked beside the land beside the cottage. Barton sat with her on the sofa, he tried to remember all of what had been said to him over the course of the afternoon. After an hour, she put her fingers to his lips to silence him.

'Enough, you have done a remarkable thing today Erich, there will be time now to decide how you want to move forward with this. For now, my love, you have achieved your goals. We need to eat, then there are people to let know that you have done very much what you set out to do. I'm going to look after you tonight, I've worried about you these past days… I've poured us both a drink, here take this,' She passed him his glass of single malt. 'So here I am, along with my toothbrush…' She sat back raising her glass, a raised eyebrow with that look upon her face which told him emphatically there could be no argument with her.

As he made his way to bed that night, Barton paused at the top of the stairs, then sat quietly at his desk for a pensive long moment thinking on the events of the day. Finally, taking the diary with the note file from his case, placed the documents along with the Iron Cross, the identity disc and coins in the desk drawer, he then purposefully turned the key, another day would come, this was not over, it may even be just the beginning of something so much bigger...

44

So it was in the last week of November, when Barton with Sheila, touched down at Flughafen Salzburg in the early first falls of the Winter snow. Picking up a car from the same Hertz care hire cabin Barton had used on the previous trip they began the two-hour drive to Österndorf. It was a surprisingly easy journey, the autobahn kept clear of snow, on reaching Wörgl turning off and up into the Brixen valley, the Winter scenery was stunning. They both were wearing sunglasses to shield their eyes from the glare of the white panorama. Already the mountains were covered with their blankets of thick snow with the promise of more to come as the Alpine December weather approached. The road Barton had driven short months before in Summer weather was still passable even as the conditions deteriorated, now he found he needed to concentrate more on the winding bends as they climbed into the reaches of the valley. Were the occasion not so sombre both would have enjoyed taking time to gaze in wonder at the magnificent scenery rising on all sides as they drove. They arrived in the village and parked the hire car at the rear of the Adlerhof hotel, there were few tourists so early in the season the hotel reception and lounge area were all but empty. Booking in Barton asked if there were any messages for him? There was one, a written note, Dorn and his wife would be joining them at two o'clock for their arranged meeting and the following ceremony. There was time to have lunch and change before the Dorn couple arrived.

They sat together in the restaurant talking about the prospective meeting with Dorn, they expected another to join them, Frau Inga Morgenstern had responded to his telephone call before leaving home saying she too intended to be with them on this day. Barton and Sheila retired to their room after their light lunch, changing into black formal clothing before their poignant meeting with the other expected guests. A little before two Dorn arrived with his wife, he shook hands warmly with Barton, took off his cap when he was introduced to Sheila bending to kiss her hand. Turning to his wife waiting behind him he beckoned her to join him.

'May I present my wife Frau Ilse Dorn, mother of my children Erich…! It's an honour to meet you too Fraulein Lewis,' he said reaching for Sheila's hand, 'this one,' Dorn gesturing towards Barton, 'has told me about you when he called, for an Englishman, strange he didn't exaggerate...' His belly laugh followed, Dorn's wife glared at her husband quickly saying to him smartly in German to remember his manners, '*You Bumpkin!*' Frau Ilse Dorn had dressed for the weather in sensible warm winter clothes, with gloves and a long thick scarf wrapped about her neck, her easy manner echoed that of her husband, something in her bright smiling features suggesting in her younger years she would have been a very pretty woman, with her flaxen hair braided in coils over her ears even now in her sixties she still had the bearing and the posture of a female half her age. They adjourned to the hotel bar, where Barton ordered hot chocolate drinks for each of them, Dorn predictably demanding a schnapps to go with his, then looked at his watch Barton and said to the Dorn.

'It's coming up to one forty-five Leon, do we need to make a move...?' As he said the words out of the corner of his eye, he noticed Inga Morgenstern enter the bar. She was dressed in black, a heavy coat with a fur lined hood, beneath, on her feet, were stout boots in contrast to her otherwise formal clothing. Inga came over to greet them with a broad smile to each in turn.

'Grüss Gott...! It's good to see you again Herr Barton, this must be your wife is it not so?' Her spoken English was laboured, Inga was searching for the right words when Sheila answered her in good passable German putting her at ease. Careful to avoid any misunderstanding Sheila explained that she was Barton's companion and friend to which Inga merely opened her eyes a little wider answering.

'Naturlich Fraulein Lewis...' and not a word more as she turned back to Dorn with a nod indicating that she was ready.

Dorn had arranged for the village priest to meet with them on the steps of the church at two o'clock, he stood waiting in black cassock as they made their way the few steps from the rear of the hotel through the church gates. Greeting the small group of five people he led the way through the churchyard to near the little memorial chapel stood. A path had been cleared through the snow to the foot of the grave, the priest stood at the bottom end whilst the others, Leon and Ilse Dorn on the right with Barton, Sheila and Inga Morgenstern gathered on the opposite side. The stone headstone held an inset photograph of Bruno Reinecke dressed in the full-dress uniform of a Kapitänleutnant of the Kriegsmarine. It had clearly been a memorable day for him when the picture was being taken, his face wore a fixed smile for the camera, yet there was pride as well in his young bearded features which reminded Barton of the last mental images he held in his mind of the old man as he walked from their meeting at the Reinecke Haus back in August.

The father gave a brief personal dedication to the man who everyone had known in the village, sprinkling some incense over the grave he concluded the liturgy with the promise of the eternal life for the departed. The group, except for Inga, making the sign of the cross as he brought the service to a close. The priest then nodded to each in turn, then leaving them with their thoughts to make his way back, with the five people Reinecke had touched in his life left standing at the graveside. Tears were coursing unashamedly down Inga's lined face, as her shoulders heaved with emotion, Sheila put her arm around her in comfort hugging the little woman to her side, she leaned aside to Barton slipped her hand in his and whispered.

'I forgot to tell you, my degree was a double barreled one, my second subject was modern languages, I took German...' The silent laugh on her lips muted by the solemnity of the occasion.

Barton knelt in the snow near the headstone his breath freezing in small clouds of vapour from his lips; taking off his gloves he reached into his black overcoat pocket bringing into the light Reinecke's worn Iron Cross, Dorn nodded his approval. Barton dug into the frost hardened soil a few inches with his fingers making a space just beneath the photograph, into this he laid the cross, carefully patted the soil back into place before standing again. It was done...

Dorn stared hard at Barton as he stood up brushing the soil from his fingers, 'Is that the end of the Reinecke diary story Erich...?' He said in his deep rumbling baritone voice.

Barton caught the pained look on Inga Morgenstern's pinched white face, expectant as her eyes closed upon his waiting for the answer. After a moment's hesitation he looked over the grave at his friend's raised eyebrows then wistfully raising his eyes against the glare of the sun in the crystal clear azure blue sky above their heads said quietly with a wry smile, 'No my friend Leon, it was only a beginning, there is more, so very much more of things yet untold to come... This, I promise you...!

Author's Historical Footnote

The original idea for the basis of the story Reinecke Diary began many years ago when I was given a small booklet recounting an incident where a German U-boat, the U-38 commanded by Kpt Max Valentiner slipped into Llandudno Bay on the night of the 14th August 1915, waited for three nights undetected to pick up three escaping prisoners of war. The attempt failed. However a little research yielded information that this was not the first incursion of this type, an earlier mission within sight of the Great Orme in June of the same year by U-27 under Korvettenkapitan Bernd Weggener is recorded, as is later on Christmas Day 1917, when the U-87 was rammed and sank of Bardsey Island.

A little more research, this time taking in the later conflict years 1939-45, revealed that on the 14th May 1945, after the German capitulation, four days after the German U-boat arm of the Kriegsmarine had been ordered to surrender by Donitz. The U-234, a type XB submarine surfaced and surrender to an American surface ship. She was found to be carrying 560 Kgs of uranium oxide and 24 tonnes of paper documents bound for Japan.

These stories began a series of 'what if?' questions in my imagination, was there the substance of a tale to be told here, would it stir the imagination of the reader? They began to unfold with visits to the sites mentioned in the Reinecke Diary coupled with some very real visits to the little chapel type buildings in the churchyards of villages in the Brixen Valley in Austria. The body of a German airman had been indeed found in 1965 when road workings were being improved near Bangor in North Wales, the airman's body had later been laid to rest at the Cannock German war cemetery with other casualties from that period. An unrelated number of photographs taken in Llandudno in 1944 and1945 of American service men billeted in the town came into my possession, these along with lengthy talks with local people who remembered the 'Yanks', the good and the bad of those experiences of those far off days, added further human touches and the idea for the Reinecke Diary was born.

The name or numbering of a specific U-boat for the story posed a problem, after much research it was found from the Kriegsmarine lists that a gap appeared between the listing of U-366 and U-368, thus in good faith, the U-367 became a creation of my imagination, to the best of my belief, no such boat ever sailed.

I have used extensive artistic license to allow the characters in the book to live and move about in a landscape which will may be recognisable to many readers, I would crave their patience in that for the purposes of this novel, it was necessary to change or to reinvent place names and to create the fictitious persona of some of the main players. There were, however, some very human foundations created from an amalgam of real people. Some, however, of necessity, are purely fictitious creations from my imagination, these the many characters and personalities who inhabit the pages of the story of the Reinecke Diary. For any potential discrepancies I readily apologise for any semblance that may be found for real people either living or dead.

For the reader who may wish to find more about the U-boat arm of the German Kriegsmarine during World War Two, I would strongly recommend two informative books on the subject.

Bishop, C. (2006) *Kriegsmarine U-Boats. 1939-1945.* Amber Books Ltd. London.

Stern, R. (1991) *Type V11 U-boats.* Arms and Armour Press. London.

I would sincerely hope that the reader will take some pleasure in the reading of this story, hopefully as much as I have experienced and enjoyed in the writing of this tale founded in elements of real and factual history laced with a sizeable seasoning of my imagination.

- Terence James. North Wales. 2020

About the Author

Terence James is a retired lecturer in the social sciences and history.

He a graduate with an MSc in Psychology having spent his professional life working in the field of mental health before returning to writing and the academic world.

A father and grandfather, Terence serves as local councillor and lives with his wife Patricia, a fellow councillor, at their home in North Wales.

Available worldwide from Amazon

———————————

www.mtp.agency

www.facebook.com/mtp.agency

@mtp_agency

Michael Terence
Publishing

Printed in Great Britain
by Amazon